GCSE maths
(foundation level)
for post-16 learners

Kevin Norley

twentyfivefiftytwo

Published by twentyfivefiftytwo

Copyright © Kevin Norley 2008, 2011, 2018

Previously published by twentyfivefiftytwo (2018) without the additional
GCSE learning materials as 'Making Britain Numerate' (3rd edition).
This 4th enhanced GCSE edition published 2018

'Making Britain Numerate' was previously published by
Imprimata 2008 (1st edition) and 2011 (2nd edition).

A CIP Catalogue record for this book is available
from the British Library

ISBN 978-1-9996653-4-0

Printed in Great Britain

In loving memory of my mother and father

Contents

Foreword for GCSE maths (foundation level) for post-16 learners

GCSE maths (foundation level) for post-16 learners has been written mainly for adult learners studying maths (GCSE or functional skills) in a range of environments including further education colleges, adult and community learning, and work-based learning providers. However, it is also suitable for 16 – 18 year-olds resitting GCSE maths whilst studying on vocational programmes in further education colleges or whilst studying in sixth-form colleges. It has been designed therefore for those who have already studied maths at school and maybe in an educational setting since school, but who have not yet, for whatever reason(s), achieved GCSE maths.

The GCSE Learning Guide within the book has been put together in such a way as to, as far as possible, allow learners to make links between topics within the GCSE maths (Foundation Tier) and to allow for the development of transferable skills across such topics. Through experience, the types of transferable skills needed by learners can be assessed via diagnostic questions that probe understanding and vary slightly through subtle changes in difficulty, whilst types of error can be anticipated and corrected when they occur. Such skills, for example, include factorising and expanding algebraic expressions, calculating algebraic terms such as ab, n^2 and pt^2 etc., forming and simplifying fractions, converting fractions to percentages (and vice-versa) and carrying out a scale conversion etc. Aside from the GCSE learning guide, the rationale for the rest of the resources in the book is outlined in the foreword and rationale in Making Britain Numerate (3rd Ed).

In 2018, the pass rate for GCSE maths in FE colleges was around 20%, similar to previous years. I believe that this stubbornly low pass rate relates to the low level of expectations of students and staff, along with the continued emphasis on student-centred learning at the expense of more teacher-centred learning and that these factors are partly responsible for the issue of the skills gaps that arise within education and society today.

Research shows that, in the context of post-16 education, those teachers with an A level in maths obtain better results in maths with their learners than those teachers without. With or without the research though, common sense dictates that in order to teach a subject, teachers themselves need to be qualified, through an examined qualification, to at least one level above (i.e. level 3) the level at which their learners are aiming to achieve. Common sense and fairness also dictate that those wishing to enter on to any teacher training course within the post-compulsory sector should have a GCSE maths qualification. The reality is however, that an A-level in maths is not a requirement to teach maths in the post-16 education sector, and a GCSE in maths has not always been a requirement to get onto a teacher training course in the sector. Such a low level of expectations of staff is only matched by the low level of expectations of students i.e. one is the concomitant of the other.

Some of the issues that teachers are generally agreed upon include a dislike of the unnecessary and increasing administrative burden that is placed on them (be that through the need to complete individual leaning plans, group profiles, electronic registers or countless other forms etc.) along with a dislike of the stress and anxiety caused by the continued use of observations and 'walk-throughs', along with their changing emphases and expectations of teachers. We need to question, I believe, what the benefits of such observations are, with their misguided concept of the need to observe learning and to see evidence of differentiation etc., when there is no apparent collective feedback from them leading to any significant and measurable improvements in GCSE maths results. Furthermore, in the context of the time spent gleaning feedback from students from a range of formal, and informal, settings and perspectives, we also need to question, I believe, its benefits and impact on any significant and measurable improvements in results.

L1 Numeracy Learning Assessment

Name: ....   **Date:** ....

The learning assessment consists of a Part A and a Part B. The guidance notes relate to Part B, and if necessary, are there to assist. You can refer to them as you carry out your assessment. If required, a tutor may guide you through them prior to you carrying out the assessment.

   The purpose of the assessment is to check any weak areas you may have, but more importantly to give you the chance to learn from it, and to develop everyday numeracy skills. Following the assessment, a tutor will mark and give you feedback on it. The focus will then be on learning from errors, carrying out corrections and having them remarked.

Part A

Tally Charts

	Morning	**Afternoon**
Monday	‖‖‖ ‖‖‖ ‖‖‖ ‖‖‖ ‖‖‖	‖‖‖ ‖‖‖ ‖‖‖ ‖‖‖ ‖‖‖
Tuesday	‖‖‖ ‖‖‖ ‖‖‖ ‖‖‖ III	‖‖‖ ‖‖‖ ‖‖‖
Wednesday	‖‖‖ ‖‖‖ ‖‖‖ ‖‖‖ ‖‖‖	‖‖‖ ‖‖‖ ‖‖‖
Thursday	‖‖‖ ‖‖‖ ‖‖‖ ‖‖‖ II	‖‖‖ ‖‖‖ ‖‖‖ ‖‖‖ I
Friday	‖‖‖ ‖‖‖ ‖‖‖ ‖‖‖ ‖‖‖ III	‖‖‖ ‖‖‖ ‖‖‖ ‖‖‖ ‖‖‖ III

Q1 The above tally chart shows the number of customers using a sports centre's new Bistro during its first week of opening. How many more customers used the Bistro during the busiest day than during the quietest day?

Pictograms

January	
February	
March	
April	
May	
June	

Key: = 50 mobiles

Q2 The above pictogram shows the number of mobile phones sold by a retailer during the first six months of 2007. How many more mobile phones were sold in June than in January?

....

Reading and Interpreting Large Numbers

Q3 It was estimated that two hundred and one thousand, nine hundred and twenty six people attended a football match. Write this number on the line below:

....

Q4 During a recent 'Save the Earth' charity concert, 23 064 tickets were sold on-line. Write 23 064 in words on the line below:

....

Graphs

The bar chart shows the speed (in miles per hour) of five different land animals:

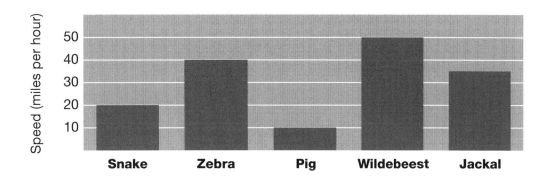

Q5 What are the units shown on the vertical axis?

....

Q6 According to the bar graph, how much faster is the jackal than the pig?

....

Q7 A pie chart is often used for showing proportions. However, what is missing from the following?

....

Proportions of vehicles (cars, buses, lorries and motorbikes) which currently use the motorways.

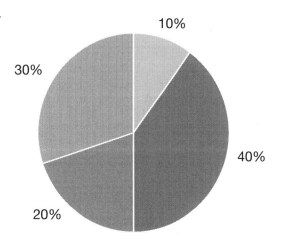

Reading Scales

$Q8$ What is the weight shown on the following scale?

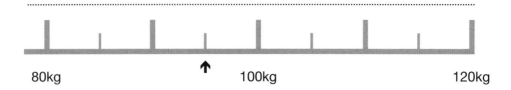

80kg　　　　　　　　100kg　　　　　　　　120kg

$Q9$ What is the measurement (in degrees Centigrade) shown on the following thermometer?

0°C　　　　　　　20°C　　　　　40°C

Rounding up/down

$Q10$ 84,648 people attended a football match. How many is this to the nearest thousand?

Timetable

$Q11$ The following timetable shows the times of trains from Leighton Buzzard to London Euston:

Leighton Buzzard	9.43	10.13	10.43	11.13
Berkhamsted	9.53	10.23	10.53	11.23
Hemel Hempstead	10.03	10.31	11.03	11.31
Watford	10.11	-	11.11	-
London Euston	10.31	10.48	11.31	11.48

A man decides to take a train from Berkhamsted to London Euston some time between 10.00 am and 11.00 am
What is the difference in the times taken by the two possible trains he can catch?

Time

Q12 A woman leaves home at twenty five past eight in the morning. It takes her twenty five minutes to cycle to the station, following which she queues up for ten minutes to buy her ticket. She then waits a further ten minutes for her train to arrive. What time does her train arrive?

....

Part B

Converting fractions to percentages to decimals

Q13 Complete the following Fractions/Percentages/Decimal Conversion Table:

	Fraction	Percentage	Decimal
	1/2 (a half)		
		25%	
			0.75
		20%	
	2/5 (two fifths)		
		60%	
			0.8
		33%	

Division

Q14 A quarter of the spectators at a golf tournament were women. If there were 220 spectators, then how many of them were women?

Q15 A man decides to save two thirds of his tax refund towards a holiday. If his refund is £180.00 then how much does he save?

Calculating average

Q16 Six teams of engineering students take part in a rowing competition. The times were recorded by a timekeeper:

	Team 1	Team 2	Team 3	Team 4	Team 5	Team 6
Time (mins)	21	29	16	22	19	25

What is the average (mean) time recorded by the timekeeper?

Calculating range

Q17 In the above example, calculate the range of times for the 6 teams in the rowing competition.

Calculating 10% of a number

Q18 There is a 10% discount on a new computer. If its normal price is £782.00 then how much is the discount?

Calculating 5%, 20%, 30% etc of a number

Q19 In a survey of 700 people carried out by a new energy company, 20% said they were considering changing supplier. How many people is this?

Q20 Annual membership of a leisure centre normally costs £110.00. As part of a promotion, the centre is offering a 30% reduction for those who join before the end of January. How much will annual membership cost with the 30% reduction?

Forming a fraction, simplifying it, then converting it to a percentage

Q21 30 contestants enter a reality TV show. After one month, there are just 6 contestants left. What percentage of the contestants are left?

Multiplying decimals

Q22 A man buys 4 muffins at £1.15 each and 2 cappuccinos at £1.80 each. How much does he spend in total?

Calculating area

Q23 A gardener wants to measure the area of a flower bed. If the length is 7m and the breadth 1.5m then what is its area?

Calculating volume

Q24 An airline passenger concerned about hand luggage restrictions at airports, measures his case to be 40cm long, 10cm wide and 30cm high. Calculate its volume.

Multiplying by 10, 20, 30 etc

Q25 A part-time catering assistant earns £6.15 an hour. How much does he earn for 30 hours work?

Rounding up/down to the nearest whole number and to the nearest tenth

Q26 A man runs a 100m in 11.147 seconds. What was his time to the nearest tenth of a second?

Q27 The length of a warehouse is measured as 28.62m. What is the length of the warehouse to the nearest metre?

Ratios

 A chef decides to try out a new recipe, 'Buttered Mussels', and uses the following ingredients:

3 cloves of garlic
70g of unsalted butter
½ lemon
a dash of tabasco
5 tablespoons of finely chopped parsley
3kg of mussels
3 finely chopped shallots
150ml of dry white wine

If the recipe is for 6 people, then how many grams of butter will he need for 24 people?

Scale drawings

 The distance between 2 towns on a scale drawing is measured as 7cm. If the drawing is drawn to a scale of 1cm : 3km then what is the actual distance between the 2 towns?

Kilograms/kilometres

Q30 If a small loaf of bread weighs 400g, what would be the weight (in kilograms) of 40 loaves of bread?

Guidance Notes

Forming a fraction

Make a note of the number of shaded parts, and the total number of parts for each pie chart. The fraction will be the number of shaded parts out of the total number of parts.

For example, 1 shaded part out of 5 parts in total = $\frac{1}{5}$ (a fifth).

Division

In order to calculate $\frac{1}{3}$ (a third) of a number, you need to divide that number by 3.

Worked example:

A bar manager carries out a smoking survey on 42 of her regular lunchtime customers, and finds out that a third of them are smokers. How many of the customers are smokers?

A third of 42 = $42 \times \frac{1}{3} = \frac{42}{3} = 3\overline{)4^12}$ (quotient 14)

14 of the customers are smokers

In order to calculate $\frac{1}{5}$ (a fifth) of a number, you need to divide that number by 5.

Worked examples:

a) Five friends go out for a meal in a restaurant. The bill at the end of the evening comes to £110.00 The friends decide to split the bill equally. How much does each friend pay?

A fifth of £110.00 = $5\overline{)11^10.00}$ (quotient 022.00) So, each friend pays £**22.00**

b) Two fifths of the passengers on a bus are children. If there are 60 passengers on the bus, how many of them are children?

To work out $\frac{2}{5}$ of 60, we can work out $\frac{1}{5}$ of 60, and then double it.

So, $\frac{1}{5}$ of 60 = $5\overline{)6^10}$ (quotient 12) Then, 2 x 12 = 24

So, **24** of the passengers are children.

Calculating the average of a group of numbers

Division is used to calculate averages:

Worked example - The weight of 4 patients was recorded by a nurse:

	patient 1	patient 2	patient 3	patient 4
Weight(kg)	79	75	79	63

To calculate the average weight of the patients, we need to add up all the weights (total), and divide by the number of patients (number).

So, average $= \dfrac{\text{Total}}{\text{number}} = $

$$
\begin{array}{r}
79 \\
75 \\
79 \\
+\ 63 \\
\hline
296 \\
\end{array}
$$

$$296 \div 4 = 4\overline{)29^16} \quad \begin{array}{r}7\,4\end{array}$$

So, the average (mean) weight of the patients is **74 kg**

Calculating the range of a group of numbers

To calculate the range of weights recorded by the nurse, we look for the highest weight and the lowest weight, then work out the difference between them.

So, range = highest number – lowest number = 79 – 63 = **16kg**

Calculating 10% of a number

Percent means out of a hundred.

So, 10% means 10 out of a hundred, which can be written as $\dfrac{10}{100} = \dfrac{1}{10}$ (a tenth)

In order to calculate $\dfrac{1}{10}$ (or 10%) of a number, you need to divide that number by 10.

To divide a number by 10, you make the number 10 times smaller by changing the place value of the numbers. For example:

$£24.50 \div 10 = \dfrac{£24.50}{10} = £2.45 \quad £8.90 \div 10 = £0.89 \quad £65.00 \div 10 = £6.50$

Calculating 5%, 20%, 30% etc of a number

In order to calculate 5% of a number, you can find 10% of that number and then halve it. For example:

> **This week only: 5% off your dry cleaning bill !**

Calculate the discount on a usual bill of £24.00

10% of £24.00 = £2.40

5% of £24.00 = £1.20

In order to calculate 20% of a number, you can find 10% of that number (as above), and then double it. For example:

> **20% off our Chartered Flights!**
> **Usual Price: £280.00**

Calculate the discount:

10% of £280.00 = £28.00

20% of £280.00 = £28.00 x 2 = £**56.00**

In order to calculate 30% of a number, you can find 10% of that number and then treble it. For example:

> **30% off trainers!**
> **Retail Price: £45.50**

Calculate the sale price of the trainers:

10% of £45.50 = £4.55

30% of £45.50 = £4.55 x 3 = £ 4.55   Sale price = £4⁴5¹⁴5¹0
                            x 3   − £13.65
                            ─────   ─────────
                            13.65   **£31.85**
                             ─   ─────────
                             1 1

Forming a fraction, simplifying it, then converting it to a percentage

Worked example:

> During a survey carried out into the eating habits of 80 young people, it was found that 20 of them described themselves as vegetarian. What percentage of the young people are vegetarian?

So, 20 out of the 80 young people are vegetarian:

$$20 \text{ out of } 80 = \frac{20}{80}$$

We can simplify this fraction, since 20 will go into 80 (4 times) and into itself (once).

So, $\dfrac{\mathbf{20}^1}{\mathbf{80}^4} = \dfrac{\mathbf{1}}{\mathbf{4}} = \mathbf{25}\%$ (see conversion table)

Calculating area

To calculate the area of a rectangular space (e.g. the floor of a room), we need to multiply its length by its width: Area = length x width

Worked example:

A garden is 7m long and 4.5m wide. Calculate its area.

Area = length x width = 7m x 4.5m =

```
      4.5
   x    7
   _____
   3 1.5 m²
      ‾
      3
```

Calculating volume

To calculate the volume of a cuboid shape (e.g. a room in a house, or a box), we need to multiply its length by its width by its height:

Volume = length x width x height

Worked example:

The kitchen in a restaurant is measured by a builder, and is found to be 8m long, 6m wide and 2.5 m high. Calculate its volume.

Volume = length x width x height = 8m x 6m x 2.5m

When you have to multiply 3 numbers together, it's best to multiply 2 of them together first, then multiply the result by the third number.

```
So,     2.5        Then, 15 x 8 =    15
      x   6                        x  8
      _____                    _____
      1 5.0                        120        Answer = 120m³
         ‾                           ‾
         3                           4
```

Volume is usually measured in m³, cm³, litres (L) or millilitres (ml).

Multiplying by 10, 20, 30 etc.

To **divide** a number by 10 we can do the following: £12.50 ÷ 10 = £1.25

To **multiply** a number by 10 we can do the following: £12.50 x 10 = £125.00

Further examples: £65.00 x 10 = £650.00 £4.05 x 10 = £40.50

To multiply a number by 20 we can multiply it by 10 and then double it.

E.g. A receptionist earns £5.25 an hour. How much does he earn for a 40 hour week?

£5.25 x 40 = £5.25 x10 x 4 = £52.50 x 4 =

$$
\begin{array}{r}
£\ \ 52.50 \\
\text{x} \quad\ \ 4 \\
\hline
£\ \mathbf{210.00} \\
\end{array}
$$
_1 2_

Rounding up/down to the nearest whole number and to the nearest tenth

A boy's weight is recorded as 46.362kg. What is his weight to the nearest kilogram?

tens	units	tenths	hundredths	
4	**6** .	**3**	**6**	**2**

When giving an answer to the nearest whole number, there should be nothing after the decimal point. If the number after the decimal point (tenths column) is below 5, the number in the units column stays as it is.
So, answer = **46**kg

What is his weight to the nearest tenth of a kilogram?

When giving an answer to the nearest tenth, there should be just one number after the decimal point. If the number in the next column is 5 or above, the number in the tenths column is rounded up to the next number.
So, answer = **46.4**kg

Converting units

Grams and kilograms

The word 'kilo' means a thousand. There are a thousand grams (g) in a kilogram (kg):

2,000g = 2kg   220g = 0.22kg   604g = 0.604kg   30g = 0.03kg   9g = 0.009kg
1kg = 1,000g   2.2kg = 2,200g   0.5kg = 500g   0.04kg = 40g   0.006kg = 6g

Metres and kilometres

There are a thousand metres (m) in a kilometre (km):

1,000m = 1km   250m = 0.25km   65m = 0.065km   408m = 0.408km
3km = 3,000m   4.4km = 4,400m   0.73km = 730m   1.02km = 1,020m

Millimetres, centimetres and metres

The word 'cent' means a hundredth part of. There are a hundred centimetres (cm) in a metre. The word 'milli' means a thousandth part of. There are a thousand millimetres (mm) in a metre and ten millimetres in a centimetre:

1m = 100cm   3.2m = 320cm   0.6m = 60cm   0.04 = 4cm
45cm = 0.45m   204cm = 2.04m   9.5cm = 0.095m   80.5cm = 0.805m
3m = 3,000mm   1.6m = 1,600mm   0.5m = 500mm   0.35m = 350mm
1,000mm = 1m   2,500mm = 2.5m   750mm = 0.75m   75mm = 0.075m
65mm = 6.5cm   105mm = 10.5cm   55cm = 550mm   30.5cm = 305mm

Millilitres and litres

There are a thousand millilitres (ml) in a litre (L):

1,000ml = 1L   500ml = 0.5L   650ml = 0.65L   70ml = 0.07L   125ml = 0.125L
10L = 10,000ml   2.5L = 2,500ml   0.1L = 100ml   4.02L = 4,020ml

Cubic centimetres (cm^3) and cubic metres (m^3)

$1cm^3$ is equivalent to 1ml. There are 1,000L in $1m^3$. Litres and millilitres are used for measuring the volume of liquids, whilst cubic centimetres and cubic metres (m^3) are used for measuring the volume of solids or spaces.

Metric and imperial units

Metric	1kg	1km	1m	1L
Imperial	2.2 lbs	0.62miles	39.37 inches	0.22 gallons

Imperial	1 lb	1mile	1foot (12inches)	1 gallon (8 pints)
Metric	0.45kg	1,61km	30.48cm	4.546L

L1 Practice Questions

You will find while trying these questions, that the methods outlined in the L1 numeracy learning assessment, combined with a good knowledge of the times tables, should really help. As you become more familiar with the methods and the times tables, it should help speed things up for you and give you greater confidence in dealing with similar problems. Do not use a calculator!

1a T-shirts are on sale for £8.65 each. A man decides to buy 3 of them. How much does he pay?

1b Check your answer by dividing it by 3 and seeing if you obtain £8.65

1c If the man started off with £50.00 in his pocket, how much change will he have left?

2 A man receives his gas bill every 3 months. If his latest bill was £44.61 how much does that work out to be per month?

3 Three quarters of the residents of a care home are over 80 years old. If there are 36 residents in the care home, then how many of them are over eighty?

4 Five friends decide to club together to buy one of their friends a wedding present. If the present they have in mind costs £85.00 how much will they each have to put in?

5 The price of a regular latte was compared in 7 different venues and recorded in the table below:

	Venue 1	Venue 2	Venue 3	Venue 4	Venue 5	Venue 6	Venue 7
Cost (£)	2.30	1.70	1.85	2.25	1.85	2.60	2.15

5a What is the average (mean) price of a latte across the 7 venues?

5b In the above example, calculate the range of prices for a latte across the 7 venues.

6a Eight hundred and twenty people attend a concert. If two fifths of them are women, then how many of the people at the concert are women?

6b Check your answer by converting two fifths to a percentage, then calculating that percentage of eight hundred and twenty.

7 A traffic engineer monitors the traffic flow through a busy town centre. He records that out of 600 cars, 30% of them have sole occupancy (one person in the car). How many of the cars have sole occupancy?

8 3/5 of the mechanics working at a garage are on an apprenticeship programme:

a 3/5 as a percentage is written as: ....

b 3/5 as a decimal is written as: ....

9 It is predicted that soon, approximately 10% of books bought in this country will be bought online:

a 10% as a decimal is written as: ....

b 10% as a fraction is written as: ....

10 A man buys 30 litres of unleaded petrol at a garage. If the cost of unleaded petrol is 108.9p per litre, how much does he pay?

11 A pane of glass measures 2.2 m by 0.5 m. Calculate its area.

12 An interior designer measures the area of a living room, and works it out to be 42m². If the length of the living room is 7m then how wide is it?

13 The kitchen in a restaurant is measured by a builder, and is found to be 8m long, 6m wide and 2.5 m high. Calculate its volume.

14 A festival organiser employs 150 part-time workers for one day. If they each work 6 hours, and are paid £6.00 per hour, then what is the total amount paid for the workers?

15 A part-time receptionist at a sport centre is paid £6.20 per hour, and works 20 hours a week. How much does he earn in 4 weeks?

16 In an engineering class, there are 42 students. If 14 of the students are female, then what percentage of the students is female?

17 In a class of 15 students, it was found that 3 of the students had a learning disability. What percentage of the students had a learning disability?

18 Usain Bolt of Jamaica won the 200m gold medal at the 2008 Olympic Games in Beijing in a world record time of 19.30 seconds. If he broke the world record by two hundredths of a second (0.02 seconds), then what was the previous world record?

19 A tailor cuts 3.4m from a 20m length of cloth. How much does he have left?

20 A man leaves his house in the morning with £50.00 and spends £22.38 in his local leisure centre. How much money does he have left?

21 A couple are saving to put down a £36,000 deposit on a house. They have £23,350 saved. How much more do they need?

22 It was reported in a newspaper in August 2008 that there were 11.58 million pensioners and 11.52 million under-16s currently living in the UK. Calculate how many more pensioners there are than under-16s:

a as a number ....

b in words ....

23 In a children's playgroup, there is one child carer for every three children. If there are 18 children, then how many child carers are there?

24 A car is found, on average, to emit 300g of carbon dioxide into the atmosphere for every kilometre it travels. How many kilograms of carbon dioxide will it emit into the air during a 30km journey?

25 If a tin of baked beans weighs 400g, what would be the weight in kilograms of a case of 30 tins of baked beans?

26 A jogger records the distance she runs one morning as 4.05km. Calculate how many metres she has run?

27 A sandwich shop owner buys a 7.5m roll of kitchen foil in order to wrap his long baguettes. If he needs 50cm of kitchen roll to wrap each one, how many can he wrap with the 7.5m roll?

28 A man is training to take part in a cross-channel swimming relay, where each swimmer needs to swim 3.5 km. He trains in his local 'Olympic-sized' swimming pool which is 50m long. How many lengths would he have to swim during his training to reach 3.5km?

29 A man weighs himself and records his weight as 65.455kg. What is his weight to the nearest kilogram?

30 The length of a field is measured as 50.272m. What is the length of the field to the nearest tenth of a metre?

L2 Numeracy Learning Guide

Name: ....   **Date:** ....

This guide is intended to assist learners in developing their everyday numeracy skills. It builds on the skills gained (and the methods used) from the L1 numeracy learning assessment and contains worked examples and practice questions.

Forming and simplifying fractions

Worked Example:

A survey was carried out in a coffee shop to find out the popularity of different types of coffee.

Type of coffee	Number of people
Latte	87
Americano	44
Machiato	65
Espresso	68

Calculate the proportion of people who chose Americano as their favourite type of coffee.

Initially, we need to find the total number of people who took part in the survey. We can do this by adding up the numbers in the table.

$$
\begin{array}{r}
87 \\
44 \\
65 \\
+\ 68 \\
\hline
\mathbf{264} \\
\end{array}
$$
2

Then, we need to form a fraction.

So **44** out of the **264** people who took part in the survey chose Americano as their favourite type of coffee.

44 out of 264 = $\dfrac{44}{264}$

We then need to simplify the fraction.

$$\frac{44}{264} = \frac{22}{132} = \frac{11}{66}$$

We can simplify further as 11 will go into the top and bottom:

$$\frac{\cancel{11}^{1}}{\cancel{66}^{6}} = \frac{1}{6} \quad \text{(a sixth)}$$

Questions – Forming and Simplifying Fractions

Q1 A new sports centre opens in Milton Keynes. The following table shows the number of visitors who used the different facilities during the opening hour of its opening day:

Facility:	Leisure pool	Table tennis	Badminton	Climbing wall
Number of visitors:	43	28	33	36

What proportion of the visitors played table tennis during the opening hour?

Q2 The following table shows the number of children who took part in a school's end of term activities:

Activity:	Number of Children:
Outdoor Sports	41
Indoor Sports	17
Board Games	20
Computer Club	41
Arts & Crafts	34

Calculate the proportion of children who chose indoor sports for their end of term activity.

Converting from fractions to percentages

To convert from a decimal (or fraction) to a percentage, we need to multiply the decimal (or fraction) by 100% so,

$$1/4 \times 100\% \;=\; \frac{100}{4} \;=\; 4\overline{)10^2 0}^{\,25} \;=\; 25\%$$

$$1/5 \times 100\% \;=\; \frac{100}{5} \;=\; 5\overline{)100}^{\,20} \;=\; 20\%$$

$$1/8 \times 100\% \;=\; \frac{100}{8} \;=\; 8\overline{)10^2 0.\!^4 0}^{\,12.5} \;=\; 12.5\%$$

$$1/6 \times 100\% \;=\; \frac{100}{6} \;=\; 6\overline{)10^4 0.\!^4 0^4 0}^{\,16.66} \;=\; 16.7\% \quad \text{(to 1 decimal place)}$$

Converting from fractions to decimals

$\dfrac{1}{4}$ is one divided by four, $1 \div 4$ or $4\overline{)1.0^2 0}^{\,0.25} \;=\; 0.25$

$\dfrac{1}{5}$ is one divided by five, $1 \div 5$ or $5\overline{)1.00}^{\,0.20} \;=\; 0.20$

$\dfrac{1}{8}$ is one divided by eight, $1 \div 8$ or $8\overline{)1.0^2 0^4 0}^{\,0.125} \;=\; 0.125$

$\dfrac{1}{6}$ is one divided by six, $1 \div 6$ or $6\overline{)1.0^4 0^4 0^4 0}^{\,0.1666'} \;=\; 0.167$

Here, we can round up to 3 decimal places (3 numbers after the decimal point), so 0.1666' recurring becomes 0.167

Converting from decimals to percentages

0 . 2 5   x 100 = 25%

0 . 2 0   x 100 = 20%

0 . 1 2 5 x 100 = 12.5%

0 . 1 6 7 x 100 = 16.7%

Converting from percentages to fractions to decimals

Percent means 'out of a hundred'.

$$25\% \quad = \quad \frac{25.}{100} \quad = \quad 0.25$$

$$20\% \quad = \quad \frac{20.}{100} \quad = \quad 0.20$$

$$12.5.\% \quad = \quad \frac{12.5}{100} \quad = \quad 0.125$$

$$23\% \quad = \quad \frac{23.}{100} \quad = \quad 0.23$$

$$68\% \quad = \quad \frac{68.}{100} \quad = \quad 0.68$$

$$17.5\% \quad = \quad \frac{17.5}{100} \quad = \quad 0.175$$

Questions – Converting from fractions to decimals to percentages (and vice-versa).

Complete the following 'Fractions/Percentages/Decimals Conversion Tables.'

Complete the Fractions column first, then use the blank pages below to convert the fractions to decimals and percentages.

For the decimals column, give your answer to 3 decimal places (3 numbers after the decimal point). For the percentages column, give your answer to 1 decimal place (one number after the decimal point):

Fractions/Percentages/Decimal Conversion Table

	Fraction	Percentage	Decimal

	Fraction	Percentage	Decimal

Calculating percentages

When you calculate 10% of a number, you make the number 10 times smaller by changing the place value of the numbers. For example:

10% of £186.00 = £18.60 (See L1 learning assessment)

To calculate 1% of a number, the number is made 10 times smaller again:

1% of £1 8 6 . 0 0 = £1.86

Then, if we wish to calculate say 23% of £186.00 we can use the following method:

10%	=	£ 18.60		1%	=	£ 1.86
20%	=	£ 18.60		3%	=	£ 1.86
		x 2				x 3
		£ 37.20				£ 5.58
		1 1				2 1

So, 23% = 20% + 3% =   37.20
                     +   5.58
                        £ **42.78**
                           1

Worked Example:

VAT @ 17.5% needs to be added to a bill of £92.00. Calculate the VAT.

10% = £9.20   1% = £ 0.92   0.5% = £0.46

7% =   0.92
   x   7
   £ 6.44
      1

17.5% = 10% + 7% + 0.5% =   9.20
                             6.44
                             0.46
                          £ 16.10
                            1 1

Questions - Calculating Percentages

Q1 There are 900 men and women at a barbecue. If 57% of the people are men, then calculate the number of women at the barbecue.

Q2 A car is valued at £16,500.00. Calculate the cost of the car after VAT (@17.5%) has been added.

Q3 Twenty three thousand six hundred people attend a free park concert. If 26% of them are children, then calculate the number of children at the concert.

Q4 In a recent survey, people were asked which of 6 cuisines (Indian, Chinese, Italian, Turkish, Mexican or Thai) they preferred. The results were presented in the following pie chart:

Pie chart (based on a survey) representing people's preferred cuisine

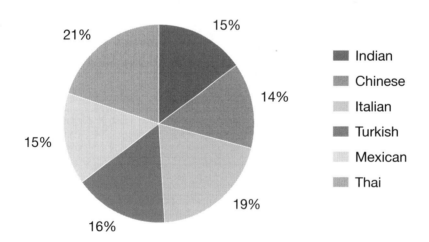

If 350 people took part in the survey, then calculate how many people chose Turkish as their preferred cuisine?

Calculating percentage increase (or decrease)

Worked example:

The table below compares electricity bills in 2006 with those in 2007 for 3 separate households:

	2006	2007
Household 1	£704	£880
Household 2	£675	£810
Household 3	£760	£798

Calculate the percentage increase in the cost of the electricity bills between 2006 and 2007 for each of the 3 households.

When calculating percentage increase, we can use the following method:

$$\frac{\text{actual increase}}{\text{original amount}} \times 100\%$$

So, for household 1, actual increase $= \begin{array}{r} 8\,^7\!8\,^1\!0 \\ -\ 7\,0\,4 \\ \hline 1\,7\,6 \end{array}$

$$\frac{\text{actual increase}}{\text{original amount}} = \frac{176}{704} = \frac{88}{352} = \frac{44}{176} = \frac{22}{88} = \frac{11}{44} = \frac{1}{4} \qquad \frac{1}{4} \times 100\% = \textbf{25\%}$$

For household 2, actual increase $= \begin{array}{r} ^7\!8\,^{10}\!4\,^1\!0 \\ -\ 6\,7\,5 \\ \hline 1\,3\,5 \end{array}$

$$\frac{\text{actual increase}}{\text{original amount}} = \frac{135}{675} = \frac{27}{135} = \frac{9}{45} = \frac{3}{15} = \frac{1}{5} \qquad \frac{1}{5} \times 100\% = \textbf{20\%}$$

For household 3, actual increase $= \begin{array}{r} 798 \\ -\ 760 \\ \hline 38 \end{array}$

$$\frac{\text{actual increase}}{\text{original increase}} = \frac{38}{760} = \frac{19}{380} = \frac{1}{20} = \qquad \frac{1}{20} \times 100\% = \textbf{5\%}$$

When calculating percentage decrease, we can use the following method:

$$\frac{\text{actual decrease}}{\text{original amount}} \times 100\%$$

Questions – Calculating percentage increase (or decrease)

The following bar chart compares the prices of 2 houses in a town in England between 2006 and 2007

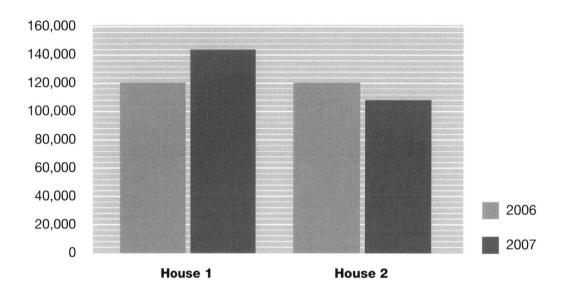

Q1a Calculate the percentage increase in the house price of House 1 between 2006 and 2007

Q1b Calculate the percentage decrease in the house price of House 2 between 2006 and 2007

Q2 In a recent bye - election, one of the main parties increased its vote from 12,500 to 16,250. Calculate the percentage increase in the party's vote.

Q3 A patient's temperature is recorded every 2 hours over a 12 hour period, and recorded in the table below:

Time:	8.00	10.00	12.00	14.00	16.00	18.00	20.00
Temperature (0C):	36.2	36.0	36.4	36.5	36.9	37.2	37.8

Calculate the percentage increase in the patient's temperature between 10.00 am and 8 pm

Calculations involving Multiplication

Worked examples:

1. A coaching assistant is paid £6.48 per hour. Calculate how much he earns in a 37.5 hour week.

£6.48 x 37.5

(37.5 = 30 + 7 + 0.5)

£6.48 x 30 = £64.80   £6.48 x 7 = £6.48   £6.48 x 0.5 = £3.24

                x   3   x   7
          ──────────   ──────────
          £194.40   £45.36
          ‾1‾2‾   ‾3‾5‾

So, £6.48 x 37.5 = 194.40

                        45.36

              +   3.24
          ──────────
          £ **243.00**
          ‾1‾1‾1‾1‾

2. A warehouse operative works 148 hours over a four week period. If she is paid £6.75 per hour, then calculate her pay over the four week period.

£6.75 x 148

(148 = 100 + 40 + 8)

£6.7 5 x 100 = £675.00   £6.75 x 40 = £67.50   £6.75

                                          x _____4   x ___8

                                          £270.00   £54.00
                                            3 2   6 4

So, £6.75 x 148 =   675
                      270
                  +   54
                  ‾‾‾‾‾‾‾‾
                    £**999**
                       1

Questions - Calculations involving multiplication

Q1 A barman is paid £5.85 per hour. Calculate how much he earns for a 36 hour week.

Q2 If the same barman works 8 hours overtime one Sunday, at time and a half, then calculate how much he earns on that Sunday.

Q3 A hotel receptionist works 42.5 hours in a week. If he is paid £6.00 per hour, calculate how much he earns in:

a) a week   b) four weeks

Q4a A chef is paid £6.30 per hour. If he works 175 hours in a month, then calculate how much he is paid for that month.

Q4b If the same chef continues to work for the same amount of hours every month over the period of a year, then calculate how much he will earn in a year.

Q5 The diagram below shows a plan of 2 adjacent lawns.

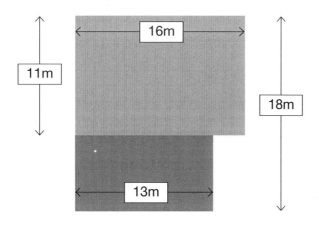

Calculate their combined areas

Q6 Calculate the area of a warehouse which is 63m long by 22.4m wide.

Q7 A gardener who maintains a nearby lawn wishes to replace the topsoil. If the lawn measures 22m by 15m and the depth of the topsoil is 20cm calculate the volume of the topsoil.

Q8 If a tin of soup weighs 450g then calculate the weight of 33 tins of soup. (Give your answer in kilograms.)

Mean, Range, Median and Mode

A company director decides to carry out a survey relating to the age of the company's 14 employees. She records the following data in order to calculate the mean, range, median and mode:

Age of employees: 22, 31, 28, 18, 22, 31, 38, 31, 23, 26, 25, 24, 31, 28

Mean

The mean (or average) of a set of data is obtained by adding up all the individual pieces of data, and dividing the total by the number of pieces of data.

So, looking at the above data, the mean = 378 divided by 14

$$= 378 \div 14 = \frac{378}{14} = 14 \overline{)37^98} \quad \text{So, the mean} = \mathbf{27}$$

$$\begin{array}{r} 027 \end{array}$$

$$\begin{array}{r} 14 \\ \times \quad 7 \\ \hline 98 \\ \hline 2 \end{array}$$

Range

The range of a set of data is obtained by finding the difference between the highest number and the lowest number within that data.

i.e. Range = highest number – lowest number = 38 – 18 = **20**

Median

The median of a set of data, is the number that occurs in the middle when the data is placed in ascending order.

18, 22, 22, 23, 24, 25, 26, 28, 28, 31, 31, 31, 31, 38

When there is an even number of pieces of data (in this case 14), then the median is the average of the two middle numbers (the 7th and 8th numbers).

So, looking at the above data, median = $\frac{26 + 28}{2}$ = **27**

Mode

The mode of a set of data is the number which occurs most frequently within that data.

Looking at the above data, **31** is the number that occurs most frequently (it occurs four times, which is more than for any other number in the data).

Questions - Mean, Range, Median and Mode

Q1 The following table records an airline's prices for flights from London to Madrid during a week in February:

Date:	4/2/08	4/2/08	5/2/08	5/2/08	6/2/08	6/2/08	7/2/08
Dep time:	9.30	16.45	7.40	16.30	9.30	16.45	7.40
Arr time:	13.00	20.15	11.10	19.55	13.00	20.15	11.10
Cost:	£43.00	£47.00	£43.00	£47.00	£43.00	£47.00	£43.00

Date:	7/2/08	8/2/08	8/2/08	9/2/08	9/2/08	10/2/08
Dep time:	16.30	9.30	16.45	7.40	16.30	7.45
Arr time:	19.55	13.00	20.15	11.10	19.55	11.05
Cost:	£53.00	£46.00	£56.00	£46.00	£61.00	£49.00

1a Calculate the average (mean) cost of the flights over the week.

1b Calculate the range of flight costs over the week.

1c Calculate the median cost from the above data.

1d Calculate the mode from the costs in the above data.

Ratios

We can use ratios to compare numbers.

Worked example:

> 546 people turn up at a local cinema for the opening night of the new, 'James Bond' film. Of these, 135 are men, 75 are women, 192 are boys and 144 are girls. Calculate the ratio of:

a) men to women

The ratio of men to women is 135 to 75 which can be written as 135 : 75
Like with fractions, we can simplify ratios by doing the same to both sides. So, for the ratio of 135 : 75 we can divide both sides by 5
Then, 135 : 75 becomes 27 : 15
We can simplify further by dividing both sides by 3
So, 27 : 15 becomes **9 : 5** (and this is its simplest form).

b) girls to boys

The ratio of girls to boys is 144 : 192 = 72 : 96 = 36 : 48
Both sides can be divided by 12 so, 36 : 48 becomes **3 : 4**

c) adults to children

$$
\begin{array}{ll}
\text{The number of adults is} \quad 135 & \text{The number of children is} \quad 192 \\
\qquad\qquad\qquad\quad + \ 75 & \qquad\qquad\qquad\qquad\quad + \ 144 \\
\qquad\qquad\qquad\quad \overline{210} & \qquad\qquad\qquad\qquad\quad \overline{336} \\
\qquad\qquad\qquad\quad {\scriptstyle 1\ 1} & \qquad\qquad\qquad\qquad\quad {\scriptstyle 1}
\end{array}
$$

So, the ratio of adults to children is 210 : 336 = 105 : 168

Both numbers can be divided by 3 (we can tell this because if we add up the digits of each number, the sums are divisible by 3).

i.e. 1 + 5 = 6 (which is divisible by 3) and 1 + 6 + 8 = 15 (which is also divisible by 3)

So, 105 : 168 = 35 : 56

Both sides can be divided by 7, so 35 : 56 becomes **5 : 8**

Questions – Ratios

Q1 The following pie chart shows the proportion of people by sector studying for an apprenticeship with a work-based learning provider:

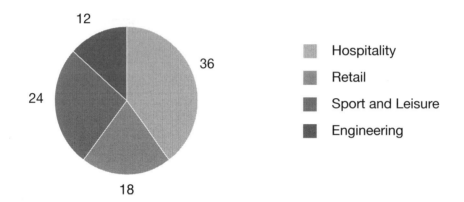

From the above data, calculate the ratio of apprenticeship trainees across the four sectors i.e. hospitality to retail to sport and leisure to engineering

Q2 Within the hospitality sector, the trainee apprentices are working towards the following NVQs;

Food and drink service (15)   Food processing (9)

Customer service (6)   Front of house (6)

From the above data, calculate the ratio of apprenticeship trainees across the 4 NVQs.

Q3 In a supermarket, the ratio of 'boxes of strawberries' to 'boxes of blueberries' sold in one day is 13 : 2
If there were 208 boxes of strawberries sold, then calculate the number of boxes of blueberries that were sold.

Q4 The following table shows the number of ascents made by climbers in 2006 on the world's five highest mountains:

Mountain:	Mount Everest	K2	Kangchenjunga	Lhotse	Makalu
Height of Mountain (ft):	29,035	28,250	28,169	27,940	27,766
Height of Mountain (m):	8,850	8,611	8,586	8,516	8,463
Number of ascents:	145	45	38	26	45

From the above data :–

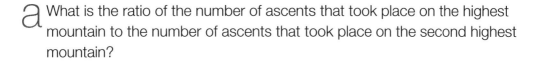 What is the ratio of the number of ascents that took place on the highest mountain to the number of ascents that took place on the second highest mountain?

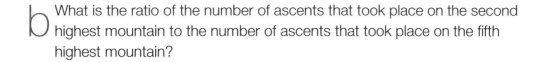 What is the ratio of the number of ascents that took place on the second highest mountain to the number of ascents that took place on the fifth highest mountain?

Priming learners for level 2 Functional Skills maths

Q1 The cost of hiring a new model of car is £199 per week. If the car is hired for more than eight weeks, then there is a discount of 15% for each additional week. Calculate the cost of hiring five new models of the car for three months.

Check one of your answers:

Q2 Five members of the public take part in a series of radio quizzes over a period of time and their mean results are recorded in the table below:

Name	Mean (%)	Range (%)
Sarah	72	20
John	79	20
Frances	60	12
Simona	67	15
Afshah	72	10

If you had to choose two of the above for your radio quiz team, which two would you choose? Give two reasons for your choices. One reason should relate to the mean and the other should relate to the range.

Q3 A classroom measures 6.5m by 4m and has carpet tiles on the floor. If each tile measures 50cm by 50cm, then calculate the number of carpet tiles there are on the floor. Show your workings.

Q4 Seven random people were asked about their savings. They gave the following answers:

£500   £718   £0   £86   £6,900   £10,000   £5,000

a Calculate the range of results

b Calculate either the mean or the median

c Check one of your results above

d Explain why you chose the mean or the median.

In another sample group of seven people, the range of results was found to be £320.

e If the person with the highest savings in this group had £915 in the bank, then calculate how much the person with the lowest savings had.

f Write a comment comparing the ranges in the two groups.

Q5 There are three beads in a bag. Two are red and one is green. If one is chosen at random from the bag, what are the chances of it being a red? Show your answer on a probability scale.

Q6 If two coins are flipped, what are the chances of both coins being a head? Show your answer on a probability scale.

Coin 1   **Coin 2**
Heads   Heads

Q7 Tim, Bill and Sarah had an investment worth £225,000 two years ago. Now the investment has grown by 10%.

a What is the value of the investment now?

b The three decide to close the business and divide the investment in the ratio of 2 : 3 : 5
   How much will each person get?

Q8 The current world record for the men's marathon is 2:02:57, set by Dennis Kimetto of Kenya on September 28, 2014, at the Berlin Marathon. The total distance for the marathon is 41.92km.

a Assuming he kept an even pace all the way round the course then what would have been his time (to the nearest second) a quarter of the way around the course?

b Calculate the distance (in km) travelled a quarter of the way around the course.

C   If 1 mile = 1.6 km, then calculate the number of miles of the marathon.

Q9 The following table shows the weights (in kg) of 20 suitcases:

10.5	7.8	20.0	7.4	20.1	9.3	19.5	11	12.4	11.0	**Total**
16.3	10.1	11.6	8.5	13.0	11.2	13.5	9.8	8.0	9.0	**240**

Calculate:

a   The mean weight of the suitcases. Show your workings.

b   The range of the weights. Show your workings.

c   The mode of the weights.

d   The median value of the weights. Show your workings.

e   Check one of your answers.

f   If one of the suitcases is chosen at random, what is the probability of its weight being higher than the mean weight? Show your answer on a probability scale.

10   A group of 20 students were asked to rate a film they had seen by giving it a mark out of ten. When the results were analysed, the range of marks was found to be 1. Write a comment about the range.

11   The value of an investment was £2,000,000. There was a 10% loss in value last year.

a What was the value of the investment at the end of last year? Show your workings.

b The owners of the investment were advised to add 15% of the original investment to the business to improve the value. How much money would need to be added to the original investment and what would the new value be? Show your workings.

12 A tiler wishes to tile a wall measuring 3m by 2.5m using square tiles of side 25cm.

a Calculate how many tiles he needs.

b If the tiles come in boxes of 50 and cost £79.50 (plus VAT @ 20%) a box, then calculate the cost of the tiles.

c Check one of your answers:

13 A retail shop made a profit of £72,122 at the end of a particular year. If the profit was to be shared amongst Peter, Sam and Vivian (the owners of the shop) in the ratio of 2 : 3 : 4 then find out how much each person will get to the nearest penny.

14 Johnny and Rash made a meal from the ingredients following the recipe given below:

	Johnny	Rash
Flour	15% of 200g	1/5 of 180g
Oil	0.2kg	190g
Sugar	75g	0.08kg
Salt	5g	0.005kg
Colouring	10% of 10g	0.5g

Determine who will use the highest weight of ingredients.

15 Table tops are made from sheets of wood:

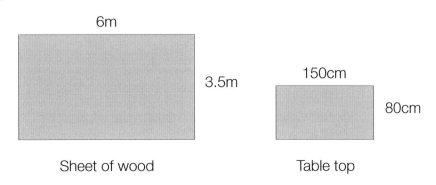

6m

3.5m

Sheet of wood

150cm

80cm

Table top

a How many sheets of wood are required to make 60 table tops?

b 250ml of varnish is needed for one coating of a table top. Varnish comes in 5L tins. If two coats are required, then calculate the number of tins of varnish needed to varnish all the table tops.

16 A metal sphere has its circumference measured and is found to be 20cm. Calculate its volume. Volume of a sphere $= \dfrac{4 \pi r^3}{3}$

17 If the exchange rate between the Euro and the pound is: 1€ = £0.91 then calculate how many Euros (to the nearest cent) you would get from £70

18 The thickness of the ten piece was increased in January 2011 from 1.7mm to 1.9mm. Calculate the percentage increase in the thickness of the coin (to the nearest whole number).

19 Two friends visit a fitness centre following which they both decide to lose some weight. Jamal weighs 94kg while his friend Byron weighs 198 pounds (lbs).
Jamal is informed that in order for his Body Mass Index to be within the 'normal' range, he must lose one eighth of his weight. Jamal is informed that in order for his Body Mass Index to be within the 'normal' range, he must lose eight percent of his weight. Calculate the difference (in kilograms) in weight between the two friends if both are successful in losing their required amount of weight.

20 Twenty one adult students across three classes, who are initially assessed at level 1, inform their tutor that they wish to achieve level 1 and level 2 functional skills maths within one academic year. If all the students initially passed their L1 functional skills maths test and went on to take the level 2 test, and if the overall pass rate for the students (including all L1 and L2 tests) was approximately 93% then calculate how many students passed the L2 functional skills maths test.

21 The following shows a scatter-graph of average temperature (°C) in the UK over a period of 8 weeks.

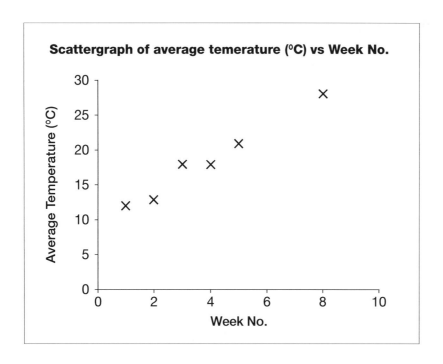

a   On the scatter graph above, plot a trend line (line of best fit).

b   Using the trend line, estimate the average temperature for week 7.

c   Write a comment about the average temperature in the UK over the period of 8 weeks.

22   The following shows a scatter-graph of sales of rowing machines over a period of 12 months.

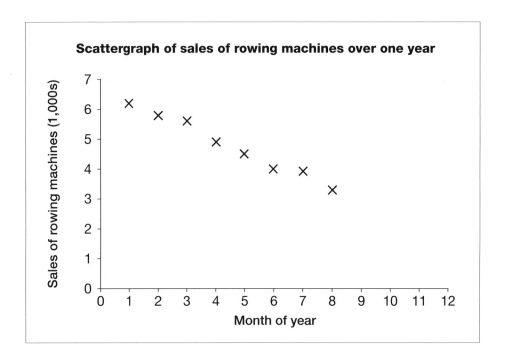

Scattergraph of sales of rowing machines over one year

Sales of rowing machines (1,000s)

Month of year

On the horizontal axis of the scatter graph above, 1 represents January and 2 represents February etc.

a   On the graph, plot a trend line (line of best fit).

b   Using the trend line, estimate the sales of rowing machines in November.

c   Write a comment about the sales of rowing machines over the course of the year.

23 Twelve plane passengers had their waiting times passing through passport control recorded at an airport. The airport's policy/target with regard to waiting time states:

"The average waiting time for passengers passing through passport control should be less than one and a half hours."

1hr 15mins	1 hr 25mins	2 hrs 10 mins	2hrs
1hr 30 mins	1hr 45 mins	1 hr 45 mins	1 hr 30 mins
1hr 45 mins	1hr 35mins	1 hr 20 mins	1hr 12 mins

a Has the airport met its target? Show your workings and explain your answer.

b Calculate the percentage of passengers that had to wait an hour and a half or longer to pass through passport control.

c Calculate the range of waiting times from the above sample.

A second sample of twelve passengers passing through passport control had their waiting times recorded. The mean waiting time was found to be one hour and forty eight minutes and the range of waiting times was found to be one hour and six minutes.

d If the lowest waiting time in the second sample was the same as in the first sample, then calculate the longest waiting time in the second sample.

e Draw a bar graph to compare the mean waiting times for the two samples of passengers, and include the airport's target for waiting times.

24 Look at the line graph below, which shows the changes in percentage obesity levels between 1993 and 2004.

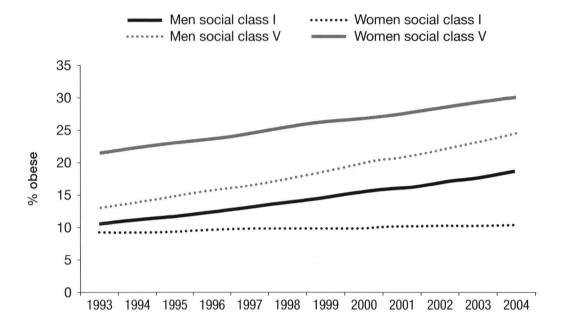

a Write a general statement about what the line graph shows.

b Write a comment comparing obesity levels of men and women.

C Write a comment comparing obesity levels of men and women of social class 1 with men and women of social class V.

25 Study the line graphs below, which show how life expectancy changed between 1972–76 and 2002–05.

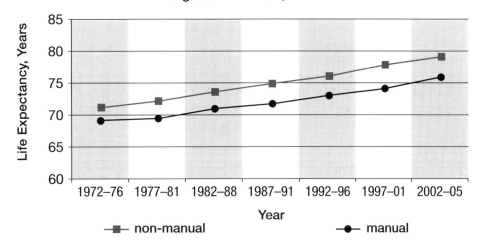

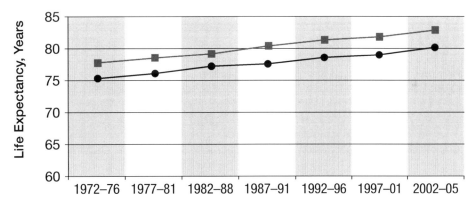

a Write a comment about the general trend of life expectancy in the UK between the years 1972 and 2005

b Write a comment comparing the life expectancy of non-manual workers with manual workers.

c Write a comment comparing the life expectancy of men with women.

26 A report by the High Pay Centre think-tank in August 2017 calculated that on average, Britain's top Chief Executive Officers (CEOs) from the FTSE 100 index (a share index of the top 100 companies listed on the Stock Exchange) were paid 130 times that of their average employee. The figures illustrate a dramatic rise in executive pay in relation to most UK workers over the past couple of decades, since in 1998, the average top executive was paid 47 times that of their average employee.

a If the average pay of the top 100 CEOs last year was four and a half million pounds, then from the above data, calculate the average pay (to the nearest pound) of the top 100 companies' employees.

b If the average annual salary of a full-time UK worker is £28,000 then calculate how long (to the nearest year) he/she would have to work to earn what an average FTSE 100 CEO is paid in one year.

27 Since the gambling industry became deregulated in 2005, **on-line gambling** has been described as Britain's biggest hidden crisis and, with 400,000 hidden addicts, a problem that disproportionately affects poor families. Furthermore, it has been argued that the surge in the habit has coincided with the inexorable rise of TV shows offering instant stardom. If gamblers using fixed odd betting machines (which have been linked to addiction, family breakdown, debt and money laundering) can wager £100 every 20 seconds, then calculate how much a gambler could lose in half an hour.

28 In 2017, an Australian human rights group, released research estimating that almost 46 million men, women and children were trapped in jobs into which they were coerced or deceived and which they cannot leave, in other words, **modern day slavery!** The report ranks incidences of slavery in 167 countries, with India, China, Pakistan, Bangladesh and Uzbekistan accounting for approximately half of the total. India is reported to have the highest number of slaves (18.4 million) while North Korea has the highest percentage of slaves per capita. This year's estimates are nearly 30% higher than in a previous report, which estimated 35.8 million people living in slavery in 2014, and more than double those by the International Labour Organisation (ILO), which estimated in 2012 that 20.9 million were trapped in modern day slavery! The human rights group says the rise is partially due to a more accurate methodology, but also that the number of people trapped in slavery is increasing year on year. Of those suffering in forced labour, around 90% are in the private economy, exploited by individuals or enterprises (through sexual exploitation and in activities such as agriculture, construction, domestic work and manufacturing), whilst around 10% work in state-imposed forms of modern day slavery, for example in prisons under conditions which violate ILO standards, or in work imposed by the state military or by rebel armed forces.
The current population of the world is estimated to be around 7.5 billion.

a Reflecting on the above statistics, estimate (to one decimal place) the percentage of people in the world who are living in slavery.

b Give your answer as a number of people (to the nearest whole number) out of a thousand.

29 It is well known that historically, disabled people have faced exclusion and discrimination. However, in August, 2017, a UN report, in the form of a 17 page document, was highly critical of the UK's record on almost every area covered by the UN convention on the rights of persons with disabilities. The report found that The UK government is failing to uphold disabled people's rights across a range of areas from education, work and housing to health, transport and social security. It drew attention to current concerns over disabled people's living conditions, including assertions that due to austerity measures, around a half a million disabled people had lost between two and three thousand pounds a year.

Based on the above figures, between which two values does the total amount of money lost by disabled people due to austerity fall?

30 **Female Genital Mutilation** (FGM), also known as female genital cutting and female circumcision, comprises all procedures that involve partial or total removal of the external female genitalia, or other injury to the female genital organs for non-medical reasons (World Health Organisation). There are no health benefits to FGM and it is recognised internationally as a human rights violation. The practice is rooted in gender inequality, attempts to control women's sexuality, and ideas about purity, modesty and beauty.

UNICEF estimated in 2016 that around 200 million women have undergone the procedures in more than 29 countries across Africa, parts of the Middle East and South East Asia, and countries where migrants from FGM affected communities live. In the UK for example, it is estimated that 137,000 girls and women are living with the consequences of FGM and that 60,000 girls under 15 are at risk.

The prevalence of FGM in females aged 15 to 49 in 29 different countries is highlighted below:

Somalia (98%) Guinea (97%) Djibouti (93%) Sierra Leone (90%) Mali (89%) Egypt (87%) Sudan (87%) Eritrea (83%) Burkina Faso (76%) Gambia (75%) Ethiopia (74%) Mauritania (69%) Liberia (50%) Guinea-Bissau (45%) Chad (44%) Côte d'Ivoire (38%) Nigeria (25%) Senegal (25%) Central African Republic (24%) Kenya (21%) Yemen (19%) United Republic of Tanzania (15%) Benin (9%) Iraq (8%) Togo (5%) Ghana (4%) Niger (2%) Uganda (1%) Cameroon (1%)

(Source: UNICEF, February 2016)

The prevalence of FGM in females aged 0 to 14 in 29 different countries is highlighted below:

Gambia (56%) Mauritania (54%) Indonesia (49%, 0–11) Guinea (46%) Eritrea (33%) Sudan (32%) Guinea-Bissau (30%) Ethiopia (24%) Nigeria (17%) Yemen (15%) Egypt (14%) Burkina Faso (13%) Sierra Leone (13%) Senegal (13%) Côte d'Ivoire (10%) Kenya (3%) Uganda (1%) Central African Republic (1%) Ghana (1%) Togo (0.3%)Benin (0.2%)

(Source: UNICEF, February 2016)

From the above data, calculate which country has the median prevalence of FGM in females aged 15 to 49

From the above data, calculate which country has the median prevalence of FGM in females aged 0 to 14

31 **Dynamic pricing**, which is the process of the fluctuation of prices for on-line goods and services, is becoming widespread across the internet and experts believe that in future, every shopper may pay a different amount for the same product as retailers use data to tailor prices to a person's buying habits or assumed wealth. It has been argued that changes can be so rapid, that it can be hard for consumers to know if they are getting a good vale for money.

The cost of a barbecue on a website is £125 If it increases by 160% as summer approaches, then calculate the new cost of the barbecue.

32 Read and engage with the following facts and statistics relating to domestic violence, mental health, and the correlation between life expectancy and working environment.

General facts on domestic violence

- 2 women are killed every week in England and Wales by a current or former partner (Office of National Statistics, 2015) – 1 woman killed every 3 days

- 1 in 4 women in England and Wales will experience domestic violence in their lifetimes and 8% will suffer domestic violence in any given year (Crime Survey of England and Wales, 2013/14)

- Globally, 1 in 3 women will experience violence at the hands of a male partner (State of the World's Fathers Report, MenCare, 2015)

- Domestic violence has a higher rate of repeat victimisation than any other crime (Home Office, July 2002)

- Every minute police in the UK receive a domestic assistance call – yet only 35% of domestic violence incidents are reported to the police (Stanko, 2000 & Home Office, 2002)

- The 2001/02 British Crime Survey (BCS) found that there were an estimated 635,000 incidents of domestic violence in England and Wales. 81% of the victims were women and 19% were men. Domestic violence incidents also made up nearly 22% of all violent incidents reported by participants in the BCS (Home Office, July 2002)

- On average, a woman is assaulted 35 times before her first call to the police (Jaffe, 1982)

General facts on mental health
Trends in mental illness

- One adult in six had a common mental disorder (CMD): about one woman in five and one man in eight. Since 2000, overall rates of CMD in England have steadily increased in women and remained largely stable in men.

- Reported rates of self-harming have increased in men and women and across age groups since 2007. However, much of this increase in reporting may have been due to greater awareness about the behaviour.

- Young women have emerged as a high-risk group, with high rates of CMD, self-harm, and positive screens for posttraumatic stress disorder (PTSD) and bipolar disorder. The gap between young women and young men has increased.

- Most mental disorders were more common in people living alone, in poor physical health, and not employed. Claimants of Employment and Support Allowance (ESA), a benefit aimed at those unable to work due to poor health or disability, experienced particularly high rates of all the disorders assessed.

- Last academic year (2015/16), more than 15,000 UK based 1st year students disclosed a mental health condition, which is more than 5 times the number it was 10 years ago.

Trends in treatment and service use

- One person in three with CMD reported current use of mental health treatment in 2014, an increase from the one in four who reported this in 2000 and 2007. This was driven by steep increases in reported use of psychotropic medication. Increased use of psychological therapies was also evident among people with more severe CMD symptoms.

- There were demographic inequalities in who received treatment. After controlling for level of need, people who were White British, female, or in mid-life (especially aged 35 to 54) were more likely to receive treatment. People in the Black ethnic group had particularly low treatment rates.

- Socioeconomic inequalities in treatment use were less evident, although people living in lower income households were more likely to have requested but not received a particular mental health treatment.

- Since 2007, people with CMD had become more likely to use community services and more likely to discuss their mental health with a GP.

Correlation between life expectancy and working environment

Research carried out within the civil service by world-renowned epidemiologist Sir Michael Marmot (2004) to look at links between how long you live, social class and how powerful and wealthy you are, concluded that people working in environments where they have a lack of control over their own positions, alongside high demands and low support, suffer greater workplace stress and, as a result, are at greater risk of heart disease, mental illness, cancer and diabetes etc. He was also able to demonstrate, based on nearly 30 years of research, that such issues are exacerbated the lower people are in an organisational hierarchy and concluded that status is not a footnote to the causes of ill health, it is the cause. He argued that health follows a social gradient i.e. that the lower people are in the hierarchy, the greater at risk they are in relation to mental illness, heart disease, cancer, alcohol and drug abuse, suicide, lung disease and susceptibility to tuberculosis etc. ☞

The difference in life expectancy gap between men in North Kensington (the location of Grenfell Tower), and South Kensington and Chelsea, is 14 years, whilst in Glasgow, the life expectancy gap between one of the wealthiest areas (Cathcart and Simshill) and one of the most socially deprived areas (Ruchill and Possilpark) is 16 years.

Principles of a bar chart

When setting and discussing questions relating to bar charts, for example in Q 23 e) above, it is good practice to emphasise the importance of following certain principles, for example:

- Give the bar chart a title. For example, 'Bar chart to show mean weights of groups A, B and C'

- Ensure that the numbers are placed going up on the vertical axis in equal increments starting from 0 for example: 0, 10, 20, 30 … or 0, 1, 2, 3 … or 0, 5, 10, 15 …etc.

- Ensure that the heights of the bars are correct, particularly when they fall between the more prominent lines on the centimetre squares.

- Ensure that the vertical axis is given a label e.g. mean weight (kg)

- Ensure that the bars are labelled beneath the bars, and that there is no labelling (or numbering) within the bars or on top of the bars.

- In addition, the bars should be separate and equally spaced.

Worked example

Table to show weights of male learners in class A

Name	Weight (kg)	Name	Weight (kg)
Kevin	78	Amir	67
Ahmed	65	Lee	75
Stephen	74	Arad	80
Harry	75	Nathan	78
Arnold	86	Michael	82
Jamie	75	Jacob	72
Shuhel	74	Simon	70

From the above table, calculate:

- The mean weight of males in class A (to one decimal place).

Mean $= \dfrac{\text{Total}}{\text{Number}} = 1{,}051 \div 14 = \textbf{75.1kg}$ (to one decimal place)

- The Range of results for class A
  Range = highest – lowest = 86kg – 65kg = **21kg**

- The Mode
  Mode = most common number = **75kg**

- The Median
  Median = 65, 67, 70, 72, 74, 74, 75, | 75, 75, 78, 78, 80, 82, 86 = **75kg**

Check one of your calculations: 65kg + 21kg = 86kg

(ps – the mean calculation should not be checked here, since as the result has been rounded down, 75.1 x 14 does not equal 1,051, it equals 1,051.4)

From your answers above, calculate the difference between the mean and the median:

75.1kg – 75kg = **0.1kg**

The mean weight of male learners in class B was found to be 74.5kg and in class C, it was 81kg. Draw a bar chart to show the mean weights of learners in classes A, B and C. Following some research, the mean weight of male adults in the UK was found to be 84kg. Show this result on the bar graph also.

Scale drawings

Scale drawing 1

In introducing the topic, I normally work through an example of a scale drawing of a small hall with a couple of doors, stage and desks. Without telling the learners which scale to use, or how to write a scale correctly, I hand a sheet of graph paper to my learners, then ask them to place it in the landscape position and write the title from the board of 'scale drawing of a small hall'. I then draw a sketch of the following on the board and ask the learners (who are hopefully equipped with a 30cm/12" ruler and a pencil) to draw it as a scale diagram and, if they're able to, to write down the scale that they've used:

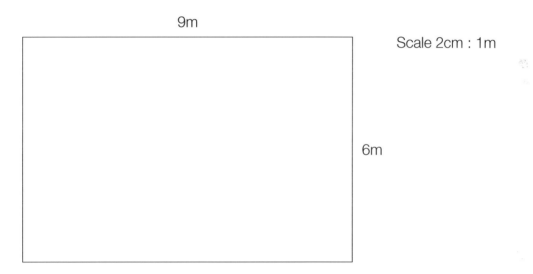

9m

Scale 2cm : 1m

6m

When the learners have completed the drawings, I normally find that some will have drawn it to a scale of 1cm : 1m whilst others will have drawn it larger, using a scale of 2cm to 1m. As I go around the class, I ensure that all the learners, whichever drawing they have done, have labelled their drawings with the correct dimensions. If they've written a scale down, I check to see if it's written correctly for the drawing they have done and if it it's not, correct accordingly. Common mistakes here will include:

- Writing the scale the wrong way round e.g. 1m : 1cm
- Writing the wrong scale e.g. writing the scale of 1cm : 1m for a scale drawing which is 2cm:1m
- Using the = sign instead of : e.g. 2cm = 1m
- Leaving out the units e.g. 2: 1 or putting units on just one side e.g. 2 : 1m
- A combination of the above
- Writing the dimensions as the drawing size rather than the actual/real life size e.g. 6cm (or 12 cm) instead of 6m

The above need to be reinforced and emphasised in all examples.

I take an example of each of two scale drawings (1cm : 1m and 2cm : 1m), hold them up to the class, and ask which one they think is the clearer diagram, with the intention of eliciting the answer of it being the larger one. I emphasise here however that provided the correct scale has been used for the relevant drawing, that both are correct, but that the larger one will be more suitable as more will be added to the diagram.

The importance of writing the scale correctly is emphasised on the basis that it determines how each part of the drawing is represented, on the one hand, and the fact that calculations to determine dimensions can be written beneath it on the other.

Once the learners have, if necessary, redrawn the scale diagram to the scale of 2cm : 1m and written the scale correctly, they can then be asked to add to the drawing. For example, doors can be added (say 1m wide and 1m in from the corner), and labelled, and dimension lines can be added, as follows:

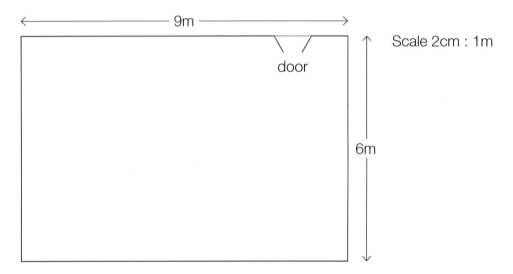

Following this, a stage can be drawn, and labelled, at one end of the hall, in the centre of the wall:

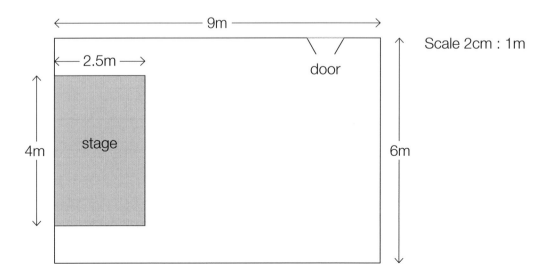

After this, the following exercise can be set:

Tables need to be set out in the hall in order to prepare for a fete. Each table needs to be at least one metre away from the walls and stage, and from each other. If each table measures 1.5m by 0.5m, then how many tables can fit into the hall. Draw the tables on the scale diagram. Label, and give the dimensions of, one of them (See answer on p232).

New carpet tiles measuring 50cm by 50cm are to be laid on the floor. If the tiles come in boxes of ten, then calculate the number of boxes required (See answer on p230):

Scale drawing 2

Scale diagram of an L-shaped field, and wigwams

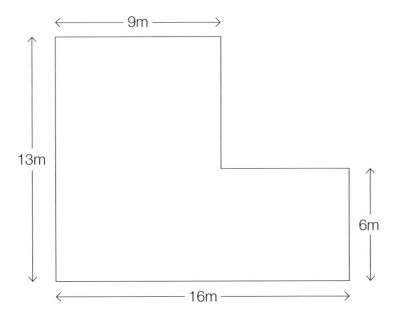

Draw a scale diagram of an L-shaped grass field from the drawing above. Give the diagram a heading, then:

- Write down the scale you have used (with units)
- Calculate the perimeter of the field (don't forget the units)
- Calculate the area of the field (don't forget the units)

The owner of the field decides to place some wigwams (circular tents) in the field. If the radius of each wigwam is 1m, then:

- Calculate the number of wigwams that can fit in the field, by drawing them on the scale diagram. They must be at least 1m apart and 1m away from the edge of the field.

- Next, calculate the area of the wigwams (remember, the area of a circle = πr² and π = 3.14)

- Calculate the area of the remaining grass

- Finally, check one of your calculations

Scale drawing 3

A classroom measuring 6.5m by 4m is to be covered with square carpet tiles with sides of 50cm.

a) Using a scale of four centimetres to represent one metre, draw a scale drawing of the classroom, including the carpet tiles. Check that the number of tiles drawn is the same as your answer on p.219

b) Check one of the distances you have measured.

Scale drawing 4

Some wasteland adjacent to an existing carpark measuring 24m by 16m is to be converted to an overflow carpark, which is to include 2 disabled bays both at the same end of the parking area, but opposite each other. If the disabled bays measure 4.8m by 3.2 m and the non-disabled bays measure 4.8m by 2.6m then calculate the number of car park spaces that can be created. Then, through drawing a scale drawing of the overflow carpark (using a suitable scale) and car park spaces, check if the number of car park spaces on the scale drawing matches the number calculated.

Two different models of car measuring 1,700mm by 3,700mm (model A) and 1,900mm by 4,600mm (model B) park in the carpark spaces. Show and label them on the scale drawing.

Scale drawing 5

A temporary outdoor stage is to be built using square blocks measuring 5 feet by 5 feet.

   a) If the stage needs to be at least 6m by 10m, then calculate the number of blocks required to build the stage: Take 1 foot = 30cm

   b) Using a suitable scale, draw a scale diagram of the stage with the blocks, then check if the number of blocks is the same as the number calculated in a).

Scale drawing 6

   a) A study of length 2.5m is to be used to store chests of drawers. If each chest of drawers measures 45cm wide by 60cm tall and can be stacked two high (directly on top of each other), then calculate how many can fit along the wall.

   b) Using a scale of 10cm:1m draw a scale drawing of the chests of drawers, and check if you have the same number as the calculation in a).

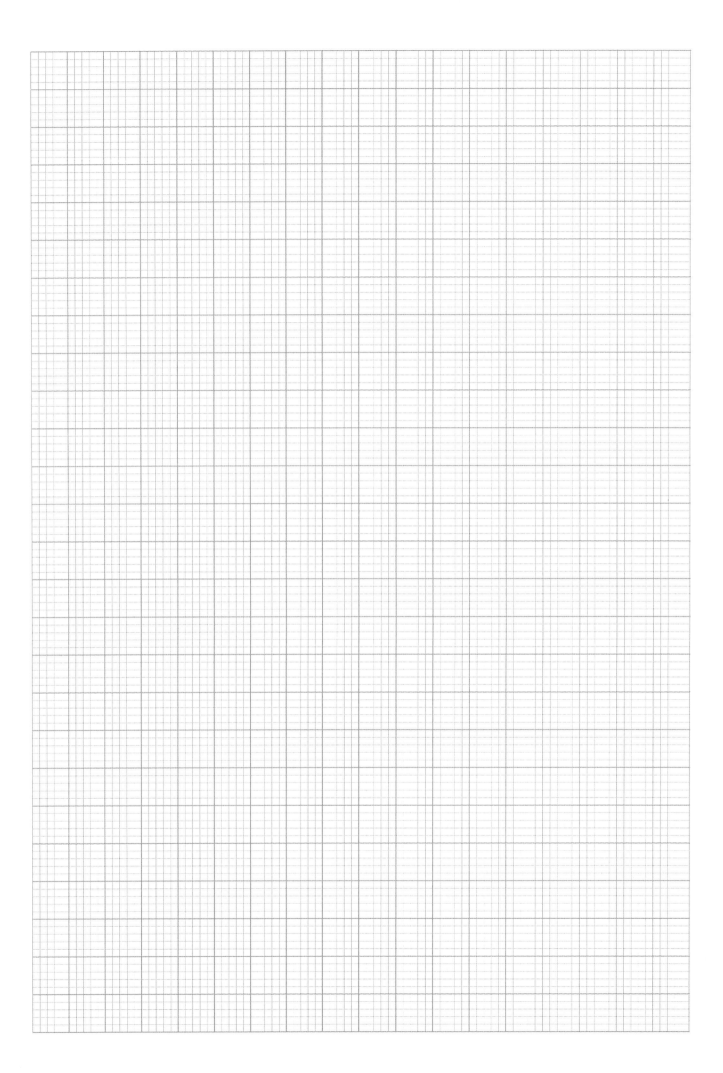

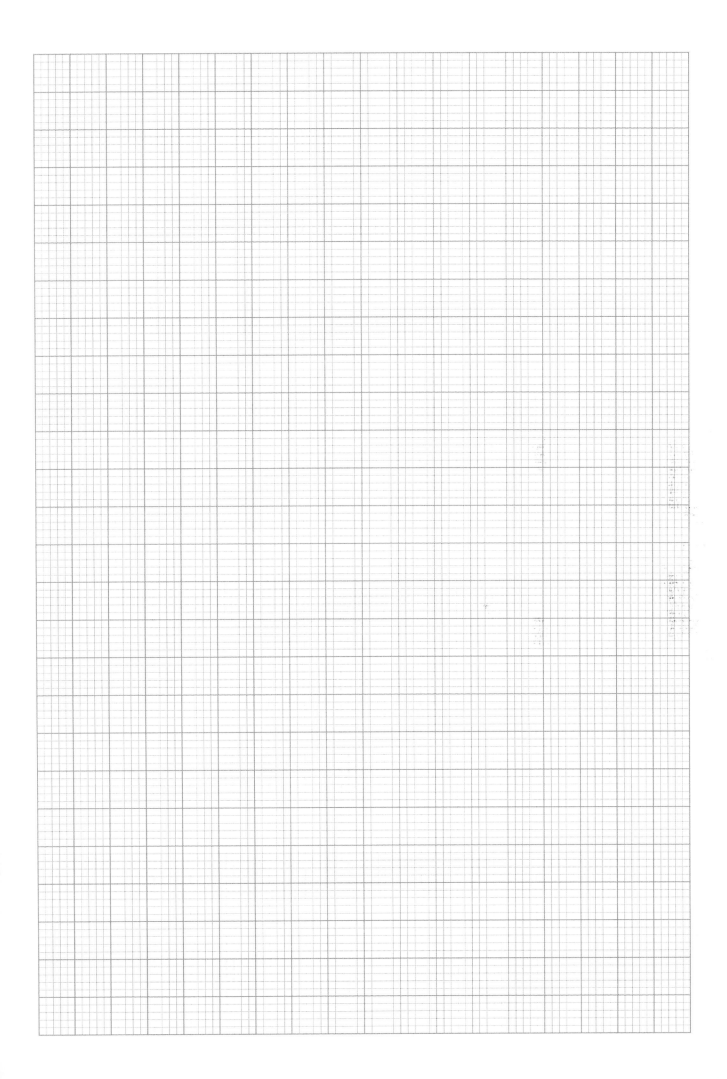

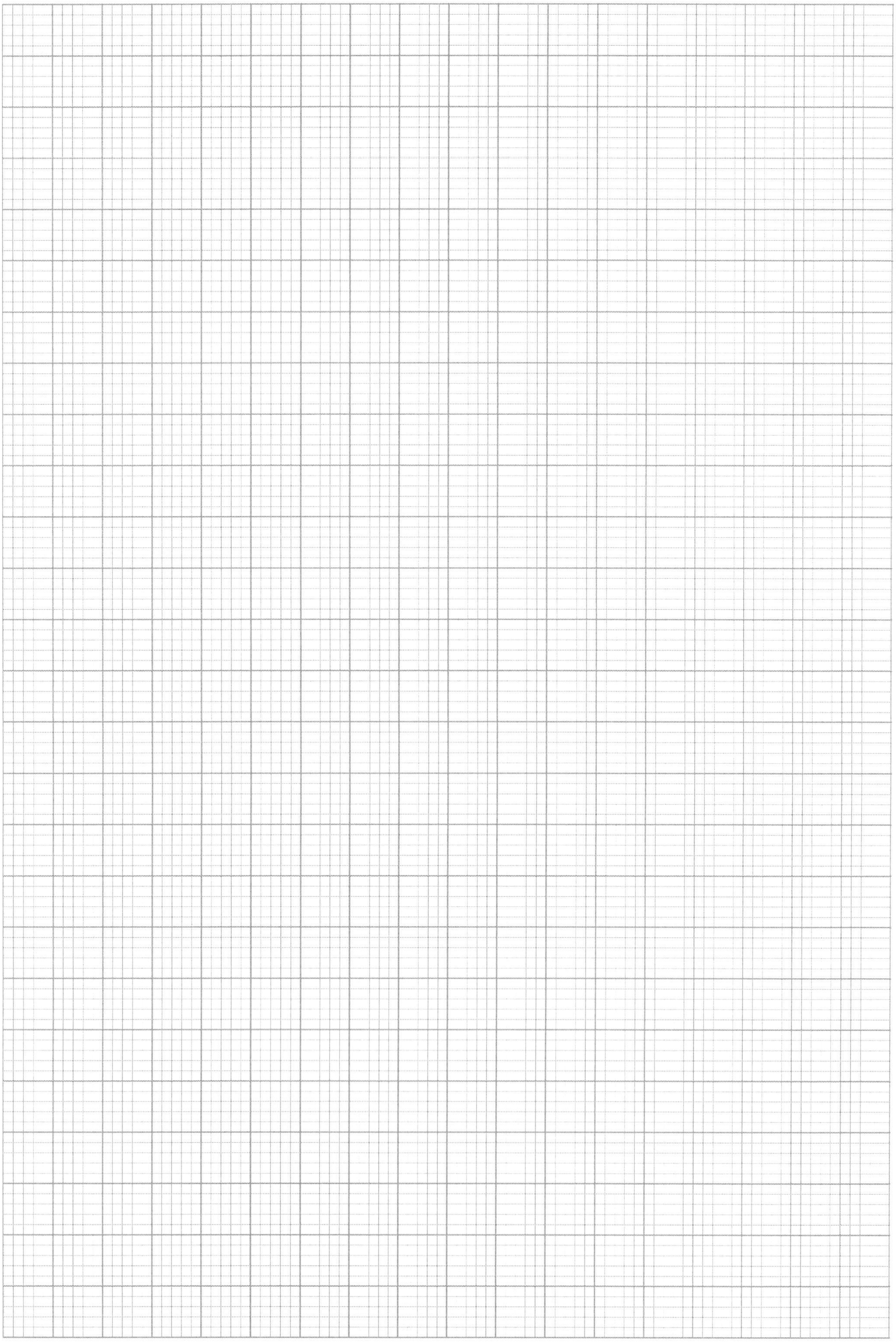

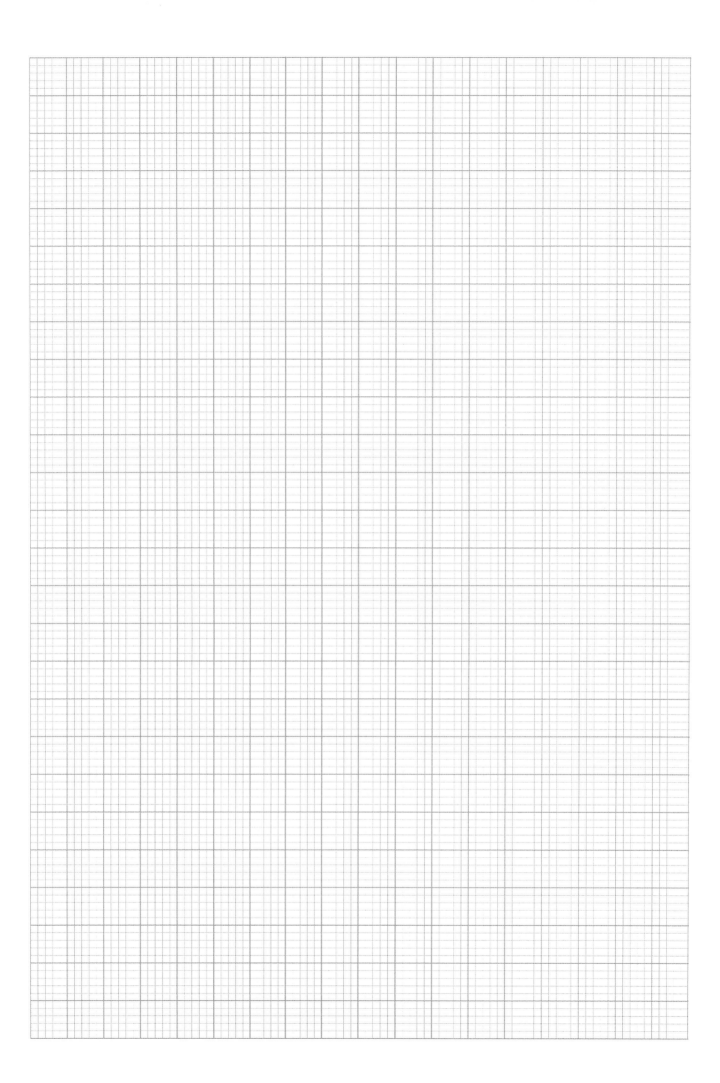

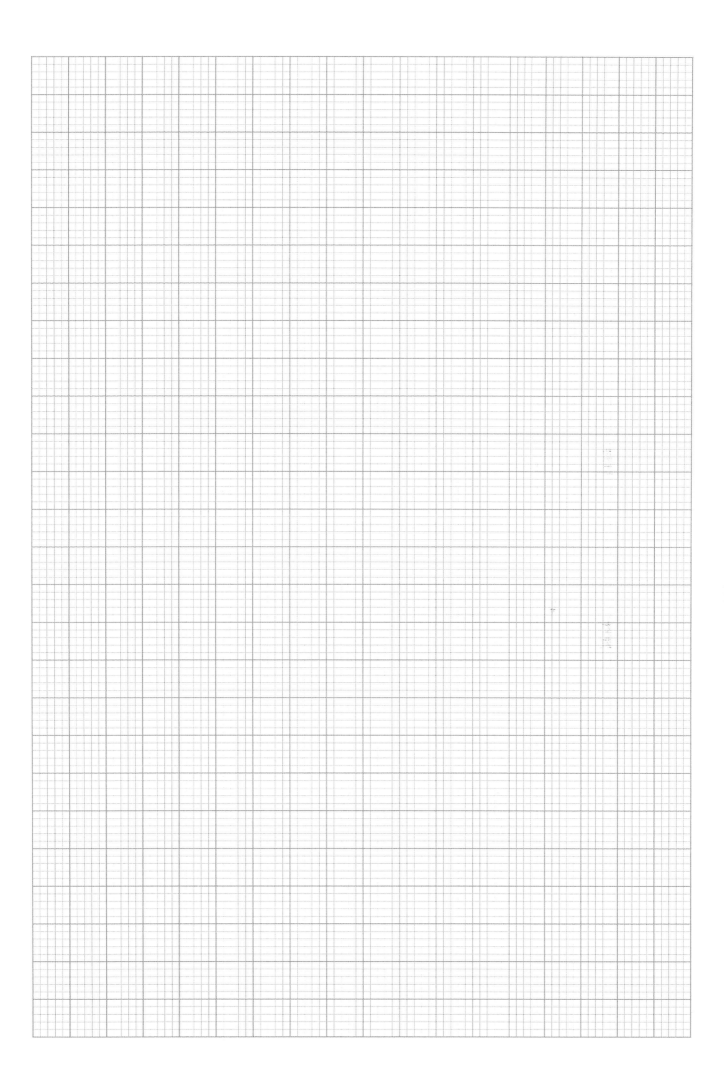

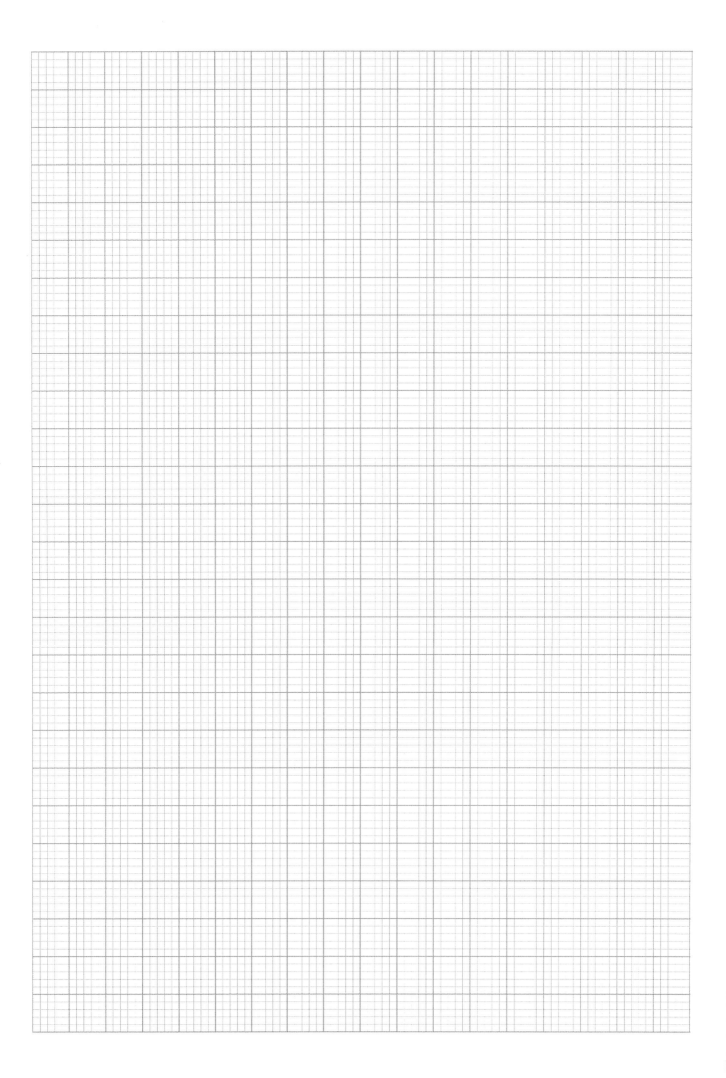

Scale conversions

With scale drawings, students also need to be able to interpret scales without units

e.g. 1 : 100 1: 20,000 etc.

The scale used in the first examples was: 2cm : 1m

To convert 2cm : 1m to a scale without units, we first need to ensure that the scale has the same units, following which we can remove them from both sides, then simplify the scale, showing the workings under the scale:

2cm : 1m
2cm : 100cm
2 : 100
1 : 50

So, the scale of 2cm : 1m is equivalent to a scale of 1 : 50

We can also convert the scale of 1 : 50 back to 2cm : 1m by giving both sides of the scale the same units, then doubling both sides and converting the 100cm back to 1m:

1 : 50
1cm : 50cm
2cm : 100cm
2cm : 1m

The scale of 2cm : 1m can be described as the 'working scale' on the basis that it is the actual scale used when calculating or measuring distances on the scale drawing.

We can apply a similar process when converting any scale with units to one without units or converting any scale without units to one with units.

Scale drawing 7

Convert the scales in the above questions to scales without units:

A scale on a local map may be 1 : 20,000 which can be converted to a 'working scale' as follows:

1 : 20,000
1cm : 20,000cm
1cm : 200m
5cm : 1,000m
5cm : 1km

If the distance between village A and village B on the drawing is measured as 7cm

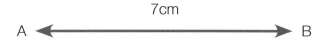

7cm

A ⟷ B

Here, the working scale could be taken as:

1cm : 200m   or   1cm : 0.2km
7cm : 1,400m (7 x 200m)   7cm : 1.4km (7 x 0.2km)
7cm : 1.4km

Scale drawing 8

A man travels by car from town A to town B where he picks up a friend. Together, they travel to town C where they pick up another friend. From town C, they travel to town D where they pick up the final person. Together then, they travel to town E, which is their destination:

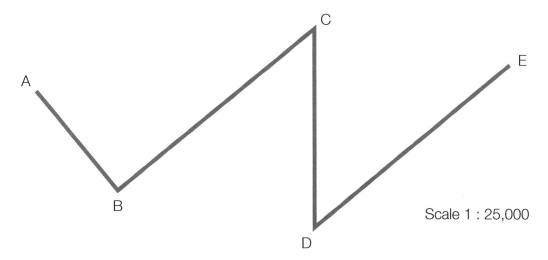

Scale 1 : 25,000

a) Using the above scale, calculate the distance (in km) the car travels.

b) Using 1km = ⅝ miles, calculate the distance the car has travelled to the nearest half a mile.

Scale drawing 9

The distance between towns P and S is 80km. How far will this be represented on a map if its scale is 1 : 500,000

Scale drawing 10

The distance between towns A and B on a map is 10cm. If the distance represents 25km, then calculate the scale (without units) of the map.

Conversion-integration methodology

Worked Example (from L2 learning guide p.76 Q7)

A gardener who maintains a lawn wishes to replace the topsoil. If the lawn measures 22m by 15m and the depth of the topsoil is 20cm calculate the volume of the topsoil.

Volume of topsoil = length x width x height

Length = 22m Width = 15m Height (or Depth) = 20cm = 0.2m = ⅕m

Volume = 22 x 15 x ⅕

15 x ⅕ = $\frac{15}{5}$ = 15 ÷ 5 = 3 22 x 3 = 66m^3 or $22 \times \cancel{15}^{3} \times \frac{1}{\cancel{5}_{1}}$ = **66**m^3

Alternatively,

Volume = 22 x 15 x 0.2 = 330 x 0.2 = 33 x 10 x 0.2 = 33 x 2 = **66**m^3

Or, 15 x 0.2 = (10 + 5) x 0.2 = (10 x 0.2) + (5 x 0.2) = 2 + 1 = 3 22 x 3 = **66**m^3

In the above case, I would argue that the first method i.e. converting 20cm to a fraction (⅕) of a metre is the more appropriate method. However, at least one other method should be shown, and understood, again in order to give learners a wider range of methods to draw upon in solving numeracy problems in general.

Q1 If a small loaf of bread weighs 400g, what would be the weight (in kilograms) of 40 small loaves of bread?

Q2 A carpenter wishes to fix together 12 pieces of wood in a straight line. If each piece of wood is 80cm long, then calculate the total length of the wood.

Q3 Bottles of water are stacked together in packs of four by five. If each bottle holds three hundred millilitres, then calculate the volume of water in four packs.

Q4 Find out the weight of a large loaf of bread, then calculate the weight of sixty large loaves.

Q5 If a bottle of water contains 0.25L, then calculate the volume of water contained in 120 bottles.

Q6 A chocolate spread comes in 200g jars and is stacked in packs of 48. Calculate the weight of 5 packs.

Q7 A well-known brand of washing powder weighs 2.5kg. Calculate the weight of 30 boxes of the washing powder.

Q8 Calculate the volume of concrete used in the construction of an industrial warehouse floor, which has the following dimensions:

Length = 25m Width = 12m Depth = 300mm

Q9 Calculate the volume of earth in a hole in the ground that measures 80cm long by 80cm wide by 25cm deep.

Q10 Calculate the volume of water (in litres) which can be held in an outdoor fish pond which is 4m long, 3m wide and 75cm deep.
$1m^3 = 1,000L$

Level 2 Functional Skills Numeracy Questions

1 In an effort to support fair trading practices in developing countries, student A buys 18 bars of 'Fairtrade' dark chocolate with spices and orange oil.

a If each bar weighs 40g, then calculate the total weight (in kilograms) of the chocolate bars.

b If each bar contains 200 calories of energy, then calculate the total energy (in kilojoules) contained in the 18 bars (1 kilojoule ≈ 240 calories).

c The food label on each bar of chocolate shows the following information:

Fat	Saturated fat	Sugar	Salt
14.5g	9.2g	16.3g	trace

From the above information, calculate the percentage of saturated fat in each bar.

d For breakfast, the student decides to try out a new cereal. The food label on the packet of cereal contains the following information:

Each 30g serving contains:

Calories	Sugars	Fat	Saturates	Salt
114	5.1g	0.5g	0.2g	0.3g
6%	6%	<1%	<1%	6%

of the guideline daily amount.

From the above information, calculate the guideline daily amount of salt that people require.

e   The packet also claims that the cereal contains less than 2% fat. Is this claim true? Show your workings.

f   The student has her friends over for dinner and decides to cook Arancini (fried rice balls), an old Sicilian dish. She checks her recipe for the dish:

10ml of olive oil
half a small shallot, finely cut
1 clove of garlic, thinly sliced
60g carnaroli risotto rice
20ml white wine
300ml vegetable stock
    Gorgonzola
10g parmesan
    walnuts
20g plain flour
1 egg
20g white breadcrumbs
vegetable oil, enough to deep fry

However, her recipe for the dish doesn't show the amount of gorgonzola or walnuts. If the ratio of rice to gorgonzola to parmesan to walnuts to flour to breadcrumbs is:

12 : 8 : 2 : 3 : 4 : 4

then calculate the amount of gorgonzola and walnuts (in grams) that she needs for her recipe.

g The following day, the student decides to check the information on the label of her bottle of olive oil:

Each 30g serving contains:

Calories	Sugar	Fat	Saturated fat	Salt
133	0g	15g	2.2g	0g
7%	0%	21%	11%	0%

of the guideline daily amount.

From the above information, calculate the approximate guideline daily amount of calories that people require.

h Check if the guideline daily amount of calories, calculated for olive oil, works out to be the same as the guideline daily amount of calories shown on the food label for the breakfast cereal.

i Whilst reading the Sunday papers, the student notices an article about the health benefits of olive oil, based on recent research. She reads that:

> *'People who cook with olive oil, add it to salads and dip their bread in it cut their risk of stroke by 41% once diet, exercise and weight are taken into account.'*

She also reads the following:

> *'It is believed that regular use of olive oil could protect against conditions such as high cholesterol, high blood pressure and heart disease.'*

Carry out some research into facts and figures associated with these claims.

j Carry out some research into facts and figures associated with food groups and food labelling.

2 Student B receives his electricity bill and decides to check the calculations:

Cost of electricity you've used this period:

Night readings

10 Mar '11 – estimated   33092
18 Apr '11 – estimated   33434

$=$ **(a)** kWh used over 40 days (estimated)

(a) x 5.296p   =   £ **(b)**

Day readings

10 Mar '11 – estimated   17531
18 Apr '11 – estimated   18024

$=$ **(c)** kWh used over 40 days (estimated)

(c) x 12.472p   =   £ **(d)**

Total cost of electricity used = (b) + (d) = (e)

From the above information, calculate:

a The estimated night reading (the difference between the readings on 18 Apr '11 and 10 Mar '11) in kWh.

b The cost (to the nearest penny) of the electricity used at night between 10 Mar '11 and 18 Apr '11 (calculated as the number of Kilowatt Hours (a) x the price per unit (5.296p).

c The estimated day reading (the difference between the readings on 18 Apr '11 and 10 Mar '11).

d The cost (to the nearest penny) of the electricity used during the day between 10 Mar '11 and 18 Apr '11 (calculated as the number of Kilowatt Hours (a) x the price per unit (12.472p).

e The total cost of electricity used (b + d).

f The average cost (to the nearest penny) of the electricity used per day over the 40 days.

Student B also receives the following information on his electricity bill:

If you continue to use energy at the same rate over the next 12 months, we estimate your cost will be £537.60 based on the following tariff breakdown:

Period	Your tariff	Projected cost
19 April '11 – 18 April '12	standard	£537.60

The cost of your electricity isn't just the price of your fuel:

5% Profit

12% Government obligation to help the environment

7% VAT and corporation tax

12% Operating costs

27% Delivery to your home

37% Wholesale electricity

g   Calculate the estimated combined cost over the 12 months of the Government obligation to help the environment, and the energy supplier's operating costs.

h   Calculate the difference in cost over the 12 months between the estimated price of the wholesale electricity and the estimated price of delivery to the student's home.

i   An alternative energy supplier claims to be able to reduce the cost of student B's electricity bill. They offer a 15% reduction on the current energy supplier's projected cost. If, however, there is an eighty five pound transfer payment to be made for changing supplier, then calculate if the student would make a saving (in the year April '11 to April '12) by changing supplier.

In order to reduce his energy costs, as well as his 'Carbon Footprint', the student decides to buy some greener living, light 'Sticks'. In terms of the carbon output, the 'Sticks' produce 6.5kg of Carbon Dioxide per 1,000 hours of use compared with conventional 60W light bulbs, which produce 34kg of Carbon Dioxide per 1,000 hours.

From the above information, calculate:

j   The approximate carbon output of the light 'Sticks' as a proportion of the carbon output of the conventional 60W light bulbs.

k   The amount of Carbon Dioxide that would be produced in a leap year by one light 'Stick' that was constantly on.

l   Carry out some research into facts and figures associated with alternative energy sources.

3a   Students A and B are debating who has the most fuel efficient car. Student A states that her car, on average, does 420 miles on a full tank of 40 litres, whilst student B states that his car, on average, does 16km/litre. Which student has the more fuel efficient car?
(1 mile ≈ 1.6 kilometres)

b   Student B's car takes 12½% more fuel in its tank than student A's car. Calculate the amount of fuel, in gallons, that is needed to fill Student B's car.
(1 gallon ≈ 4.5 litres)

The two students decide to travel from their flat in London to Edinburgh for the weekend, with two of their friends, in the more fuel efficient car.

c   The car's Sat-Nav shows the distance to their destination in Edinburgh as 420 miles. One of the students decides to check this distance by making an estimation using a map. If the scale of the map is 1 : 2,000,000 and she measures the distance as 33 cm, then calculate the difference between the estimation and the Sat-Nav reading.

d | The four friends decide to share the cost of the petrol equally. If the cost of petrol is 133.9p per litre, then calculate, to the nearest 10p, the cost of petrol that each of the friends have to pay.

Before the trip, one of the students decides to check on the weather report:

Weather Report for June 1st, 2011:

	Sun (hrs)	Rain (mm)	Temp (°C) High/low		Weather (noon)
Aberdeen	8.3	0.1	17	7	Showers
Aberystwyth	1.9	0.4	15	11	Cloudy
Aviemore	6.9	1.4	13	5	Showers
Barrow in Furness	4.9	0.6	15	11	Sunny
Belfast	5.3	1.4	14	9	Sunny
Birmingham	2.7	0.0	20	12	Cloudy
Bognor Regis	0.9	0.0	16	8	Cloudy
Bournemouth	1.4	0.0	17	12	Cloudy
Bristol	2.2	0.2	17	12	Rain
Cardiff	0.2	0.7	15	12	Rain
Cork	5.1	0.0	14	10	Cloudy
Cromer	3.2	0.0	19	12	Cloudy
Dublin	3.1	0.1	17	10	Sunny
Durham	3.1	0.0	17	9	Cloudy
Edinburgh	7.9	0.9	14	8	Showers
Eskdalemuir	5.0	6.2	13	6	Showers
Glasgow	7.9	4.6	13	7	Showers
Guernsey	0.4	0.0	15	12	Cloudy
Holyhead	0.8	0.1	15	12	Cloudy
Hove	2.2	0.0	16	13	Cloudy
Huntingdon	5.4	0.0	19	12	Cloudy
Ipswich	2.9	0.0	21	12	Cloudy
Isle of Mann	4.3	0.4	15	10	Sunny
Isle of Wight	1.0	0.0	14	12	Cloudy
Jersey	0.8	0.0	16	12	Cloudy
Kilkenny	4.7	1.2	14	7	Cloudy
Kinlochewe	5.4	17.5	11	7	Rain
Kirkwall	0.9	11.5	11	7	Cloudy
Leeds	3.2	3.4	17	10	Rain
Leuchars	8.9	0.0	16	7	Sunny
Liverpool	2.9	0.0	16	12	Cloudy

London	3.3	0.0	20	13	Cloudy
Malin Head	5.3	5.0	13	8	Cloudy
Manchester	0.3	0.5	16	11	Rain
Margate	7.6	0.0	20	12	Sunny
Morecambe	4.8	0.2	16	11	Cloudy
Nottingham	0.3	0.0	17	12	Cloudy
Okehampton	1.5	0.4	16	11	Cloudy
Oxford	4.5	0.2	17	12	Cloudy
Plymouth	5.6	0.3	15	12	Cloudy
Portsmouth	3.9	0.1	15	13	Showers
Prestwick	4.6	4.4	13	8	Showers
Shannon	3.8	0.9	14	11	Cloudy
Shrewsbury	1.8	0.0	16	12	Cloudy
Skegness	4.2	0.0	17	11	Cloudy
Southend	6.1	0.0	20	13	Sunny
Stornoway	3.5	6.8	11	6	Rain
Swansea	4.0	1.6	14	12	Cloudy
Tiree	0.0	2.6	12	8	Showers
Valentia	0.3	1.0	13	11	Fair

Sun & Moon

Sun rises: 04 52

Sun sets: 21 04

Moon rises: 03 11

Moon sets: 18 56

e Calculate the temperature range across the five capital cities shown in Britain and Ireland (i.e. London, Cardiff, Dublin, Belfast and Edinburgh).

f Calculate the average rainfall across the five capital cities.

g Which place, shown on the weather report, had the highest recorded temperature range?

h   Which place, shown on the weather report, had the highest amount of sunshine?

i   Calculate the amount of daylight there was on June 1st.

j   One of the students is a keen athletics fan. He applies on-line for a ticket for the 100m men's sprint final in the London Olympics. Unfortunately, however, there are only thirty thousand tickets available and approximately one million people have applied. Approximately what percentage of those people applying for tickets on-line, will not be successful in their application for tickets for the 100m men's sprint final?

k   Overall, one million and nine hundred thousand people applied on-line for tickets of their choice for the London Olympics. Of those, one million and two hundred thousand people were not successful in the ticket allocation the first time round. Those who were successful, on average, received 5 tickets each at a cost, again on average, of £75 a ticket. Calculate the income generated from the on-line sale of tickets, the first time round, for the London Olympics.

l   Carry out some research into facts and figures associated with fuel prices.

m   Carry out some research into facts and figures associated with climate change.

4   Student A usually cycles to her local supermarket (Safeburies) to do her shopping. However, she hears that a new supermarket (Morose) has opened up, approximately 8 miles from where she lives, which claims to offer better value for money for shoppers. She makes a list of typical items that she buys on a regular basis, and decides to compare prices:

Product	Supermarket	
	Safeburies	**Morose**
1 Litre of skimmed milk	£0.83	£0.86
2 x 1 litre cartons of orange juice	£1.75 per carton	£1.95 per carton
Broccoli (335g)	£1.27	£1.35
Organic spinach	£1.00	£1.10
Large wholemeal loaf of Bread (800g)	£1.36	£1.38
600g bag of apples	£1.67	£1.70
2 kg of bananas	35p/lb	35p/lb
1 kg of carrots	30p/lb	35p/lb
Peppered steak (435g)	£4.00	£4.00
Pork loin steaks (0.66kg)	£4.00	£4.00
Chicken (1.45kg)	£4.00	£4.00
Original coffee granules (200g)	£4.00	£3.85
Pure vegetable oil (1L)	£1.10	£1.25
Salted butter (750g)	£0.98	£0.94
12 free range medium eggs	£2.73	£2.80
Milk chocolate digestives	£1.00	£1.10
Easy cook rice	£1.06	£1.06
3 in 1 Shampoo	£2.20	£2.45
TOTAL		

(1 kg = 2.2 lb)

The following deals/offers at the supermarkets apply:

Safeburies:
1L Cartons of orange juice – 2 for £2.50

Morose:
1L cartons of orange juice – buy 1, get one free
Portions of peppered steak (435g), pork loin steaks (0.66kg) and chicken (1.45kg) - £4.00 each or any 3 for £10.00

Calculate:

a   Calculate which of the two supermarkets would be more economical for student A to shop in (bearing in mind the cost of petrol used in driving to the Morose supermarket).

b   The student notices that supermarkets up and down the country have checkouts which state '10 items or less.' Why is this statement incorrect?

c   The student reads an article which states that in 2006, the average food shopping bill was 40% less than it is in June 2011. If that's the case, then calculate what the student's shopping bill would have been at Safeburies in 2006.

d   In order to attract more custom, both supermarkets decide to start an 'on-line' shopping option for its customers. They decide to start with the following offers:

Safeburies: 10% off any order above £30.00

Morose: 5% off any order above £30.00

Calculate, with the above offers, which of the two supermarkets would Student A's shopping have been cheaper on-line.

e Student A wants to update her mobile phone and decides to go on-line to check some Phone deals for the new AI Phone models:

	Model A	Model B	Model C	Model D	
AI Phone:					
	£5 a month for first 3 Months followed by £10 a month thereafter	First 3 months free followed by £15 a month	£15 a month with £50 cashback	£20 a month for first year followed by £10 a month for second year	Phones on a 24 month contract when you sign up on-line.
	200 mins	300 mins	500 mins	600 mins	Mins to all UK Mobiles & UK Landlines (starting 01, 02,03)
	500 texts	Unlimited texts	Unlimited texts	Unlimited texts	Standard UK texts
	250MB	250MB	500MB	500MB	UK mobile internet a month

She wishes to obtain the best phone she can (in terms of memory and number of minutes per month), with unlimited texts, up to a maximum price of £350 over the two years. Which model should she choose?

f Carry out some research into facts and figures associated with on-line shopping.

g Carry out some research into facts and figures associated with mobile phone tariffs.

5 The following table shows the level 2 Functional Skills results for two groups of students:

Group 1

Student	Presentation	Discussion	Reading	Writing	Maths
Tommy Cooper	F	P	P	P	P
James Paxton	P	P	P	P	F
Harry Kamboni	P	P	P	P	P
Chris Parsloe	P	P	P	P	P
Robert John	A	P	P	F	P
Jennifer Kerans	P	P	P	P	F
Heather Slater	F	P	P	P	P
Nigel Osatch	P	P	P	P	F

Group 2

Student	Presentation	Discussion	Reading	Writing	Maths
Christine White	P	P	P	P	P
Ian Wall	A	A	P	P	P
Rob Harris	P	P	P	P	F
Simon Fudge	P	P	P	P	P
Peter Brightman	F	P	F	F	F
Neil Barney	P	P	P	P	P
Letchimi Nair	P	P	P	P	P
Kevin George	P	P	P	P	F
Steve McDaniel	P	P	P	F	P
Andrew James	P	P	P	P	P
Clive Dean	P	P	P	P	F

Key: P = Pass   F = Fail   A = Absent

a Calculate the fraction of students from the 2 groups combined who have completed all the requirements of the Functional Skills level 2 English (i.e. presentation, discussion, reading and writing).

b Calculate the difference between the percentage pass rate in maths between the two groups.

C Calculate the overall percentage pass rate in maths of the two groups combined.

d The maths resit is taken, and two more people pass, one from group A and one from group B. Calculate the new overall percentage pass rate in maths of the two groups combined.

e Carry out some research into facts and figures associated with GCSE and A-level pass rates over recent years.

The following table shows a comparison of the number of short-term and long-term unemployed people in the UK across three different age brackets, as recorded in May 2011:

UK Unemployment

		Short-term (Less than a year)	Long-term (More than a year)
18 – 24 years	Male	299,000	135,000
	Female	226,000	85,000
25 – 49 years	M	332,000	281,000
	F	328,000	155,000
50+ years	M	136,000	134,000
	F	79,000	50,000
Total	M	767,000	550,000
	F	633,000	290,000

f What is the ratio of the total number of short-term unemployed people to the total number of long-term unemployed people?

g   In the 50+ age range, how many more short-term unemployed adults are there than long-term unemployed adults?

h   In the 18 – 24 years old age range, how many more male unemployed adults are there than female unemployed adults?

Unemployment in the UK 1992–2011

Number, millions

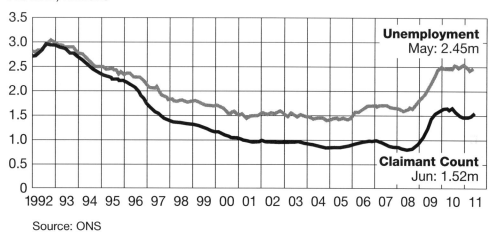

Source: ONS

i   From the above line graph, state, in words, the approximate difference between the level of unemployment and the claimant count in 2001.

j   Carry out some research into facts and figures associated with levels of unemployment.

6 A new novel 'The Berlinesque' is released on to the market. The following data table shows the number of books sold per hour in a bookshop in the first week following its publication:

	Mon	Tues	Weds	Thurs	Fri	Sat	Sun	Total
9 – 10	1	0	4	3	1	5		
10 – 11	4	5	7	5	3	5	3	
11 – 12	4	6	7	8	5	4	4	
12 – 1	6	9	10	6	3	7	4	
1 – 2	5	8	9	9	8	9	8	
2 – 3	7	6	10	10	8	9	6	
3 - 4	8	3	8	9	8	6	4	
4 - 5	4	5	5	4	4	5		
5 - 6	6	5	9	8	7	6		
6 - 7				6	5	2		
7 - 8				4	3	3		
Total								

a From the above data, calculate:
The average number of books sold per hour on the first day of its sale.

b The average number of books sold per day.

c The average number of books sold between 1 and 2pm during the first week of its sale.

d The range of books sold per hour during the week.

e On which day the median occurred for the total number of books sold per day.

f   The average number of books sold per hour on this day.

g   During the second week of sales, 420 books were sold in the bookstore. Calculate the percentage increase (to one decimal place) in the number of books sold during the second week of sales.

h   The books are stored in boxes (6 per box) which are 35cm long by 25cm wide by 20cm tall. The boxes are stored in a space in a warehouse which measures 1.4m long by 1.25m wide by 1.6m tall. Calculate the maximum number of books that can be stored in the space.

If the results shown in the data table were represented in a pie chart, then calculate:

i   the number of degrees that Thursday's sales would represent (to the nearest whole number).

j   the percentage of the pie chart that Monday's sales would represent on the pie chart (to the nearest whole number).

k In the space below, draw a bar chart of the results in the data table (days of the week along the X-axis, and total number of books sold per day along the Y-axis).

l In the space below, draw a line graph to compare the hourly book sales on Thursday and Friday (hour intervals along the X-axis (9 - 10, 10 – 11 etc) and number of books sold per hour along the Y-axis).

j Carry out some research into facts and figures associated with the increasing popularity of E-books.

7 New research shows that there are currently approximately 3.5 million home workers in the UK, and that approximately 60% of new businesses are started from home.

A business woman is considering setting up a business to support 'home-working' social entrepreneurs who require collaborative working office spaces to match their needs, as an alternative to working from home. As such, she is looking to rent some premises, and is considering the following three options:

Site A   Area = 48 m²   Rent per month = £420
Site B   Area = 42 m²   Rent per month = £360
Site C   Area = 54 m²   Rent per month = £468

a The woman chooses the site which offers the best value for money in terms of the cost per square metre.
She plans to charge her clients £20/day to use her office, for which they will have use of a shared desk area, together with wi-fi, and tea and coffee. She plans to open her office from Monday to Friday, and estimates, based on the interest shown by local entrepreneurs in her business, that on average six people per day will use the facilities.
Calculate how many weeks it will take before she is able to cover the cost of the annual rent i.e. 'break even.'

A plan is drawn of the office using a scale of 1 : 25

Below are some measurements and real life sizes of areas within the plan:

	DRAWING SIZE	REAL LIFE SIZE
Office area	(c) x (d)	7m x (b)
Comfy chair area	11cm x 9cm	(e) x (f)
Desk area (g)	(h) x (i)	4m x 1.5m
WC/bathroom	7cm x 5cm	(j) x (k)
Kitchen (7 m²)	(m) x (n)	(l) x 2m

Calculate the following:

b)

c)

d)

e)

f)

g)

h)

i)

j)

k)

l)

m)

n)

O Carry out some research into facts and figures associated with changing property prices.

P Using a scale of 1 : 50 draw a plan of the office (including comfy chair area, desk area, WC/bathroom and kitchen) in the space below:

8 On Thursday, May 5th, there was a referendum in the United Kingdom on the introduction of an Alternative Voting System in the country. Approximately nineteen million, two hundred thousand people of voting age voted in the referendum, the result being as follows:

32% in favour of the Alternative Vote (Yes campaign).
68% opposed to the Alternative Vote (No campaign).

Given the above result, calculate the following:

a The approximate number of people who voted in favour of the alternative voting system (to the nearest one hundred thousand).

b The number of people who opposed the alternative voting system (to the nearest one hundred thousand).

c If the turnout for the vote was roughly 42% of the population, then calculate the approximate number of eligible voters in this country (to the nearest one hundred thousand).

d If the current population of the United Kingdom is approximately 60 million, but is predicted to rise to 71 million by the year 2033, then calculate the percentage increase in the country's population (to one decimal place).

e In 2009, the estimated population of Britain was 61,113,205 and on June 15th 2011, it was estimated at 60,432,098 Based on these figures, calculate the reduction in the population of Britain between these times.

f   In April 2011, 30 million people in Britain had a Facebook account. However, by the end of May 2011, that number had decreased by 100,000 (as people apparently become bored with the site and concerns grow over privacy issues etc). If this decrease was to continue at the same rate (i.e. at 100,000 people per month), then calculate when the number of people with a Facebook account will have reduced by 10% from its peak of 30 million.

g   The Gender Identity Research & Education Society (a UK wide organisation whose purpose is to improve the lives of trans and gender non-conforming people of all ages, including those who are non-binary and non-gender) estimates that about 1% of the British population are gender nonconforming to some degree. In 2016, the estimated population of the UK was 65.64 million. Using these figures, estimate, to the nearest ten thousand, the number of people in the UK who are gender nonconforming to some degree.

h   The black minority ethnic (BME) population of England is estimated as 11%. Taking the population of England to be 50,760,000, calculate the approximate non-BME population of England (to the nearest one hundred thousand).

i   The population of Bedford is approximately 80,000. If the BME population of Bedford is approximately 10,000 then calculate whether or not Bedford has a higher, or lower, than average BME population within England.

j   In Bedfordshire 14.3% of people have a disability, health problem or long-term illness. If the population of Bedfordshire is approximately 382,000 then calculate the approximate number of people in Bedfordshire who have a disability, health problem or long-term illness.

K   In 2009/10, there were an estimated 555,000 new cases of work-related ill health:

- Stress, depression or anxiety – 234,000 cases
- Musculoskeletal disorders (MSD) – 188,000 cases
- Other illnesses – 133,000 cases

In addition, the estimated number of injuries at work in the same year (which met the criteria to be reportable under the RIDDOR regulations) was 233,000

From the above information, using Microsoft Office Excel, create a pie chart showing the percentages of each of the four categories of Health and Safety incident (i.e. Stress, MSD, other illnesses and Injury), then sketch it in the area below:

Comparison of work-related incidents of ill health and injury – 2009/10

l   In 2009/10, there were an estimated 23.4 million working days lost as a result of work-related ill health:

- Stress, depression or anxiety – 9.8 million
- Musculoskeletal disorders (MSD) – 9.3 million
- Other illnesses – 4.3 million

In addition, there were an estimated 5.1 million working days lost in 2009/10 due to workplace injuries.

From the above information, using Microsoft Office Excel, create a pie chart showing the percentages of each of the four categories of working days lost due to work-related ill health and injury (i.e. Stress, MSD, other illnesses and Injury), then sketch it in the area below:

Comparison of days lost due to work-related ill health and injury – 2009/10

m   Scientists researching into human evolution have recently claimed that 30,000 years ago, Cro-Magnon man, the earliest modern human, had a brain volume of approximately 1,500 cubic cm. On the basis that the average brain size of man today is approximately 1,350 cubic cm, calculate the percentage decrease in man's brain size since Cro-Magnon man.

n   Find out the population of your home town. Has the population there been increasing or decreasing over recent years?

O Find out the population of a country that you have visited or where a friend, or colleague of yours, is from. Has the population there been increasing or decreasing over recent years?

p Whilst the actual number of substantiated cases of child abuse is not known, the approximate number of children in the UK known to be at risk is (i.e. those appearing on the child protection register). Find out this number. Also, find out the percentage of young adults who were severely maltreated during childhood.

q Carry out some research on the internet into facts and figures associated with equal opportunities.

9 A college employee receives his payslip at the end of the month, only to find that parts of it are missing:

Organisation
A1 College

Employee Name
Lucky Jim

Employee Number
012345

Pay and Allowances		**Deductions**		**Period Details**	
Salary	2345.00	Income Tax	349.00	Date Paid	26/**(a)**/2010
Project Allowance	90.00	National Insurance	183.27	Tax Period	08
Travel-862 miles @ 40p/mile	**(b)**	Teacher's Pension (6.4%)	**(c)**	Tax Code	647L

National Ins No.
AB 12 34 56 C

PAYE Reference
123 D45678

Total Pay
(d)

Total Deductions
(e)

NET PAY
(f)

Annual Salary
(g)

From the above information, calculate:

a The exact date the employee was paid (bearing in mind that the tax year begins in April).

b The employee's travel allowance.

c The employee's pension contribution.

d The employee's total (or gross) pay (= Salary + Project Allowance + Travel Expenses).

e The employee's total deductions (= Income Tax + National Insurance + Teacher's Pension).

f The employee's net pay (Total Pay – Total Deductions).

g The employee's annual salary (monthly salary x number of months in year).

h Carry out some research into facts and figures associated with minimum pay rates and average earnings.

10 Examine the Body Mass Index (BMI) chart below:

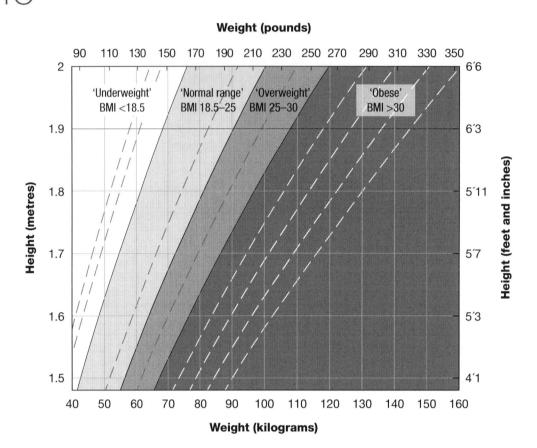

Weight (pounds)

Weight (kilograms)

a Student D measures his height as 1.70m and weight as 90kg. Using the above table, plot the student's Body Mass Index, and state which category his BMI falls under (i.e. underweight, Normal Range, Overweight or Obese).

Body Mass Index can also be calculated using the following formula:

$$BMI = \frac{Body\ Weight\ (in\ Kg)}{(Height\ (in\ m))^2}$$

b Calculate Student D's BMI (to the nearest whole number) using the above formula, and check if it's in the same category as the value plotted on the BMI chart.

C   Student C knows her height and weight in Imperial measurements. If her height is 5 feet and 9 inches, and her weight is 11 stone and 6 pounds, then plot her Body Mass Index on the above table, and state which category her BMI falls under.
(1 stone = 14 lbs)

d   Plot your own Body Mass Index on the above chart.

e   Calculate your Body Mass Index using the above formula, and check if it's in the same category as the value plotted on the BMI chart.

f   Carry out some research into facts and figures associated with childhood obesity rates.

g   The expression '20/20 vision' relates to a measurement of the clarity of eyesight. What do the numbers 20/20 actually mean though?

h   What is the average blood pressure for a healthy adult? What do the numbers refer to?

i   Find out your own blood pressure, and record your reading below. Is it high, average or low? Give an example of a high blood pressure reading and a low blood pressure reading.

j How many teeth does an adult have? What are the types of teeth, and how many of each does an adult have? How many teeth make a complete set of primary (baby) teeth?

k A high waist circumference (the distance around your abdomen) is associated with an increased risk of Type 2 diabetes, high cholesterol, high blood pressure and heart disease. Men shouldn't let their waist size go above what value (in inches). What is the value for a woman's waist size?

l How much moderate exercise (in minutes) should adults take each day?

m Lung capacity is measured in air flow as you breathe. What is the ideal peak flow for a healthy, non-smoking young man?

n What is the unit used to measure noise, and what is its range?

o What is the circumference of the earth (in miles, and kilometres) at the equator (to the nearest whole number)?

p What is the average distance (in miles, and kilometres) between the earth and the moon?

q   What is the distance (in miles, and kilometres) between the Earth, and Mars when it is nearest to the Earth?

r   What is the average distance (in miles, and kilometres) between the earth and the sun?

s   What is the speed of sound?

t   What is the speed of light?

u   What is the speed of a neutrino?

L3 Numeracy Learning Guide
(Going Further)

Name: ....

The following guide outlines a range of methods for solving numeracy problems at level 3. Its purpose is to develop skills gained from the L1 learning assessment and the L2 learning guide and has been put together to assist learners gain a level three application of number qualification. Read them through carefully, and try the practice questions at the end.

Conversions

As you look through level 3 application of number practice papers, you will see that within many of the questions, you need to convert from one unit to another. For example:

with distance (kilometres to miles, or yards to metres etc)

with speed (miles/hour to metres/second, or knots to miles/hour etc)

with area (mm^2 to m^2, or square feet to square metres etc)

with volume (gallons to litres, or m^3 to mm^3 etc)

with money (Euros to Pounds, or pounds to Swiss Francs etc) and all vice-versa.

In each case you will be given the conversion (e.g. 1 Euro = 0.626 Sterling), it's just a case of using it correctly within the problem.

Worked examples

a) If 1 Euro = 0.626 Sterling, how much sterling (to the nearest penny) would you get for 226.3 Euros?

226.3 x 0.626 = 141.6638 = **£141.66** (to the nearest penny)

However, you could be given the amount of Sterling, and asked to calculate the amount of Euros.

If 1 Euro = 0.626 Sterling, how many Euros (to the nearest Euro) would you get for £1010.58?

1 Euro = 0.626 Sterling

If we divide both sides by 0.626, then $\frac{0.626}{0.626}$ Sterling = $\frac{1}{0.626}$ Euro

So, 1 Sterling = $\frac{1}{0.626}$ Euro = 1.597 Euro (to 3 decimal places)

Then, 1010.58 Sterling = 1010.58 x 1.597 Euro = 1,613.896 Euro = **1,614** Euros (to the nearest Euro).

b) If 1 mile = 1.6103 kilometres, then how many metres are run in a marathon, which is 26.2 miles?

1 mile = 1.6103 km So, 26.2 miles = 26.2 x 1.6103 km = 42.18986 km

1 km = 1000 m so to convert from km to m, you need to multiply by 1000. When you multiply by a thousand, you move the decimal point 3 points to the right.

So, 1.6103 km = 1,610.3 m

1 mile = 1,610.3 m 26.2 miles = 26.2 x 1,610.3 m= 42,189.86 m = **42,190 m** (to the nearest m)

c) One lap of a horse race is 1 mile and 1 furlong (there are 8 furlongs in a mile). If a horse runs 6½ laps in 20 minutes and 17 seconds, then what is his average speed in metres per second (to 3 decimal places)?

Average speed = distance travelled ÷ time taken = $\frac{\text{distance travelled}}{\text{time taken}}$

The answer needs to be in m/s, so we need to calculate the distance in metres and the time in seconds.

Distance = 6.5 x 1.125 miles (1 furlong = 1/8 mile = 0.125 miles) = 7.3125 miles

(1 mile = 1,610.3 m) So, 7.3125 miles = 7.3125 x 1,610.3 m = 11,775 m
Time = 20 mins and 17 secs = (20 x 60) + 17 = 1200 + 17 = 1,217 secs

So, average speed = $\frac{\text{distance}}{\text{time}}$ = $\frac{11,775}{1,217}$ m/s = 9.675 m/s (to 3 d.p.)

d) A car is recorded driving along the A507 (where the speed limit is 60 miles/ hour) at 26 metres per second. Is the driver breaking the speed limit?

We need to convert 26 m/s into miles/hour

1,610.3 m = 1 mile   So, $\frac{1,610.3 \text{ m}}{1,610.3}$ = $\frac{1}{1,610.3}$ miles = 0.000621 miles

1 m = 0.000621 miles and 26 m = 26 x 0.000621 miles = 0.016146 miles

So, a speed of 26 metres per second = 0.016146 miles per second

In other words, the driver travels 0.016146 miles in one second

There are 3,600 (60 x 60) seconds in an hour, so in one hour the driver would travel

3,600 x 0.016146 miles = 58.1256 miles

The driver's speed is therefore **58.1256 miles/hour**, which is not breaking the speed limit.

e) The following diagram shows a lawn drawn to a scale of 1:250

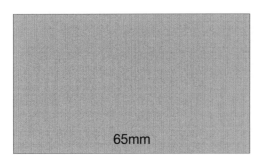

37mm

65mm

Calculate the area of the actual lawn in square metres (to 2 d.p.)

Length of lawn = 65mm x 250 = 16,250mm = 16.25m (1m = 1000mm)
Width of lawn = 37mm x 250 = 9,250mm = 9.25m

Area = length x width = 16.25 x 9.25 = 150.3125 = **150.31m²** (to 2 d.p.)

f) The area of a circular pond is measured and found to be 51.38m²

If a scale drawing of the pond was made using a scale of 1:125 then what would the diameter of the pond be on the scale drawing (to the nearest mm)?

Area of circular pond = πr^2 = 51.38m² (π = 3.14)

so, 3.14 x r^2 = 51.38 and $r^2 = \dfrac{51.38}{3.14}$ = 16.363m and r = $\sqrt{16.363}$ = 4.045m

Diameter = 2 x radius = 4.045 x 2 = 8.09m

On a scale drawing of 1 : 125   8.09m would be shown as 8.09 ÷ 125 = 0.06472m

0.06472m = 64.7mm = **65mm** (to the nearest mm)

g) How many cubic millimetres (mm³) are there in 4.72 cubic metres (m³)?

First we need to calculate how many mm³ are in 1m³

1m = 1000mm (milli = a thousandth) and 1m³ = 1m x 1m x 1m

So, 1m³ = 1000mm x 1000mm x 1000mm = 1,000,000 x 1,000 = 1,000,000,000mm³

i.e. 1m³ = a thousand million mm³ or 1 billion mm³ and 4.72m³
= **4.72 billion mm³**

Writing very large and very small numbers in standard form

The moon is 384,400,000.0m from the earth.
This is a rather large and cumbersome number, so we can write it in what is called 'standard form'. We do this so that very large (or very small) numbers can be more clearly expressed and compared.

- Place the decimal point after the first digit (3.844), then look at how many places the decimal point has moved to the left (or how many places the digits have moved to the right)

- To compensate for each place moved, we need to multiply by 10. In this example, the decimal point has moved 8 places to the left, so we need to multiply the above number by 10, eight times (i.e. 10×10×10×10×10×10×10×10). We can express this as 10 to the power 8 (10^8) i.e. 10 multiplied by itself 8 times.

- The above number can now be written in standard form as
  3.844 × 10^8

- On a calculator, this can be inputted as **3.844** followed by **Exp** (which stands for 'exponential' or 'x 10 to the power of …') followed by **8**

Looking at the numbers in the above example (g):

1,000,000 (1 million) = 1 x 10^6 or just 10^6 and 1,000,000,000 (1 billion) = 1 x 10^9 or 10^9

and 4,720,000,000 (4.72 billion) = 4.72 x 10^9

As well as very large numbers, we also need to work with very small numbers:

1 millimetre = 0.001m 1 micrometre = 0.000001m and 1 nanometre = 0.000000001m

The diameter of large bacteria is approximately 2 micrometres or 0.000002m

- Place the decimal point after the first digit (2.0), then look at how many places the decimal point has moved to the right (or how many places the digits have moved to the left)

- To compensate for each place moved, we need to divide by 10. In this example, the decimal point has moved 6 places, so we need to divide the above number by 10, six times i.e. $\dfrac{2.0}{10 \times 10 \times 10 \times 10 \times 10 \times 10} = \dfrac{2.0}{10^6}$

$\dfrac{1}{10}$ (or 0.1) can be written as 10^{-1}

$\dfrac{1}{10^2}$ (or 0.01) can be written as 10^{-2} and so on

- So, the above number can be written in standard form as **2.0 x 10⁻⁶**

Also, 0.001m (1mm) expressed in standard form is 1.0 x 10⁻³ m

Percentages

The whole notion of percentages (like any other part of numeracy I guess) can cause confusion amongst learners. Before tackling any level 3 application of number question on percentages first ensure you are familiar with the methods outlined in the L1 numeracy learning assessment and L2 numeracy learning guide.

Year	1960	1970	1980	1990	2000	2007
Population of the world (in 1000s)	3,021,475	3,692,492	4,434,682	5,263,593	6,070,581	6,573,338

The above table shows the population increase of the world from 1960 to 2007

Calculate the percentage increase in the world population from 1970 to 2000

$$\% \text{ increase in population 1970 to 2000} = \frac{\text{increase in population}}{\text{population in 1970}} \times 100\%$$

$$= \frac{6,070,581 - 3,692,492}{3,692,492} \times 100\% = \frac{2,378,089}{3,692,492} \times 100\% = \textbf{64.4\% (to 1d.p.)}$$

Trigonometry of a right angled triangle (i.e. Pythagoras, sine, cosine and tangent)

Pythagoras:

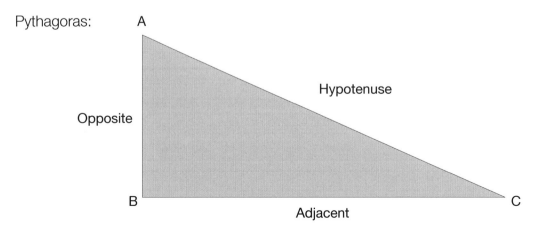

Pythagoras's theorem states that:

The square of the Hypotenuse is equal to the sum of the squares of the other two sides

In other words,   **(AC)² = (AB)² + (BC)²**

So, if AB = 6.2cm and BC = 12.2cm,

then (AC)² = (6.2)² + (12.2)² = 38.44 + 148.84 = 187.28

(AC)² = 187.28 and therefore AC = $\sqrt{187.28}$ (the square root) = 13.69cm
(to 2 d.p.)

Sine, Cosine and Tangent

Sine

For a given angle ACB, the ratio between the side opposite the angle and the hypotenuse is constant.

This ratio is called the Sine (Sin) of the angle and is equal to the opposite over the hypotenuse:

$$\text{So, Sin (ACB)} = \frac{\text{Opposite}}{\text{Hypotenuse}} = \frac{AB}{AC} = \frac{6.2}{13.69} = 0.453 \text{ (to 3 d.p.)}$$

If Sin (ACB) = 0.453 then angle ACB = 26.9° (to 1 d.p.)

Cosine

For a given angle ACB, the ratio between the side adjacent to the angle and the hypotenuse is constant.

This ratio is called the Cosine of the angle (Cos) and is equal to the adjacent over the hypotenuse:

$$\text{So, Cos (ACB)} = \frac{\text{Adjacent}}{\text{Hypotenuse}} = \frac{BC}{AC} = \frac{12.2}{13.69} = 0.891 \text{ (to 3 d.p.)}$$

If Cos (ACB) = 0.891 = then angle ACB = 26.9° (to 1 d.p.)

Tangent

For a given angle ACB, the ratio between the side opposite to the angle and the side adjacent to the angle is constant.

This ratio is called the Tangent of the angle (Tan) and is equal to the opposite over the adjacent:

So, Tan (ACB) $= \dfrac{\text{Opposite}}{\text{Adjacent}} = \dfrac{AB}{BC} = \dfrac{6.2}{12.2} = 0.508$ (to 3 d.p.)

If Tan (ACB) = 0.508 = then angle ACB = 26.9° (to 1 d.p.)

Looking at the above examples, it might sound obvious, but it is important that you are familiar with how to use your scientific calculator.

Looking at Sine for example, you first work out 6.2 divided by 13.69 = 0.453

On my calculator then, I press **2nd F** followed by **sin⁻¹** followed by 0.453 to obtain the angle 26.9° (to1 dp)

Similarly, for cosine it's **2nd F** followed by **cos⁻¹** followed by 0.891 to obtain the angle.

and for tangent it's **2nd F** followed by **tan⁻¹** followed by 0.508 to obtain the angle.

In order to calculate angle BAC:

There are 180° in a triangle, so angle BAC = 180° − (90° + 26.9°) = 180 -116.9 **= 63.1°**

Angle BAC could also be found by finding the sine, cosine or tangent of the angle.

In these cases however, relative to angle BAC, side BC would now be the opposite side, and side AB would be the adjacent side (with AC remaining as the hypotenuse):

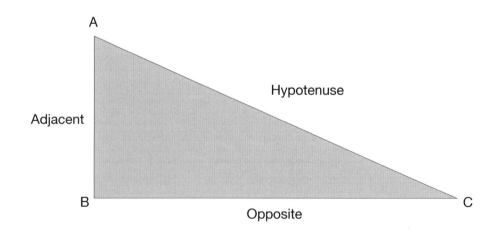

Now, Sin(BAC) $= \dfrac{\text{Opposite}}{\text{Hypotenuse}} = \dfrac{BC}{AC} = \dfrac{12.2}{13.69} = 0.891$

If Sin(BAC) = 0.891 then angle BAC = 63.1° (**2nd F** ; **sin⁻¹** ; 0.891)

And, Cos(BAC) = $\dfrac{\text{Adjacent}}{\text{Hypotenuse}}$ = $\dfrac{AB}{AC}$ = $\dfrac{6.2}{13.69}$ = 0.453

If Cos(BAC) = 0.453 then angle BAC = 63.1° (**2nd F**; **cos^{-1}**; 0.453)

And, Tan(BAC) = $\dfrac{\text{Opposite}}{\text{Adjacent}}$ = $\dfrac{BC}{AC}$ = $\dfrac{12.2}{6.2}$ = 1.968

If Tan(BAC) = 1.968 then angle BAC = 63.1° (**2nd F**; **tan^{-1}**; 1.968)

In some cases, the angle may be given, and one of the sides needs to be calculated:

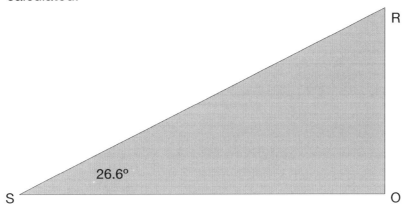

For example, a woman walks at an average speed of 0.9m/s for 1hr 17mins from village O to S then continues towards village R at the same speed. Calculate:

a) the distance from village S to village R in kilometres.

b) the total time taken if she carries on her journey, at the same speed from R back to O

a) From O to S, speed = 0.9m/s and time = 1hr 17mins
  (= 1.283hrs = 1.283 x 3600s)

Speed = $\dfrac{\text{Distance}}{\text{Time}}$ so, Distance OS = Speed x Time

= 0.9m/s x 1.283 x 3600s = 4,156.92m = 4.15692km = 4.157km (to 3d.p.)

(it is important during calculations to be aware of the units you are working in)

To calculate SR,

Cos(26.6) = $\dfrac{\text{Adjacent}}{\text{Hypotenuse}}$ = $\dfrac{OS}{SR}$ = $\dfrac{4.157}{SR}$ = 0.894 So, SR = $\dfrac{4.157}{0.894}$ = **4.650 km**

(to obtain Cos(26.6) on the calculator, I press **cos** followed by **26.6** followed by **=**)

b) From S to R Speed = $\dfrac{\text{Distance}}{\text{Time}}$ so, Time = $\dfrac{\text{Distance}}{\text{Speed}}$ = $\dfrac{4{,}650\text{m}}{0.9\text{m/s}}$ = 5,167s

5167s = $\dfrac{5167}{3600}$ hrs = 1.435 hrs (to 3d.p.)

The distance RO can be calculated using pythagoras's theorem:

$(SR)^2 = (OS)^2 + (OR)^2$ $(4.65)^2 = (4.157)^2 + (OR)^2$ $(OR)^2 = (4.65)^2 - (4.157)^2$

$(OR)^2 = 21.623 - 17.281 = 4.342$ So, OR = $\sqrt{4.342}$ = 2.084 km

(The distance RO could also be calculated by:

$\text{Sin}(26.6) = \dfrac{OR}{4.65} = 0.448$ then, OR = 0.448 x 4.65 = 2.084 km)

Then, Speed = $\dfrac{\text{Distance}}{\text{Time}}$ & Time = $\dfrac{\text{Distance}}{\text{Speed}}$ = $\dfrac{2{,}084}{0.9}$ = 2,315s

= $\dfrac{2{,}315}{3{,}600}$ hrs = 0.643hr

Total time = 1.283 + 1.435 + 0.643 = **3.361hrs**

Forming and solving equations (Algebra)

Worked example:

A man decides to sell his old LPs and singles at a car boot sale for £4.50 and £2.50 respectively. He sells 34 records at the sale and his total takings are £113.00

a) Use this information to form two equations about the LPs and singles sold at the car boot sale.

Let the number of LPs sold = A and the number of singles sold = B

Then, **A + B = 34** (Equation 1)

and, **4.50A + 2.50B = 113.00** (Equation 2)

b) Use the equations to calculate the number of LPs and the number of singles sold at the car boot sale.

If A + B = 34 then A = 34 – B

We can now substitute A = 34 – B into equation 2:

So, 4.5(34 – B) + 2.5B = 113

Next, we expand the brackets:

4.5 x 34 – 4.5B + 2.5B = 113

$153 - 2B = 113$

$153 - 113 = 2B$

$40 = 2B$ therefore **B** = **20**

We can now substitute B = 20 into equation 1

$A + 20 = 34$ therefore **A** = **14**

So, the man sold **14** LPs and **20** singles

Practice Questions

Q1 In 2008, it was estimated that the UK's assets were worth approximately £337,104,120,000

a) Write down this figure in standard form.

b) If a painting is valued at twenty three and a half million pounds, what percentage of the UK's assets is the painting worth? (Give the answer in standard form to 4 decimal places.

Q2 If the diameter of an atom is in the order of 10^8 cm, then what would be the length of one hundred and fifty thousand atoms lying side by side (give the answer in standard form in metres).

Q3 A driver travels 63 miles from town A to town C, then travels at 42 miles per hour for 42 minutes from town C to town B. In town B the driver buys a new car.

a) If the new car emits 270g of carbon dioxide for every kilometre driven, then how many kilograms of carbon dioxide will the new car emit on its journey back to A? (1km = 0.621miles).

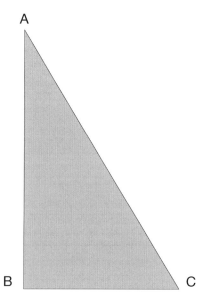

A

B   C

b) Calculate the angle BAC. Check your answer by an alternative method.

Q4 A farmer is planning to use one of his fields for growing rapeseed and wishes to make a scale drawing of the field. If the area of the field is 0.18 Hectares, and the length of the field is twice its width, then:
a) What are the actual dimensions (in metres) of the field?
(1 Hectare = 10,000m²)

b) What will be the dimensions of the field on the scale drawing, if he chooses a scale of 1 : 200?

Q5 A travel company decides to sell its return flights to France and Germany on the internet. The flights to France are sold for £33.50 and the flights to Germany for £37.00. During the first week, the company sells 380 flights. The total takings for the flights are £13,629.50

a) Use this information to form two equations about the return flights to France and Germany sold on the internet.

b) Use the equations to calculate the number of return flights to France and Germany sold on the internet during the first week.

GCSE Learning Guide

Factorising

Factor trees: worked examples

The number 63 has two factors, 9 and 7 i.e. 9 x 7 = 63 or (9)(7) = 63

In a factor tree, factors of each number are written beneath until we are left with prime numbers at the end of the 'branches' of the tree:

These prime numbers then, when multiplied together, should give us the original number:

So, 3 x 3 x 7 = 63 or 3^2 x 7 = 63

The number 60 has several factors, 30 and 2, 12 and 5, 15 and 4, and 10 and 6.
10 and 6 also have factors. 10 has factors of 5 and 2, and 6 has factors of 3 and 2. Therefore, the factor tree of 60 could look like:

The numbers left at the bottom of the factor tree will always be prime numbers.

We can write 5 x 2 x 3 x 2 = 60 or 5 x 3 x 2^2 = 60

We could also write (5 x 2) (3 x 2) = 60 which is the same as 10 x 6 = 60

Here then, the factors are (5 x 2) and (3 x 2)

Questions on factor trees

Q1.   Complete a factor tree for 135

Q2.   Complete a factor tree for 235

Factors of algebraic expressions

As with numbers, algebraic expressions and quadratic equations can also have factors.

Worked examples:

The algebraic expression $8x + 4$ can be factorised by looking at the two terms and working out what is common to both. In this case, it is 4, which is then one of the factors. The other factor is worked out by forming a bracket and calculating what the 4 needs to be multiplied by to form the expression $8x + 4$

So, $8x + 4 = 4(2x + 1)$ where 4 and $(2x + 1)$ are the factors.

This can be checked by expanding the brackets: $4(2x + 1) = 8x + 4$

For the algebraic expression $15p + 10$ the number 5 is common to both terms. The factors then will be $5(3p + 2)$, which when expanded $= 15p + 10$

Questions on factors of algebraic expressions

Find the factors of the following algebraic expressions:

1        $6n + 2$

2        $9y + 6$

3        $7p + 21$

4        $18a + 4$

5        $56y + 14$

6        $64b + 24$

Expand the following factors to form algebraic expressions:

1. $3(4x + 2)$

2. $-2(5x + 3)$

3. $4(-x + 2)$

4. $6(4x + 6)$

Factors of quadratic expressions

If an expression contains the term x^2, then it is known as a quadratic expression.

Worked examples:

Factorise the quadratic expression $x^2 + 3x + 2$

The factors will need to include x as it is common to the terms x^2 and 3x (and because x multiplied by itself) gives us x^2

$(x +\ )(x +\ )$

The number 2 can only be formed by 2 x 1, so the factors will need to contain 2 and 1 also. So, (x + 2) and (x + 1) are the factors of the equation. This can be checked by expanding the brackets, whereby the terms in the second bracket are multiplied by the terms in the first bracket separately, then added together:

$(x + 2)(x + 1) = x(x + 1) + 2(x + 1) = x^2 + x + 2x + 2 = x^2 + 3x + 2$

In the example, $x^2 + 4x + 4$ the 4 can be formed by its factors 4 and 1, or 2 and 2

So, if we try 4 and 1 first, we get: (x + 4) and (x + 1)

If we expand these brackets, we get:

$(x + 4)(x + 1) = x(x + 1) + 4(x + 1) = x^2 + x + 4x + 4 = x^2 + 5x + 4$

But, $x^2 + 5x + 4 \neq x^2 + 4x + 4$ so (x + 4) and (x + 1) are not the correct factors

If instead we take 2 and 2 as the multiples of 4, then we get (x + 2) and (x + 2)

When we expand the brackets we get:

$(x + 2)(x + 2) = x(x + 2) + 2(x + 2) = x^2 + 2x + 2x + 4 = x^2 + 4x + 4$

So, (x + 2) and (x + 2) are the correct factors.

To avoid 'trial and error' in finding the factors of quadratic expressions, the resultant x term that is formed by the expansion of factors also needs to be calculated in advance.

$2x^2 + 8x + 8 = (2x + 4)(x + 2) = 2x(x + 2) + 4(x + 2) = 2x^2 + 4x + 4x + 8 = 2x^2 + 8x + 8$

Questions on factors of quadratic expressions

Q1.   Find the factors of the following quadratic expressions:

        a) $3x^2 + 4x + 1$

b) $2x^2 - 7x + 6$

c) $4x^2 - 10x - 14$

d) $4x^2 + 8x - 12$

e) $3x^2 - 4x - 4$

f) $5x^2 + 3x - 2$

Q2. Expand the following factors to form quadratic expressions:

a) $(2x + 3)(4x + 1)$

b) $(2x + 2)(x + 1)$

c) $(5x - 3)(x - 1)$

d) $(3x + 3)(2x - 2)$

e) $(2x + 3)^2$

f) $(x - 2)(5x + 3)$

g) $(3x - 4)(2x - 2)$

h) $(x + 1)(6x - 5)$

Solving quadratic equations

Worked examples:

In the above examples, if the quadratic expressions are made into equations (through being given a value), they can be solved i.e. values of x can be calculated:

E.g. If $x^2 + 3x + 2 = 0$ then its factors $(x + 2)(x + 1) = 0$

For this to be true, x = -2 or -1

This can be checked by substituting the values into the equation.

So, for x = - 2: $(-2)^2 + 3(-2) + 2 = 4 - 6 + 2 = 0$

And for x = -1: $(-1)^2 + 3 (-1) + 2 = 1 - 3 + 2 = 0$

If $x^2 + 4x + 4 = 0$ then $(x + 2)(x + 2) = 0$

For this to be true, x = -2

$(-2)^2 + 4(-2) + 4 = 4 - 8 + 4 = 0$

If $2x2 + 8x + 8 = 0$ then $(2x + 4) (x + 2) = 0$

For this to be true, 2x + 4 = 0   2x = -4 $x = \dfrac{-4}{2} = -2$ or x + 2 = 0   x = -2

Solve the following quadratic equations:

Q1 $x^2 + 7x + 12 = 0$

Q2 $3x^2 + 12x + 9 = 0$

Q3 $4x^2 + 5x + 1 = 0$

Q4 $4x^2 - 10x + 4 = 0$

Q5 $5x^2 + 3x - 2 = 0$

Q6 $6x^2 - 6 = 0$

Inequalities

If algebraic equations do not equal zero, but rather they represent values that are greater than or less than a given value, or that lie between given values, then they can still be solved or represented on a number line.

Worked examples. Solve the inequalities:

a) $7x - 7 \geq 21$ $7x \geq 28$ $x \geq \dfrac{28}{7}$ $x \geq 4$

b) $3y + 5 < 14$ $3y < 9$ $y < \dfrac{9}{3}$ $y < 3$

Inequalities can be represented on a number line.
For example, $-2 < x \leq 4$

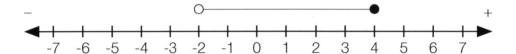

In the above example, the ○ means that the number (-2) is not included (as $-2 < x$), whereas the ● means that the number (4) is included (as $x \leq 4$). The integer values of x then that satisfy the inequality are -1, 0, 1, 2, 3 and 4

In the worked example a) above, $x \geq 4$ can be represented by the following number line:

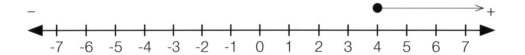

In the worked example b) above, $y < 3$ can be represented by the following number line:

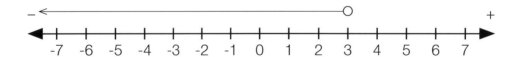

Questions on inequalities

1) Solve the following inequalities:

a) $5p + 2 \leq 17$

b) $2.5m - 1.5 > 6$

c) $7x + 6 < 13$

d) $y + 10 \geq 3$

2) Show each of the above inequalities on the following number lines:

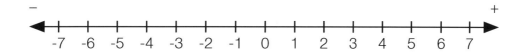

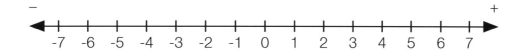

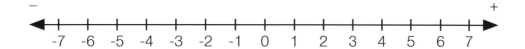

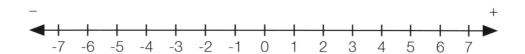

3) On the number line below, show the inequality $-5 \le y \le 4$

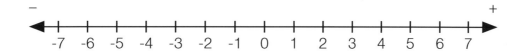

4) On the number line below, show the inequality $-1 < x < 4$

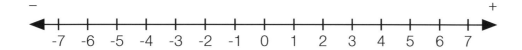

5) Write down the inequality, in x, shown on the number line below:

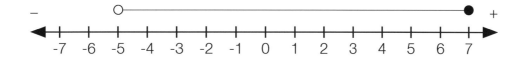

6) Write down the inequality, in y, shown on the number line below:

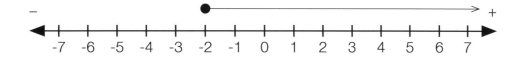

7) Write down the inequality, in p, shown on the number line below:

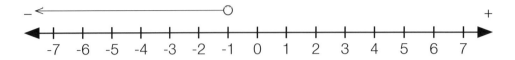

8) If t is an integer, write down all its possible values for $1 < t < 7$

9) If r is an integer, write down all its possible values for $-6 \leq r < -1$

10) If x is an integer, write down all its possible values for $-4 < x \leq 5$

Adding and subtracting fractions

When adding or subtracting fractions, we need to find the lowest common denominator, then divide each denominator (bottom number of the fraction) into the common denominator and multiply by its numerator (top number of the fraction). If necessary, the resultant fraction should be simplified.

Worked examples:

$$\frac{2}{5} + \frac{1}{3} = \frac{6+5}{15} = \frac{11}{15} \qquad \frac{1}{8} + \frac{3}{12} = \frac{3+6}{24} = \frac{9}{24} = \frac{3}{8}$$

$$\frac{5}{6} - \frac{1}{4} = \frac{20-6}{24} = \frac{14}{24} \qquad \frac{9}{10} - \frac{2}{3} = \frac{27-20}{30} = \frac{7}{30}$$

If improper fractions are added, we can add the integers (whole numbers) first, then add the fractions separately:

$$2\tfrac{1}{4} + 3\tfrac{1}{5} = 5 + \frac{5+4}{20} = 5\tfrac{9}{20}$$

Similarly, if improper fractions are subtracted, we can subtract the integers first, then subtract the fractions separately, but provided the fraction in the second term is smaller than the fraction in the first term. For example:

$$8\tfrac{1}{4} - 3\tfrac{1}{5} = 5 \text{ and } \frac{5-4}{20} = 5\tfrac{1}{20}$$

If however, the fraction in the second term is larger than the fraction in the first term, we need to convert both improper fractions into fractions. For example:

$$4\tfrac{1}{3} - 1\tfrac{2}{5} = \frac{13}{3} - \frac{7}{5} = \frac{65-21}{15} \quad \frac{44}{15} = 2^{14}/_{15}$$

Questions on adding and subtracting fractions

1) $\dfrac{1}{8} + \dfrac{7}{12} =$

2) $\dfrac{7}{9} + \dfrac{2}{3} =$

3) $3\tfrac{3}{4} + 5\tfrac{1}{3} =$

4) $\dfrac{3}{7} - \dfrac{3}{8} =$

5) $\dfrac{2}{3} - \dfrac{3}{8} =$

6) $5\tfrac{1}{8} - 2\tfrac{1}{5} =$

Multiplying and dividing fractions

When two fractions are multiplied, the numerators and denominators are multiplied separately. If possible, the fractions should be simplified before multiplying.

Worked examples

$$\frac{4}{5} \times \frac{3}{7} = \frac{12}{35} \qquad \frac{4^1}{5} \times \frac{3}{4^1} = \frac{3}{5}$$

When multiplying improper fractions, they should be converted to proper fractions first, then multiplied and converted back to an improper fraction. For example:

$$2\tfrac{1}{3} \times 3\tfrac{1}{4} = \frac{7}{3} \times \frac{13}{4} = \frac{91}{12} = 7^7/_{12}$$

When two fractions are divided, the second fraction is inverted, and the division sign changed to the multiplication sign. For example:

$$\frac{3}{4} \div \frac{2}{5} = \frac{3}{4} \times \frac{5}{2} = \frac{15}{8} = 1\tfrac{7}{8} \qquad 9 \div 3 = 3 \text{ or } \frac{9}{1} \div \frac{3}{1} = \frac{9}{1} \times \frac{1}{3} = \frac{9}{3} = 3$$

When dividing improper fractions, they should be converted to improper fractions first before inverting the second fraction and multiplying. For example:

$$6\tfrac{1}{4} \div 2\tfrac{3}{8} = \frac{25}{4} \div \frac{19}{8} = \frac{25}{4^1} \times \frac{8^2}{19} = \frac{50}{19} = 2^{12}/_{19}$$

Questions on multiplying and dividing questions

Q1. $\dfrac{4}{5} \times \dfrac{3}{4} =$

Q2. $\dfrac{7}{8} \times \dfrac{4}{11} =$

Q3. $2\tfrac{1}{5} \times 4\tfrac{3}{8} =$

Q4. $\dfrac{2}{3} \div \dfrac{1}{6} =$

Q5. $\dfrac{7}{8} \div \dfrac{4}{11} =$

Q6. $2\tfrac{1}{5} \div 4\tfrac{3}{8} =$

Solving simultaneous equations

With simultaneous equations, we need to try and solve two unknowns (e.g. x and y, or a and b) which are in each of two different equations.

Worked example

1) $2x + y = 7$ 2) $3x + 2y = 12$

Method 1: By substitution

Find an expression for y (or x) in one of the equations, then substitute it into the other equation

$2x + y = 7$ So, $y = 7 - 2x$

Substituting into equation 2), $3x + 2(7 - 2x) = 12$ which leaves us with just one unknown.

Then, expanding the brackets gives us: $3x + 14 - 4x = 12$

Rearranging the terms gives us: $14 - 12 = 4x - 3x$ So, $x = \mathbf{2}$

Then, substituting x back into equation 1 gives us:
$2(2) + y = 7$ i.e. $4 + y = 7$ $y = 7 - 4 = \mathbf{3}$

This can be checked by putting the values for x and y into the second equation:

$3x + 2y = 12$

$3(2) + 2(3) = 12$ i.e. $6 + 6 = 12$

Method 2: By equating

       1) $2x + y = 7$ 2) $3x + 2y = 12$

If the terms in equation 1) are doubled, we obtain $4x + 2y = 14$

Now, both equations contain the term 2y

In 1) $2y = 14 - 4x$ and in 2) $2y = 12 - 3x$

So, putting the equations together:

$14 - 4x = 12 - 3x$

$14 - 12 = -3x + 4x$

$\mathbf{2} = x$ which we can substitute into equations 1) or 2) in order to obtain y (as above).

$2x + y = 7$ $(2 \times 2) + y = 7$ $4 + y = 7$ $y = 7 - 4 = 3$

Questions on solving simultaneous equations

Solve the following simultaneous equations:

1) $4x - 3y = 5$ and $2x + y = 15$

2) $2x - y = 5$ and $2y - 3x = -6$

3) $4x - 3y = -1$ and $x - 2y = 1$

4) $5x - 3y = 1$ and $3x + y = 2$

Sequences

In a sequence of numbers, n represents any term in the sequence (e.g. first term, second term, third term, nth term etc.) and an expression can be given for the sequence in terms of n.

For example, in the sequence 2, 4, 6, 8, 10 … the 3rd term = 6 and the 4th term = 8

So, the expression for any term in the sequence can be represented by 2n

The 6th term then would be 2n = 2(6) = 2 x 6 = 12 etc.

In the sequence 3, 6, 9, 12, 15, 18, … the 2nd term = 6 and the 3rd term = 9

So, the expression for any term in the sequence can be represented by 3n

The 6th term then would be 3n = 3(6) = 3 x 6 = 18 etc.

In the sequence 4, 8, 12, 16, 20 … the 2nd term = 8 and the 3rd term = 12

So, the expression for any term in the sequence can be represented by 4n

The 6th term then would be 4n = 4(6) = 4 x 6 = 24 etc.

In the sequence 1, 5, 9, 13, 17 … the 2nd term = 5 and the 3rd term = 9

In other words, 3 is subtracted from each term in the previous sequence

So, the expression for any term can represented by $4n - 3$

Whereby the 2nd term = $4(2) - 3 = 8 - 3 = 5$ and the 3rd term = $4(3) - 3 = 12 - 3 = 9$

The 6th then would be $4(6) - 3 = (4 \times 6) - 3 = 24 - 3 = 21$ etc.

Looking at the above examples, if the numbers go up in steps of 3, $3n$ will be a part of the expression for all the terms and if they go up in steps of 4, $4n$ will be part of the expression for all the terms etc.

In the sequence 6, 11, 16, 21, 26 … the numbers are going up in steps of 5

So, $5n$ will be part of the expression for all the terms.

For the 1st term, $6 = 5(1) + 1 = 5 + 1 = 6$

For the 3rd term, $16 = 5(3) + 1 = 15 + 1 = 16$

The expression then for any term in the above sequence can be represented by $5n + 1$

For the 6th term, $5n + 1 = 5(6) = 1 = 30 + 1 = 31$ etc.

In the sequence 72, 69, 66, 63, 60 … the numbers are going down in steps of 3

So, $-3n$ will be part of the expression for all terms.

For the 1st term, (n = 1), the starting point of the expression needs to be 3 higher than the first term 72

So, the expression is $75 - 3n$ which should be valid for any other term.

For the 2nd term (n = 2), $75 - 3(n) = 75 - 3(2) = 75 - 6 = 69$

For the 5th term (n = 5), $75 - 3(n) = 75 - 3(5) = 75 - 15 = 60$

For the 6th term (n = 6), $75 - 3(n) = 75 - 3(6) = 75 - 18 = 57$ etc.

In the previous sequences, the same number is either added or subtracted to find the next term. They are known as **arithmetic sequences**.

However, there are other types of sequences. For example, each term can be multiplied or divided by the same number each time. These are known as **geometric sequences**:

3, 12, 48, 192, … The rule here is that the previous term is multiplied by 4

2, 10, 50, 250, … The rule here is that the previous term is multiplied by 5

810, 270, 90, 30, …The rule here is that the previous term is divided by 3

1,296, 216, 36, 6, ... the rule here is that the previous term is divided by 6

If a series of numbers is formed by adding together the two previous terms, it is known as the **Fibonacci sequence**.
The sequence runs 0, 1, 1, 2, 3, 5, 8, 13, 21 ...

If a series of numbers is formed by increasing the number you add on by one each time, it is known as the **sequence of triangular numbers** because it is generated from a pattern of dots that form a triangle. By adding another row of dots and counting all the dots we can find the next number of the sequence:

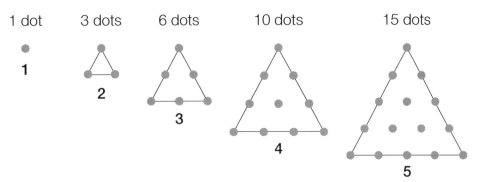

So, the sequence runs 1, 3, 6, 10, 15, ...

Questions on sequences

Q1. For the following sequences, complete the next 3 terms and find an expression for the nth term;

   a) 6, 9, 12, 15, 18, 21, 24 ...

   b) -2, 5, 12, 19, 26 ...

   c) 6, 12, 18, 24, 30 ...

   d) 1, 5, 9, 13, 17 ...

   e) 49, 46, 43, 40, 37 ...

   f) 9, 8, 7, 6, 5 ...

   g) 7, 1, -5, -11, -17 ...

   h) 0, -4, -8, -12, -16 ...

Q2. Find the value of the seventh term of the expression $5n - 8$

Q3. Find the value of the eleventh term of the expression $9 - 3n$

Q4. Find the value of the 6th term of the quadratic expression $n^2 - 6$

Q5. Find the value of the 5th term of the quadratic expression $14 - 2n^2$

Q6.   Which term of the expression 7n + 7 gives a value of 42?

Q7.   Which term of the expression 9n – 15 gives a value of 39?

Q8.   Which term of the expression 5 – 3n gives a value of -19?

Q9.   Which term of the expression – 8 – 4n gives a value of – 40?

Q10. Which term of the quadratic expression n^2 + 7 gives a value of 43?

Q11. Complete the next 2 terms of the following sequences:

   a)   4, 12, 36, 108 ...

   b)   2, 8, 32, 128 ...

   c)   12500, 2500, 500, 100 ...

   d)   880, 440, 220 ...

Q12. Calculate the 7th and 8th terms of the following sequence:
      1, 3, 6, 10, 15 ...

Q13. Calculate the 11th and 12th terms of the following sequence:
      1, 1, 2, 3, 5, 8, 13, 21 ...

Q14. Calculate the 8th and 9th terms of the following sequence:
      1, 4, 9, 16, 25 ...

Q15. Calculate the 6th and 7th terms of the following sequence:
      1, 8, 27, 64 ...

Stem and leaf diagrams

Data can be represented in an ordered stem and leaf diagram.

Worked example:

Below are the weights (in kg) of 15 students in a class:

58 62 82 75 74

61 63 55 72 59

59 68 70 66 60

Below is an ordered stem and leaf diagram showing this information:

Stem	Leaf
5	5 8 9 9
6	0 1 2 3 6 8
7	0 2 4 5
8	2

Key: 5/8 = 58kg

The median can be calculated from the above diagram = 63kg
i.e. the middle (8th) number of the 15 numbers.

The range can also be calculated = 82 − 55 = 27kg

Questions on stem and leaf diagrams

A student records the times (in minutes) that it takes for the pupils in his class to get to school:

5, 8, 9, 10, 11, 12, 12, 15, 15, 16, 17, 19, 20 21, 21, 24, 25, 25, 27, 31

Draw an ordered stem and leaf diagram to represent this information.

Stem	Leaf

Key:

Calculate the median:

Calculate the range:

Frequency tables

Data can also be represented in a frequency table:

Worked example 1

A student measured the length of 17 beetles and recorded her results in a frequency table:

Length (in cm)	Number of beetles (frequency)		
2	3	2 x 3	6cm
3	4	3 x 4	12cm
4	1	4 x 1	4cm
5	5	5 x 5	25cm
6	4	6 x 4	24cm

Number = 17   Total length = 71cm

In this example, the mean length of the beetles is calculated by multiplying each separate length by the number (frequency) of beetles of that length, then calculating the total length and dividing by the total number of beetles:

So, Mean Length = $\dfrac{\text{Total Length}}{\text{Number}} = \dfrac{71\text{cm}}{17} = $ **4.2cm** (to one decimal place)

There are 17 beetles, so the Median Length will be the 9th one (the one in the middle when there's an odd number). The 9th beetle's length is **5cm**

The Modal (most common) Length = **5cm**

The Range of lengths of beetles = 6 − 2 = **4cm**

Worked example 2

A student recorded the heights of the 20 pupils in her school form and placed the results in a frequency table:

Height (h cm) of pupils	frequency
$130 \le h < 140$	4
$140 \le h < 150$	7
$150 \le h < 160$	5
$160 \le h < 170$	3
$170 \le h < 180$	1

Total = 20

135 x 4 =   540
145 x 7 = 1015
155 x 5 =   775
165 x 3 =   495
175 x 1 =   175
2,900
1 3 2

In these types of examples, results are grouped together in intervals. For example, the first line shows that 4 pupils have a height of between 130cm and 140 cm (including 130cm but not 140cm), whilst the second line shows that 7 pupils have a height between 140cm and 150cm (including 140cm but not 150cm) and so on.

The mean height of the students in the class is calculated by first multiplying the middle number of each separate interval by the number of students (frequency) who have heights within that interval. For example, in the first line (shown above), 135 x 4 = 540

Then, the total height is calculated and divided by the total number of students.

So, Mean Height = $\dfrac{\text{Total Height}}{\text{Number}} = \dfrac{2,900}{20} = $ **145cm**

Note that the mean height will be an estimate, as the individual results are not given, but grouped together in intervals.

The Modal Interval (the interval containing the highest frequency)
= **140 ≤ h < 150**

The interval that contains the Median is **140 ≤ h < 150**
(because it contains the tenth and eleventh heights)

Questions on frequency tables

Q1. A ballet teacher has 20 pupils in her mixed age class.
     She decides to records their ages in a frequency table:

Ages (in years)	Number of children (frequency)
3	4
4	4
5	3
6	6
7	3

a) Calculate the mean age of the children.

b) State the median age of the children.

c) State the modal age of the children.

d) Calculate the age range of the children.

Q2. A student recorded the distances (in miles) of 15 different towns from
     his home town and placed her results in the following grouped frequency
     table:

Distance (d miles)	frequency
$0 < d \le 10$	3
$10 < d \le 20$	3
$20 < d \le 30$	1
$30 < d \le 40$	3
$40 < d \le 50$	5

a) Calculate an estimate for the mean distance of the towns from the
    student's home town.

b) Why is the answer an estimate?

c) Find the interval that contains the median.

d) Write down the modal interval.

Q3.   A student recorded the cost of a cappuccino at 16 different cafes.
His results were placed in the following grouped frequency table:

Cost (c £) of coffee	frequency
$1.70 < c \le 1.90$	2
$1.90 < c \le 2.10$	4
$2.10 < c \le 2.30$	3
$2.30 < c \le 2.50$	5
$1.50 \le c \le 2.70$	2

a)   Calculate an estimate for the mean cost of a cappuccino.

b)   Why is the answer an estimate?

c)   Find the interval that contains the median.

d)   Write down the modal interval.

Venn diagrams

A set of data can be represented in a venn diagram in order to separate and
compare, different pieces of information from that data. In questions relating to
venn diagrams, you are generally required to calculate missing information from
the data.

Worked example

In a class of 30 students, it was found that 16 had GCSE maths, 18 had GCSE
English and 8 had neither. Calculate how many students had both GCSE
maths and English, and complete the following venn diagram:

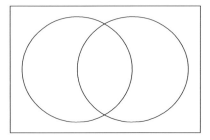

In venn diagram 1), circle A represents all the students who have GCSE maths.
In 2), circle B represents all the students who have GCSE English, whilst in
3), the area where they intersect, (A ∩ B), represents all the students who
have both GCSE maths and English. In venn diagram 4), A' represents the

complement of set A i.e. all those students who are not in set A (and do not have GCSE maths, whilst in diagram 5), B' represents the complement of set B i.e. all those students who are not in set B (and do not have GCSE English. In venn diagram 6), A ∪ B represents all those who have maths and/or English, whilst in diagram 7), (A ∪ B)' represents the complement of A ∪ B i.e. those students who have neither GCSE maths nor English and who, as part of the class, are inside the box, but outside the two circles

1) A   2) B   3) A ∩ B

4) A'   5) B'   6) A ∪ B

7) (A ∪ B)

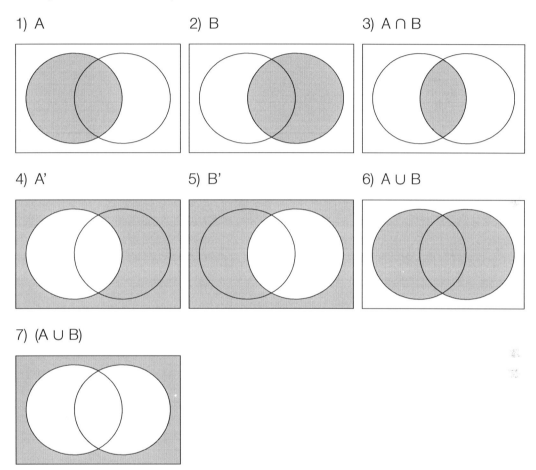

In venn diagram questions, like with questions on ratios, we are given some information and expected to find unknowns with that information. In the above example, 8 out of the 30 students, had neither GCSE maths or English, which means that 22 (30 – 8) had GCSE maths and/or English. Out of that 22 (A ∪ B), 16 had GCSE maths (A), meaning that 22 – 16 = 6 students had English GCSE only (B[1]). As 18 had GCSE English (B), then 18 – 6 = 12 students must have had both English and maths (A ∩ B). As 16 students had GCSE maths, then 16 – 12 = 4 students had GCSE maths only (A[1]). The venn diagram can now be completed:

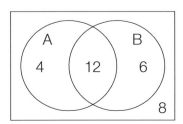

Questions on venn diagrams

Q1. In a survey, twenty five teenagers were asked about their use of the social media sites Instagram and Snapchat. The number of teenagers using Instagram only was found to be the same as the number using Snapchat only. If 12% of those surveyed said they used neither Snapchat nor Instagram and if the number using Snapchat was fifteen, then complete the following venn diagram:

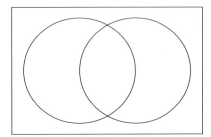

Q2. A group of students were asked if they had been to France or Spain. From the results it was found that all had been to at least one of the two countries, 8 had been to both countries and ten had been to Spain. If the number of people who had been to France was twice the number of people who had been to Spain, then complete the following venn diagram and calculate the total number of students who took part in the survey:

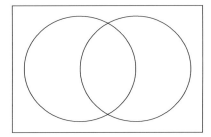

Q3. A group of 110 year 11 school pupils are asked if they play football and cricket. A tenth of the pupils stated they played neither whilst twice as many stated that they played football only than cricket only. Complete the following Venn Diagram. If one of the pupils from the group is chosen at random, what is the probability that they will meet the condition 'Football ∩ Cricket'?

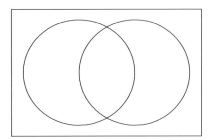

Indices

$8 = 2 \times 2 \times 2 = 2^3 \qquad 4 = 2 \times 2 = 2^2$

$8 \times 4 = 32 \qquad$ So, $(2 \times 2 \times 2) \times (2 \times 2) = 32 = 2^5$ (2 multiplied by itself 5 times)

Therefore, $2^3 \times 2^2 = 2^5$ where 2 is the base, and 5 is the indice (or power).

In other words, when indices with the same base are multiplied together, the answer is obtained by adding the indices. This is called a law of indices.

So, $2^3 \times 2^3 = 2^6$ i.e. $(2 \times 2 \times 2) \times (2 \times 2 \times 2) = 8 \times 8 = 64$
(2 multiplied by itself 6 times)

In another example, $3^2 \times 3^2 = 3^4$ i.e. $(3 \times 3) \times (3 \times 3) = 9 \times 9 = 81 = 3^4$
(3 multiplied by itself four times).

Other examples: $2a^3 \times a^4 = 2a^7$ and $3y^4 \times 4y^5 = 12y^9$

$$\frac{16}{8} = 2 \text{ or } \frac{2 \times 2 \times 2 \times 2}{2 \times 2 \times 2} = 2 \text{ or } \frac{2^4}{2^3} = 2^1 = 2$$

$$\frac{81}{9} = 9 \text{ or } \frac{3 \times 3 \times 3 \times 3}{3 \times 3} = \frac{3^4}{3^2} = 3^2$$

In other words, when indices with the same base are divided, the answer is obtained by subtracting the indices. In the first example, $4 - 3 = 1$ and in the second example, $4 - 2 = 2$

Other examples: $y^7 \div y^3 = y^{(7-3)} = y^4 \quad \dfrac{3P^8}{P^2} = 3P^6 \quad \dfrac{7a^3b^5}{2ab2} = 3.5a^2b^3$

Questions on indices

Q1 $y^4 \times 2y^3 =$

Q2 $2y^4 \times y^{-3} =$

Q3   Calculate $7^5 \times 7^{-3} =$

Q4   Calculate the following to 3 significant figures:

     a) $5^3 \times 5^2 =$

     b) $4^{-4} \div 4^{-2} =$

     c) $(2.1)^2 + (2.1)^3 =$

Angle rules

Intersecting lines: worked example

A line AB is drawn and a point C is placed somewhere along it. A protractor is then lined up along AB with its centre on point C, an angle of 24° is measured and a point is drawn. Then, a line DE is drawn passing through the points intersecting the line AB (as shown on the diagram below). Now the angle ECB can be measured by placing the protractor along the line DE with its centre on point C. It should equal 24°.

This is because, when you have two intersecting lines, **Vertically opposite angles are equal**

If the protractor is placed again along the line AB and the angle DCB measured, it should equal 156°

This is because, **Angles in a straight line add up to 180°** (24° + 156° = 180°).

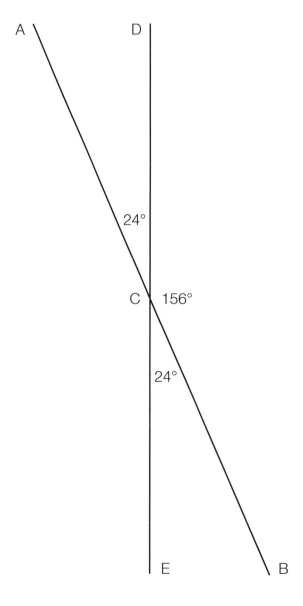

Parallel lines: worked example

In the following diagram, AC and DF are parallel lines and GH is a straight line that intersects them at B and E

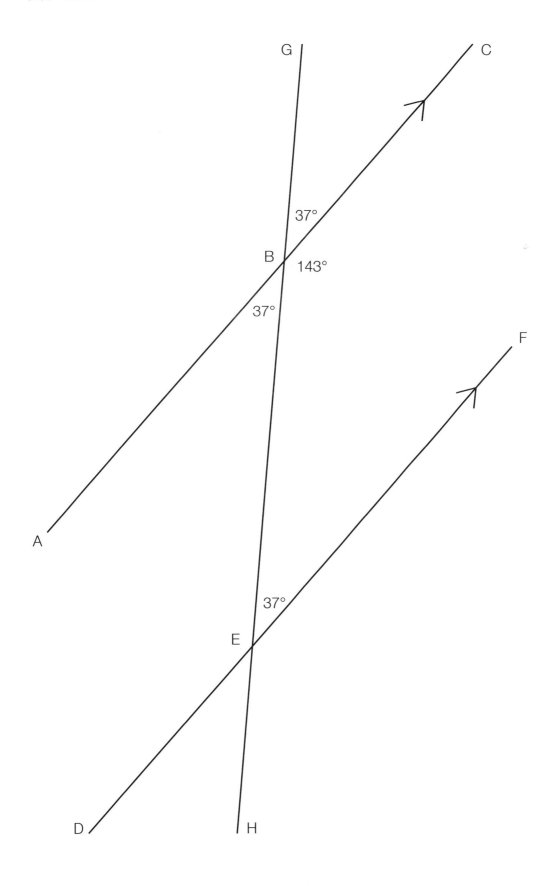

Placing a protractor along the line DEF with its centre at point E, angle BEF measures 37°. Then, placing the protractor along the line CBA with its centre at point B, angle ABE also measures 37°. So, the rule here is that for lines that intersect parallel lines, **alternate angles are equal**. If now, the protractor is turned around and placed along the line ABC with its centre at B, angle GBC should measure 37° also. The rule here is that for lines that intersect parallel lines, **corresponding angles are equal** (i.e. GBC = BEF). We can also say that ABE = GBC (**vertically opposite angles are equal**).

In addition, if the protractor is placed along the line GBE with its centre at B, angle EBC should measure 143°. The rule here is that **allied angles add up to 180°** (i.e. BEF + EBC = 180°). We can also say that EBC = 180° - 37° = 143° (**angles in a straight line add up to 180°**).

Exterior angles of a polygon (multi-sided shape): worked example

In the following diagram of a regular pentagon, if the base line of a protractor is placed along the line FB (with its centre at point A) and the exterior angle FAE measured, it should be 72°. There are five sides in a pentagon, so it has 5 exterior angles. 72° x 5 = 360°
So, the rule here is, **the exterior angles of a polygon add up to 360°**
Also, EAB = 180° – 72° = 108° (**angles in a straight line add up to 180°**)
If angles AEB and ABE are measured, they should be 36°
Triangle AEB is an isosceles triangle as it has two equal sides (EA = AB)
So, the rule here is, **the angles at the base of an isosceles are equal**

This can be checked:

AEB + ABE + 108° = 180° (**angles in a triangle add up to 180°**)

AEB + ABE = 180° - 108° = 72°

Therefore, AEB = ABE = $\dfrac{72°}{2}$ = 36°

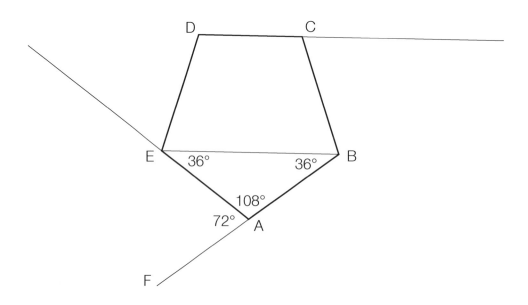

Questions on angle rules:

Q1   Look at the diagram below, of two intersecting lines. State the values of the angles x and y, and give reasons for your answers:

a)   x =   Reason:

b)   y =   Reason:

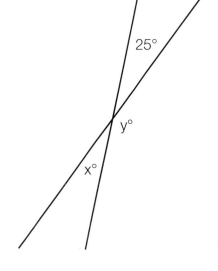

Q2   In the space below, and following the example of the first worked example above, draw 2 intersecting lines, with an angle of 48° between them:

Q3   In the diagram below, measure the angle x° between the two intersecting lines:

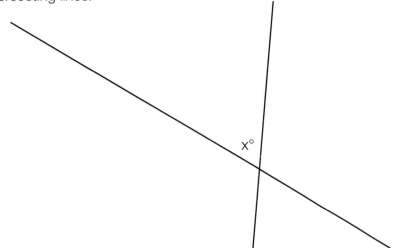

Q4 In the diagram below, AB and CD are parallel lines. Line EF intersects these lines at points G and H. If angle CHG = 120° then calculate the angle FGB. State which angle rules you have used at each stage in obtaining your answer.

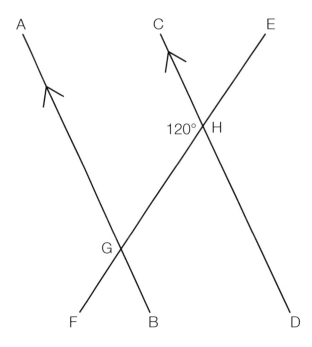

Q5 In the diagram below, AC and DE are parallel lines. If angle BDE = 37° then calculate the angle DBC. State which angle rule you have used in obtaining your answer.

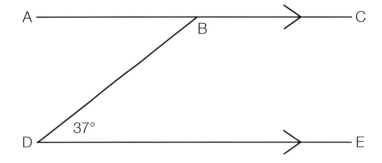

Q6 In the diagram below, 0 represents the centre of the circle.

Calculate the value of x and state which angle rules you have used at each stage in obtaining your answer.

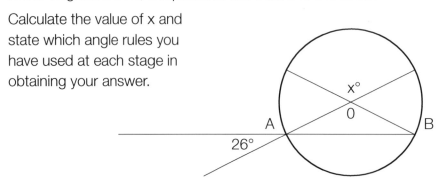

Q7   Lines AB and CD are parallel lines. Using angle rules, show that the angles in the triangle EFG (a + b + c) add up to 180°

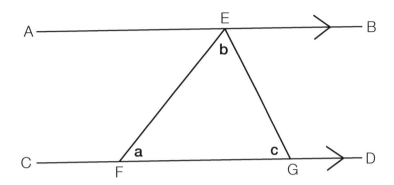

Q8   The shape below is a regular octagon. Calculate the value of the angle x and state which angle rules you have used at each stage in obtaining your answer.

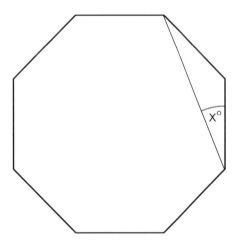

Q9   State the name of the shape below. Calculate the value of x to one decimal place and state the angle rule you have used to obtain your answer.

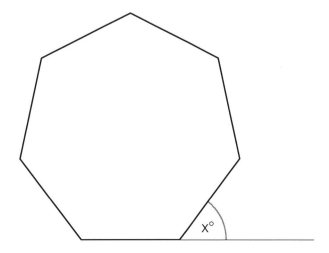

Q10   The new one pound coin has 11 sides. Calculate to one decimal place the exterior angle of the coin.

Q11   This is a regular hexagon.
Using rules of angles, show that triangle ABC is an equilateral triangle.

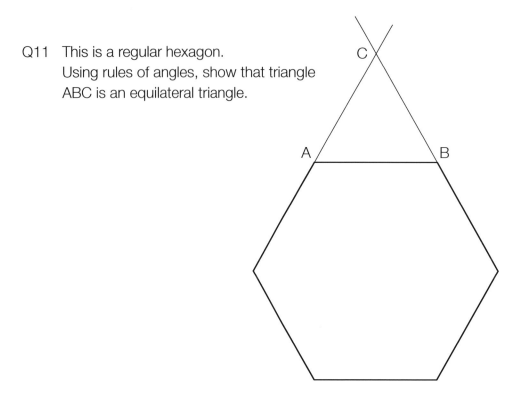

Straight line graphs

Worked examples:

Straight line graphs can be represented by the general equation **y** = **mx** + **c** where **m** is the gradient (the number of squares up or down on the y-axis for every one square across on the x- axis) and c is the y intercept (the point at which the straight line crosses the y axis.

For example, for the line **y** = **2x** – **1** (shown on G1), m= 2 and c = -1

A gradient of 2 means that for every one square across on the x-axis (from any point on the line), there are 2 squares up on the y-axis.

For the line y = **-0.5x** + **4** (also shown on G1), m = -0.5 and c = 4

A gradient of -0.5 means that for every one square across on the x-axis (from any point on the line), there is half a square down on the y-axis.

Questions on straight line graphs

Q1.   The points (-3, -9) and (1, 7) are on a straight line graph. Plot the points on a graph, draw the straight line, then work out the formula for the line and write it on the graph.

Q2.   Complete the following table for the straight line y = 3x − 1
Plot the points on a graph, then draw the straight line.

x	-4	-3	-2	-1	0	1	2	3	4
y									

Q3.   Look at the straight line graph on G2 and from it, work out the formula for the line, write it on the graph and complete the following table:

x	-4				0				4
y									

Q4.   On G3, draw and label the following straight line graphs:

a)   y = x + 4

b)   y = -2x - 2

c)   y = 2.5x

d)   y = -x + 4

Solving simultaneous equations through the drawing of straight line graphs

If we look at G1 from the worked example above, we can see that the two straight lines (y = 2x − 1 and y = -0.5x + 4) cross at the point x = 2, y = 3 i.e. at (2, 3).

The two lines can be seen as simultaneous equations, as they both contain two unknowns, x and y.

So, we have y = 2x − 1 and y = -0.5x + 4

Therefore, 2x − 1 = -0.5x + 4

Rearranging the equations gives us:

$$2x + 0.5x = 4 + 1$$
$$2.5x = 5$$
$$x = \frac{5}{2.5} = \mathbf{2} \quad \text{Substituting into above gives } y = 2(2) − 1 = 4 − 1 = \mathbf{3}$$

So, the drawing of straight line graphs and finding the co-ordinates of the point where they intersect, can be used to solve simultaneous equations.

Questions on solving simultaneous equations through the drawing of straight line graphs

Q1   On G4, draw straight line graphs of the simultaneous equations $2x + y = 7$ and $3x + 2y = 12$ and find the co-ordinates of the point where they intersect.

Point of intersection =

Q2   On G4, draw straight line graphs of the simultaneous equations $2x - y = 5$ and $2y - 3x = -6$ and find the co-ordinates of the point where they intersect.

Point of intersection =

Note: For each of the above questions, start by putting the equations into the form $y = mx + c$.

Check if your answers match the answers to the solving of the simultaneous equations on p142 (worked example) and p143 (question 2).

Quadratic Graphs

If equations have the term x^2 in them (e.g. $y = x^2 + x + 2$), i.e. if they are quadratic equations, then graphs drawn to represent these equations are known as quadratic graphs.

Like with straight line graphs, a table of values for x and y can be drawn for a quadratic equation, and the points plotted on a graph. So, for $y = x^2 + x + 2$

x	-4	-3	-2	-1	0	1	2	3	4
y	14	8	4	2	2	4	8	14	22

And, for $y = -x^2 + 2x + 1$

x	-4	-3	-2	-1	0	1	2	3	4
y	-23	-14	-7	-2	1	2	1	-2	-7

When the quadratic equations are plotted (see G5), we can see that the graphs are both smooth curves which are symmetrical about a 'turning point', with the graph with the x^2 term in the form of a ∪ shape, and the graph with the $-x^2$ term in the form of a ∩ shape.

Note how the scales on the x and y axes have been adjusted to accommodate all the values in the table i.e. on the x-axis, 2cm represents 1, whilst on the y-axis, 1cm represents 2.

Cubic graphs

If an equation contains the term x^3, then it can be represented by a cubic graph, which can be drawn after making a table of values.
For example, $y = x^3 - 2x$ on G6.

x	-3	-2	-1	0	1	2	3
y	-21	-4	1	0	-1	4	21

Questions on quadratic graphs, cubic graphs and reciprocal graphs

Q1. Complete the table below for the quadratic equation $y = 2x^2 - 2x - 2$
then plot the quadratic graph on G7

x	-3	-2	-1	0	1	2	3	4
y								

Q2. Complete the table below for the quadratic equation $y = -2x^2 + 4x + 1$
then plot the quadratic graph on G7

x	-3	-2	-1	0	1	2	3	4
y								

Q3. Complete the table below for the equation $y = -x^3 + 1$ then plot the
cubic graph on G8

x	-3	-2	-1	0	1	2	3
y							

Q4. Complete the table below for the reciprocal graph $y = \dfrac{1}{x}$ then plot the
graph on G9

x	-4	-3	-2	-1	-0.5	-0.25	0	0.25	0.5	1	2	3	4
y													

On the graph, plot the two lines of symmetry for the two symmetrical curves.

Transformations

If a shape is converted to a different position, we say that it goes through a transformation. There are four types of transformation that we should know about, namely translations, reflections, rotations and enlargements.

Translations - Worked example:

In a translation, the movement of any point on a shape is given by a column vector, in the form $\begin{pmatrix} x \\ y \end{pmatrix}$ where x represents the horizontal shift and y represents the vertical shift.

In the example on G10, triangle A has the co-ordinates (3,2), (5,2) and (5,5)

The transformation from A to B is a translation by the vector $\begin{pmatrix} 3 \\ 5 \end{pmatrix}$ i.e. each point on the triangle moves across (on the x-axis) three places to the right and up (on the y-axis) five places.

The transformation from A to C is a translation by the vector $\begin{pmatrix} -7 \\ 1 \end{pmatrix}$ i.e. each point on the triangle moves across (on the x-axis) seven places to the left and up (on the y-axis) one place.

The transformation from A to D is a translation by the vector $\begin{pmatrix} 0 \\ -7 \end{pmatrix}$ i.e. each point on the triangle moves across (on the x-axis) zero places and down (on the y-axis) seven places.

The transformation from C to B is a translation by the vector $\begin{pmatrix} 8 \\ 4 \end{pmatrix}$ i.e. each point on the triangle moves across (on the x-axis) eight places to the right and up (on the y-axis) four places.

Rotations – worked example:

When a shape is rotated, it 'turns' in a given direction (anti-clockwise or clockwise), about a given point (e.g. the origin (0,0)), and by a given angle (e.g. 90° or 180°).

In the example on G11, triangle A has the co-ordinates (3,2), (7,2) and (7,4)

The transformation from A to B is an anticlockwise rotation of 90° about the origin. Notice that when each point is rotated, its co-ordinates are swapped around and the new x co-ordinate changes its sign. So, the point (3,2) becomes (-2, 3), the point (7, 2) becomes (-2, 7) and the point (7, 4) becomes (-4, 7).

The transformation from B to C is an anticlockwise rotation of 90° about the origin. Notice that when each point is rotated, its co-ordinates are again swapped around with the new x co-ordinate changing its sign. So, the point (-2,3) becomes (-3, -2), the point (-2, 7) becomes (-7, -2) and the point (-4, 7) becomes (-7, -4).

The transformation from A to C is a rotation of 180° (anticlockwise or clockwise) about the origin. Notice that when each point is rotated, its co-ordinates just change sign. So, the point (3,2) becomes (-3, -2), the point (7, 2) becomes (-7, -2) and the point (7, 4) becomes (-7, -4).

The transformation from A to D is a clockwise rotation of 90° about the origin. Notice that when each point is rotated, its co-ordinates are swapped around and the new y co-ordinate changes its sign . So, the point (3,2) becomes (2, -3), the point (7, 2) becomes (2, -7) and the point (7, 4) becomes (4, -7).

Reflections – worked example:

For a shape to be reflected, there needs to be a straight 'mirror-line' across which its co-ordinates are reflected.

In the example on G12, triangle A has the co-ordinates (3,2), (7,2) and (7,4)

The transformation from A to B is a reflection about the line y = 0

The transformation from A to C is a reflection about the line x = 0

The transformation from A to D is a reflection about the line y = x

The transformation from A to E is a reflection about the line y = -x

Notice that triangle E, which is a reflection of triangle A about the line y = -x is in the same position as triangle C in the worked example above, of the 180° rotation of triangle about the origin. In other words, a rotation of 180° about the origin is the same transformation as a reflection about the line y = -x

Enlargements – worked example:

In order to describe an enlargement of a shape, a scale factor and the centre of enlargement are needed. The scale factor is the factor by which the sides of the new shape have increased by (or decreased by) from the original shape, whilst the centre of enlargement is the point where lines that are drawn through matching corners of the original and enlarged shapes cross.

In the example on G13, the transformation from A to B is an enlargement of scale factor 2 with centre of enlargement (0, 0) i.e. the origin. The scale factor can be worked out from:

$$\frac{\text{new length}}{\text{old length}} = \frac{a^1b^1}{ab} = \frac{4}{2} = 2 \text{ or } \frac{b^1c^1}{bc} = \frac{2}{1} = 2$$

The transformation from C to D is an enlargement of scale factor 2 with centre of enlargement (3, -9).

Note: In the case of translations, reflections and rotations, the shapes remain **congruent** i.e. they remain the same size and shape. In the case of enlargements, the shape is the same, but the sizes is different i.e. the shapes are **similar**. This means that all the angle match up and that the sides are proportional.

Questions on transformations

Q1   Looking at the translations on G10, describe the transformation:

    a) From D to B
    b) From D to C

Q2   On G14, plot the following co-ordinates of a rectangle: (-7, 1), (-5, 1) (-5, -2) and (-7, -2). Then, carry out a translation of the rectangle by the vector $\begin{pmatrix} 9 \\ -4 \end{pmatrix}$ and plot the new co-ordinates of the rectangle.

Q3.   On G15, plot the following co-ordinates of a triangle: (2, 4), (4, 6) and (1, 7) and label it A.
Then, carry out a 90° anticlockwise rotation about the origin of triangle A, write the co-ordinates and label it B.
Then, carry out a 90° anticlockwise rotation about the origin of triangle B, write the co-ordinates and label it C.
Carry out a 90° clockwise rotation about the origin of triangle A, write the co-ordinates and label it D.
Then, carry out a 90° clockwise rotation about the origin of triangle D.
Do you end up with the same co-ordinates as triangle C?
Describe a single transformation that maps triangle A onto triangle C.

Q4.   On G16, describe the transformation that maps:

    a) Shape A onto shape B.
    b) Shape C onto shape D.
    c) Shape E onto shape F.

Q5.   On G17, reflect the triangle A:

    a) About the line y = 0, write the co-ordinates and label it B.
    b) About the line x = 0, write the co-ordinates and label it C.
    c) About the line y = x, write the co-ordinates and label it D.
    d) About the line y = -x, write the co-ordinates and label it E.

Q6.   On G18, describe the transformation that maps triangle A onto triangle B

Q7.   On G18, if triangle C is diminished by a fractional scale factor of 1/3 with the centre of enlargement at (-8, -12), then plot the co-ordinates of, and draw, the diminished triangle.

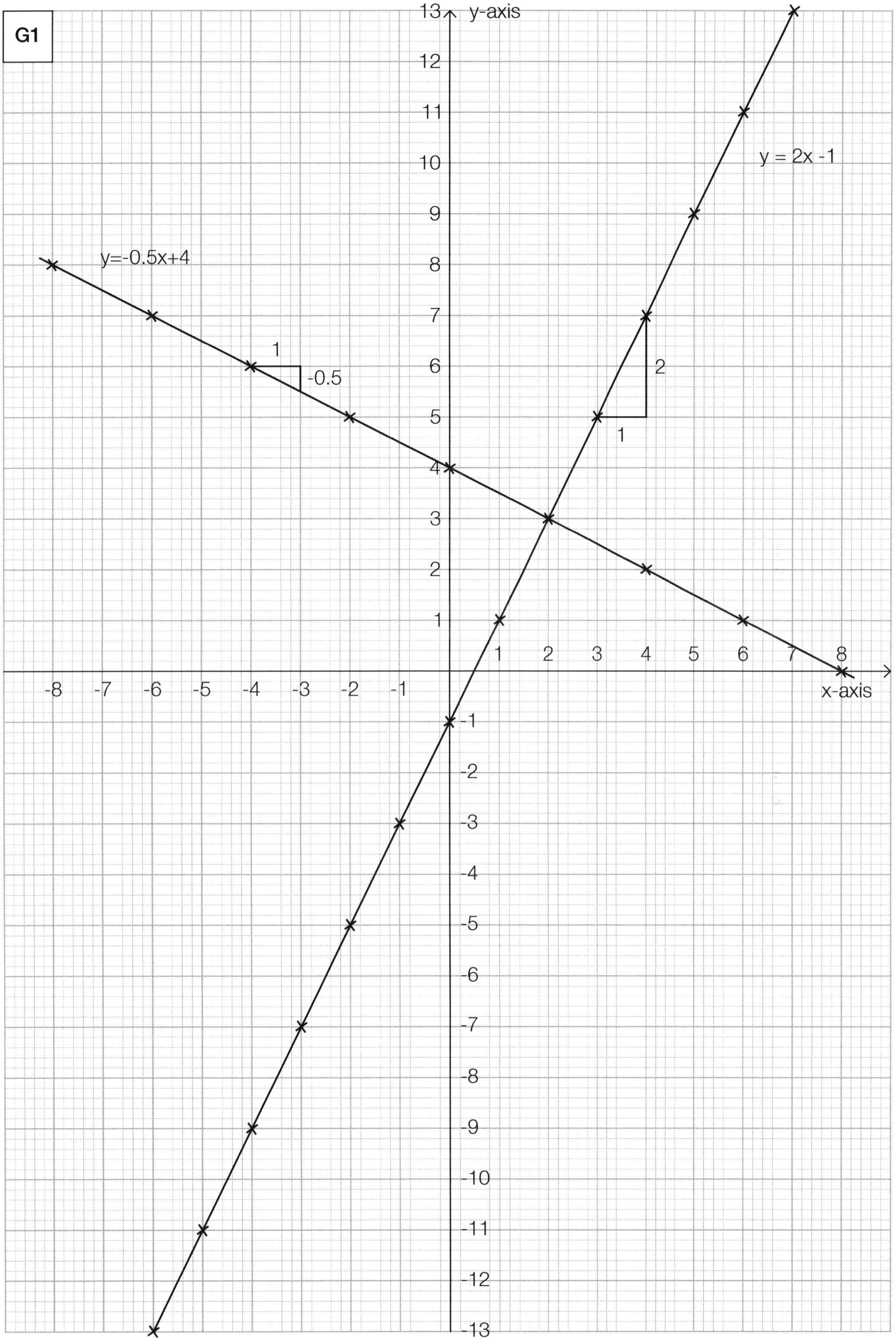
G1
y-axis
x-axis
y = 2x -1
y=-0.5x+4
1
-0.5
2
1

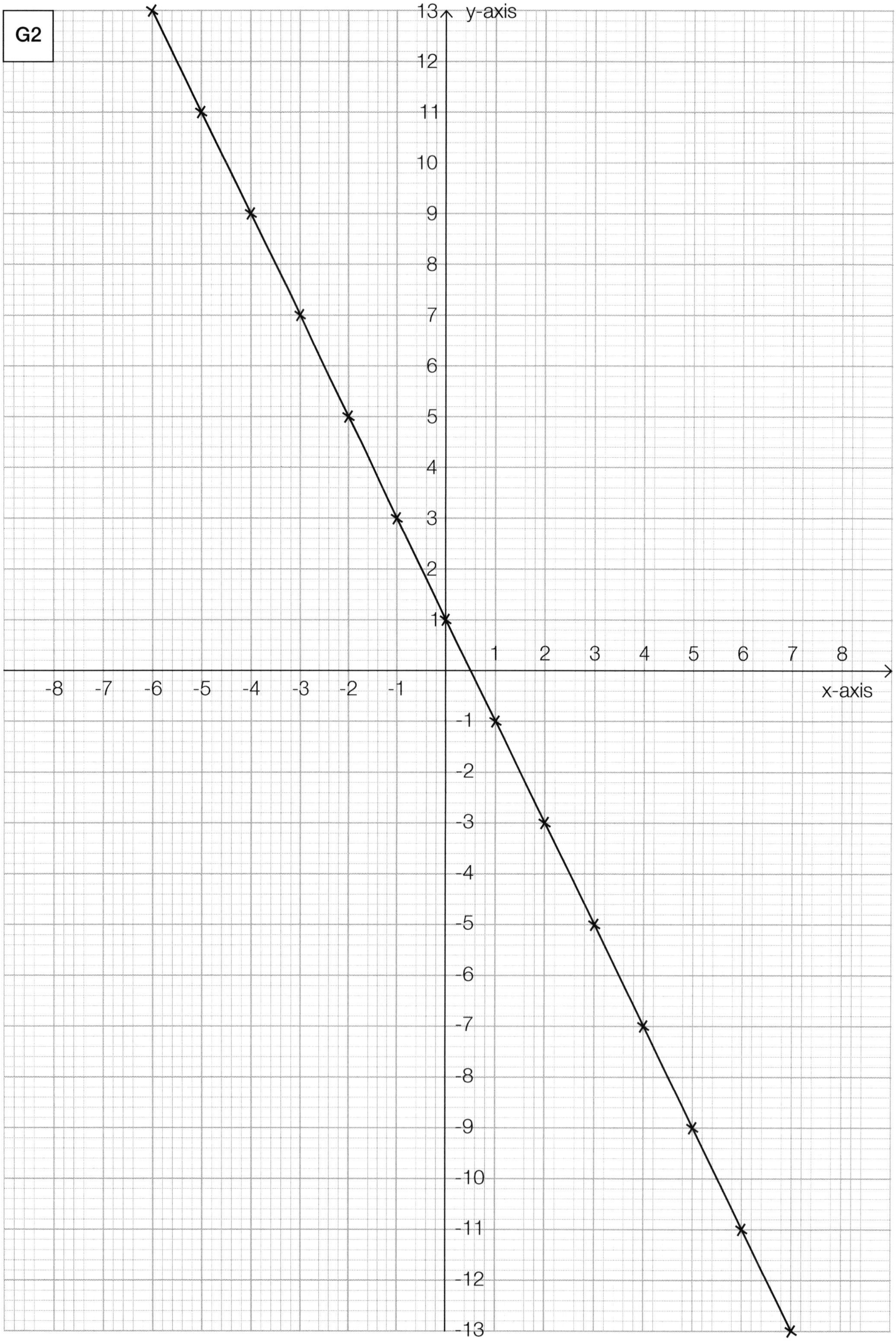
G2
y-axis
x-axis
13
12
11
10
9
8
7
6
5
4
3
2
1
-1
-2
-3
-4
-5
-6
-7
-8
-9
-10
-11
-12
-13
-8
-7
-6
-5
-4
-3
-2
-1
1
2
3
4
5
6
7
8

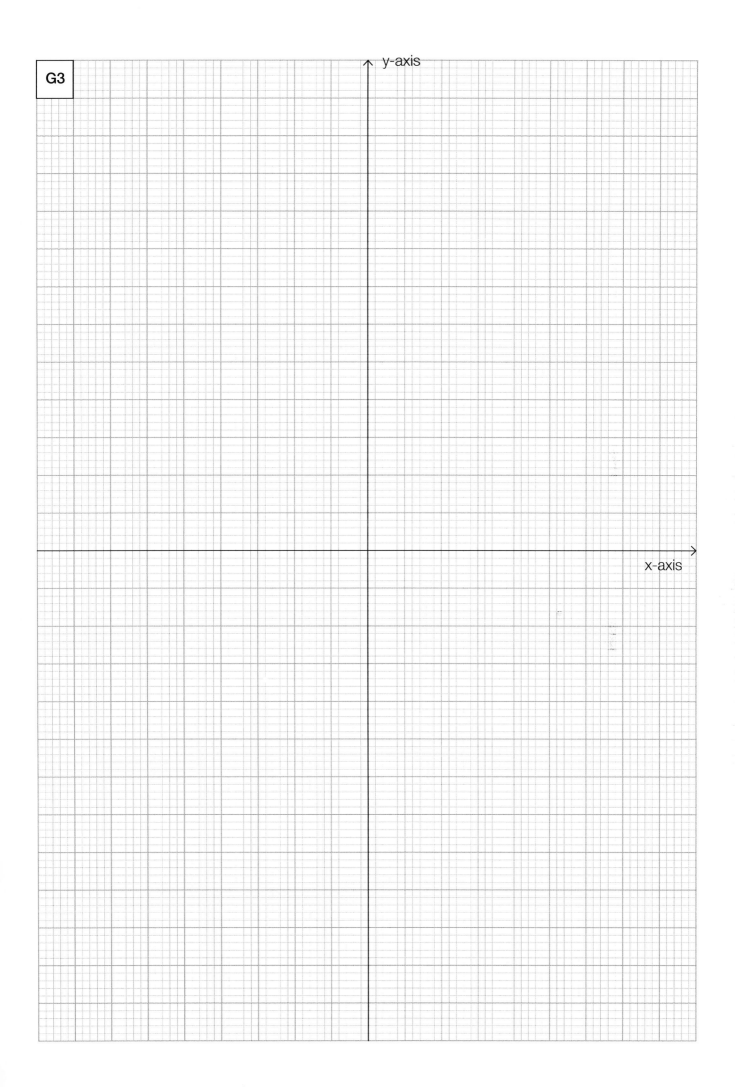

G3

y-axis

x-axis

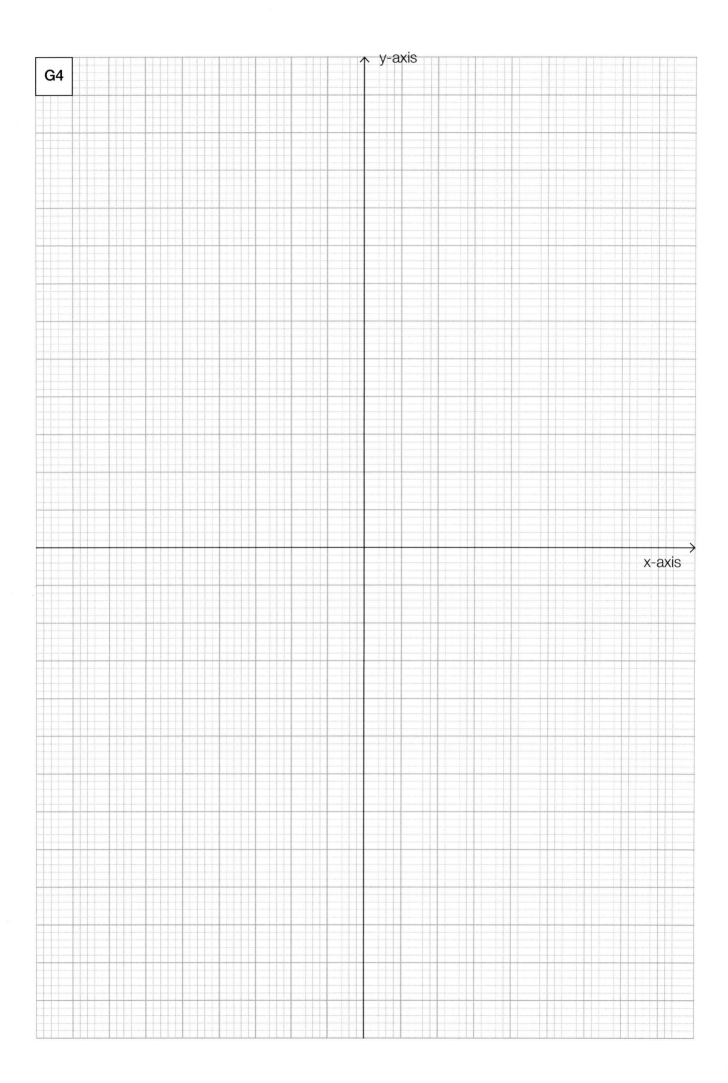

G4

y-axis

x-axis

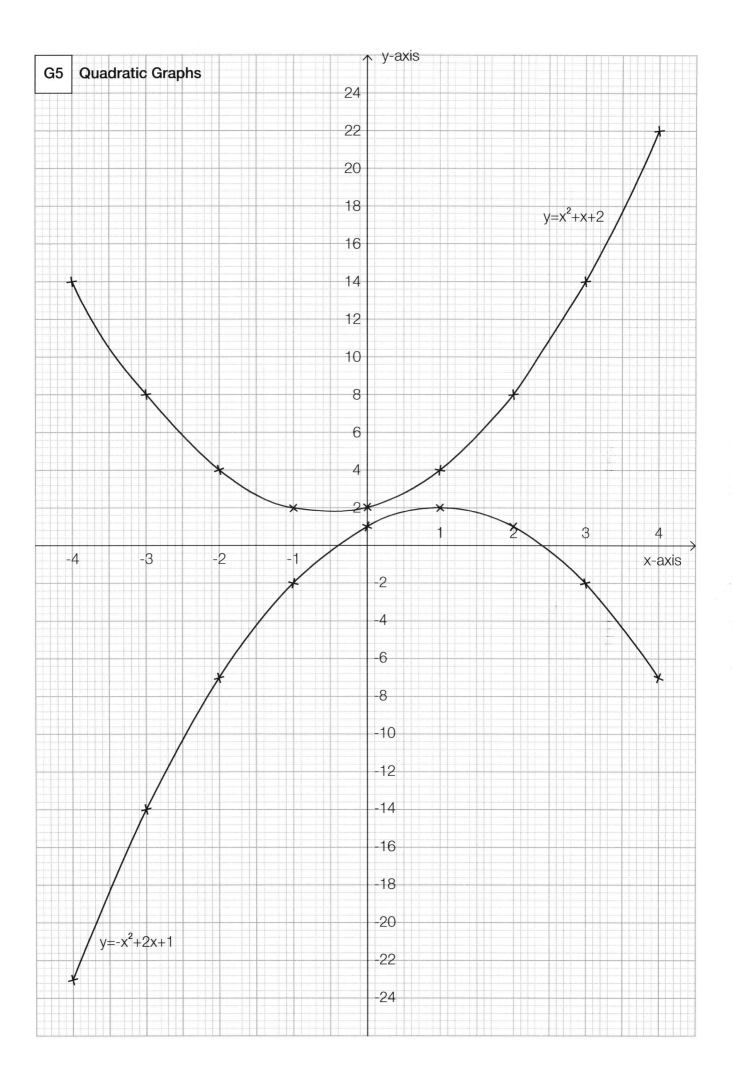

G5 | Quadratic Graphs

y-axis

$y=x^2+x+2$

$y=-x^2+2x+1$

x-axis

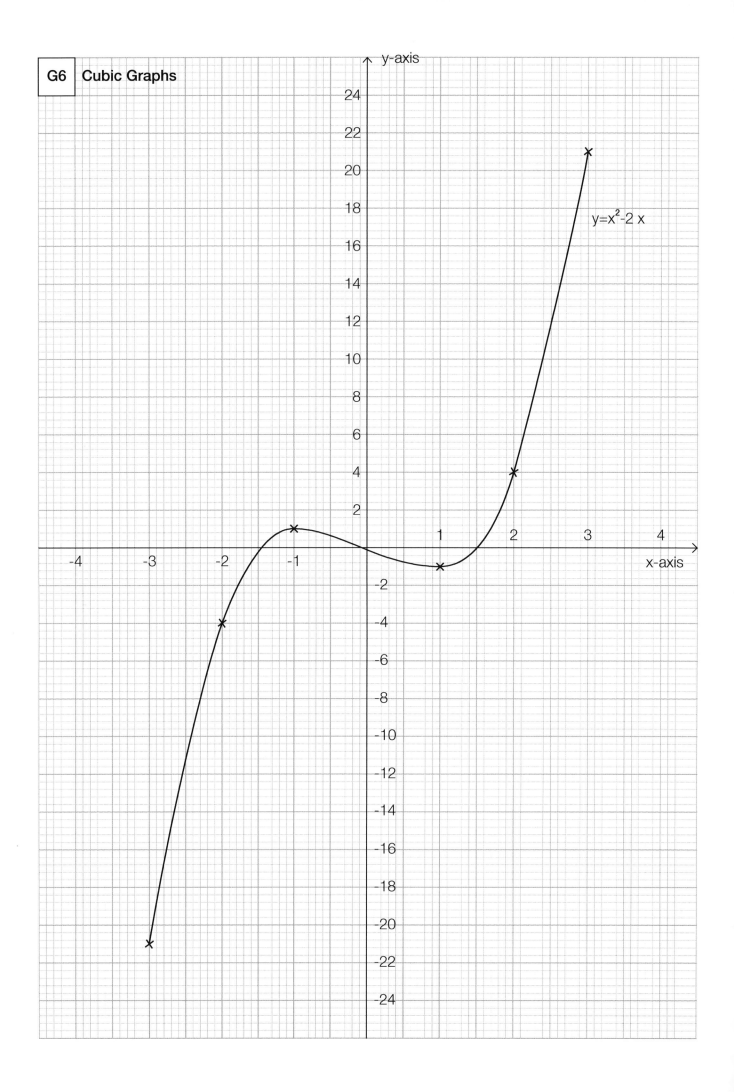

G6 | Cubic Graphs

y-axis

$y=x^2-2\,x$

x-axis

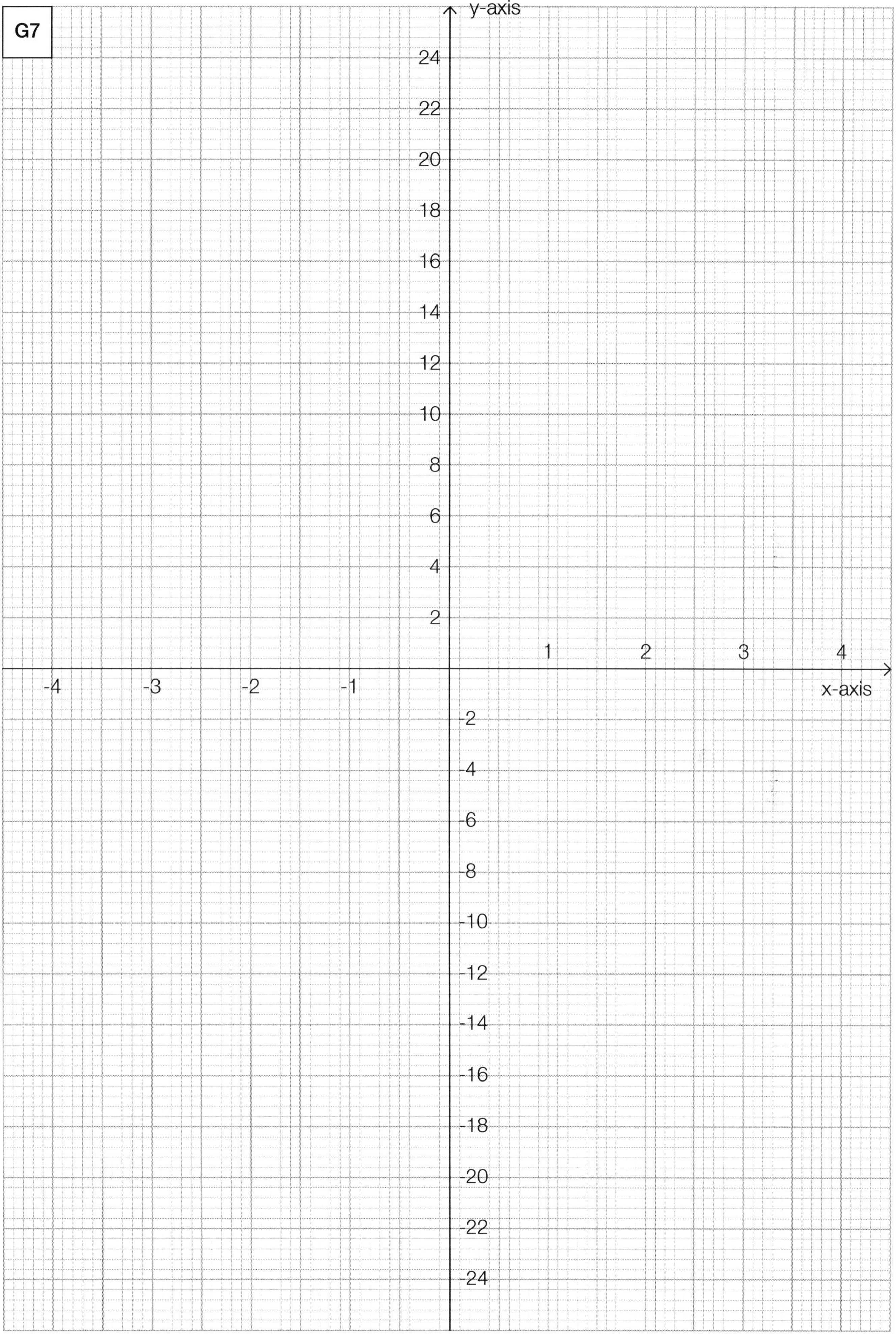
G7
y-axis
x-axis
24
22
20
18
16
14
12
10
8
6
4
2
-2
-4
-6
-8
-10
-12
-14
-16
-18
-20
-22
-24
-4
-3
-2
-1
1
2
3
4

G8

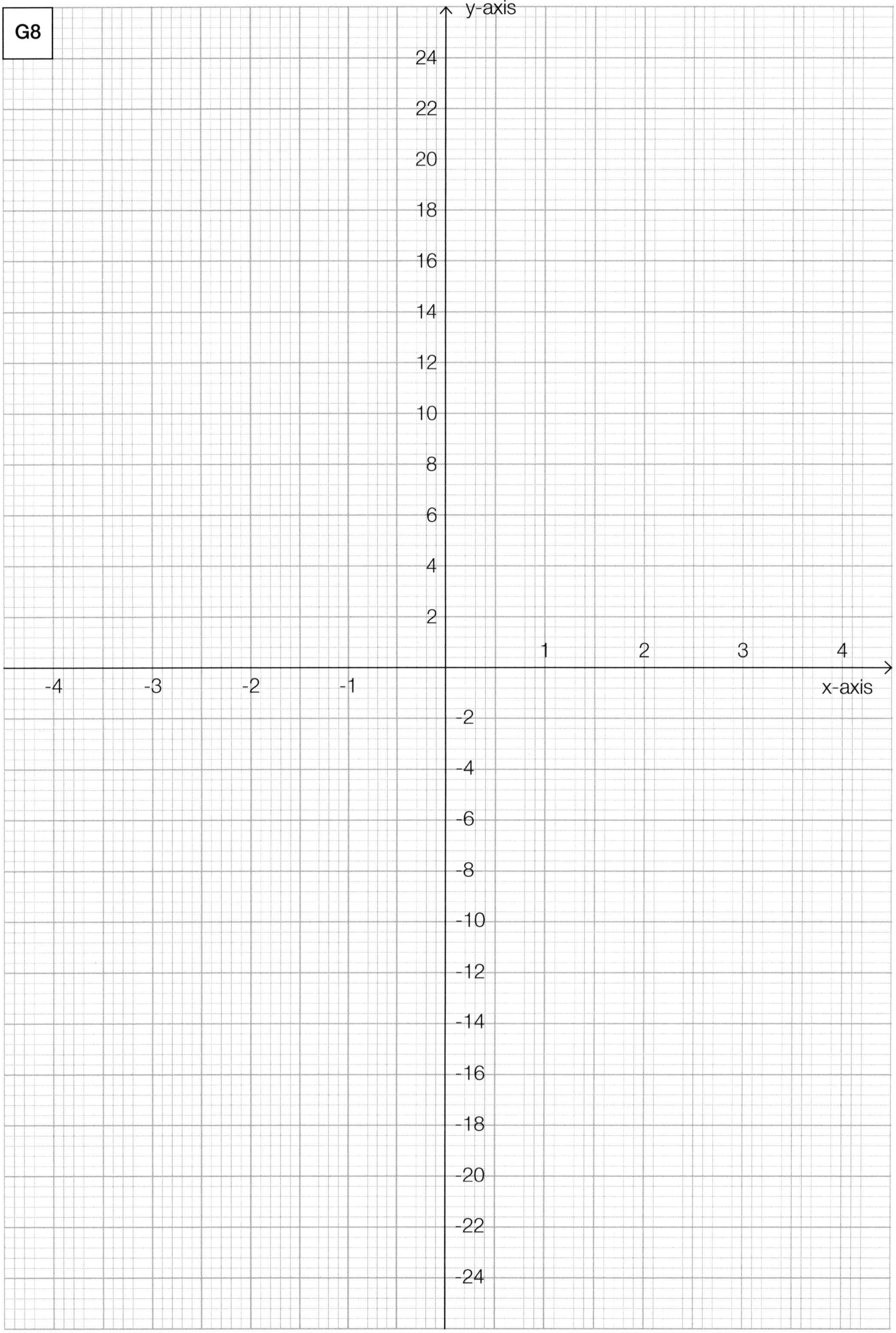

y-axis
x-axis
24
22
20
18
16
14
12
10
8
6
4
2
-2
-4
-6
-8
-10
-12
-14
-16
-18
-20
-22
-24
-4
-3
-2
-1
1
2
3
4

G9

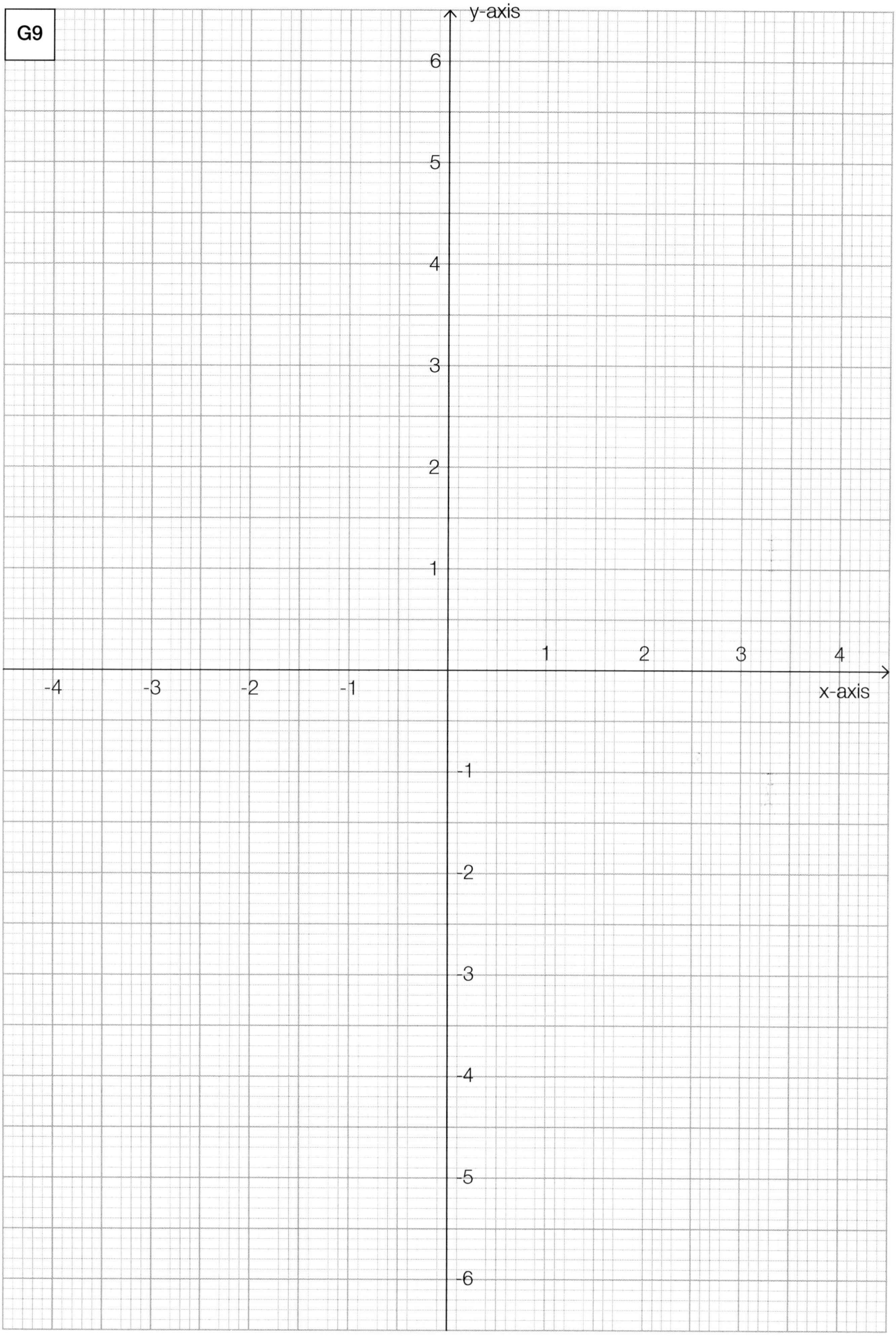

y-axis
6
5
4
3
2
1
1
2
3
4
-4
-3
-2
-1
x-axis
-1
-2
-3
-4
-5
-6

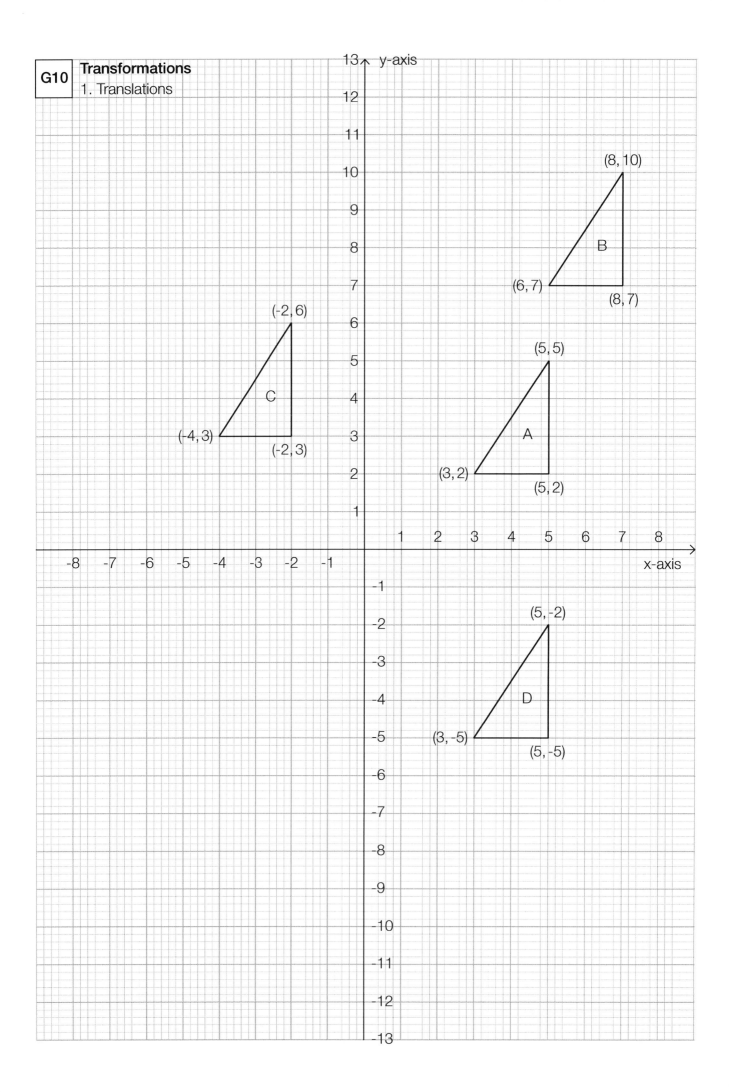

G10 **Transformations**
1. Translations

G11

Transformations

2. Rotations

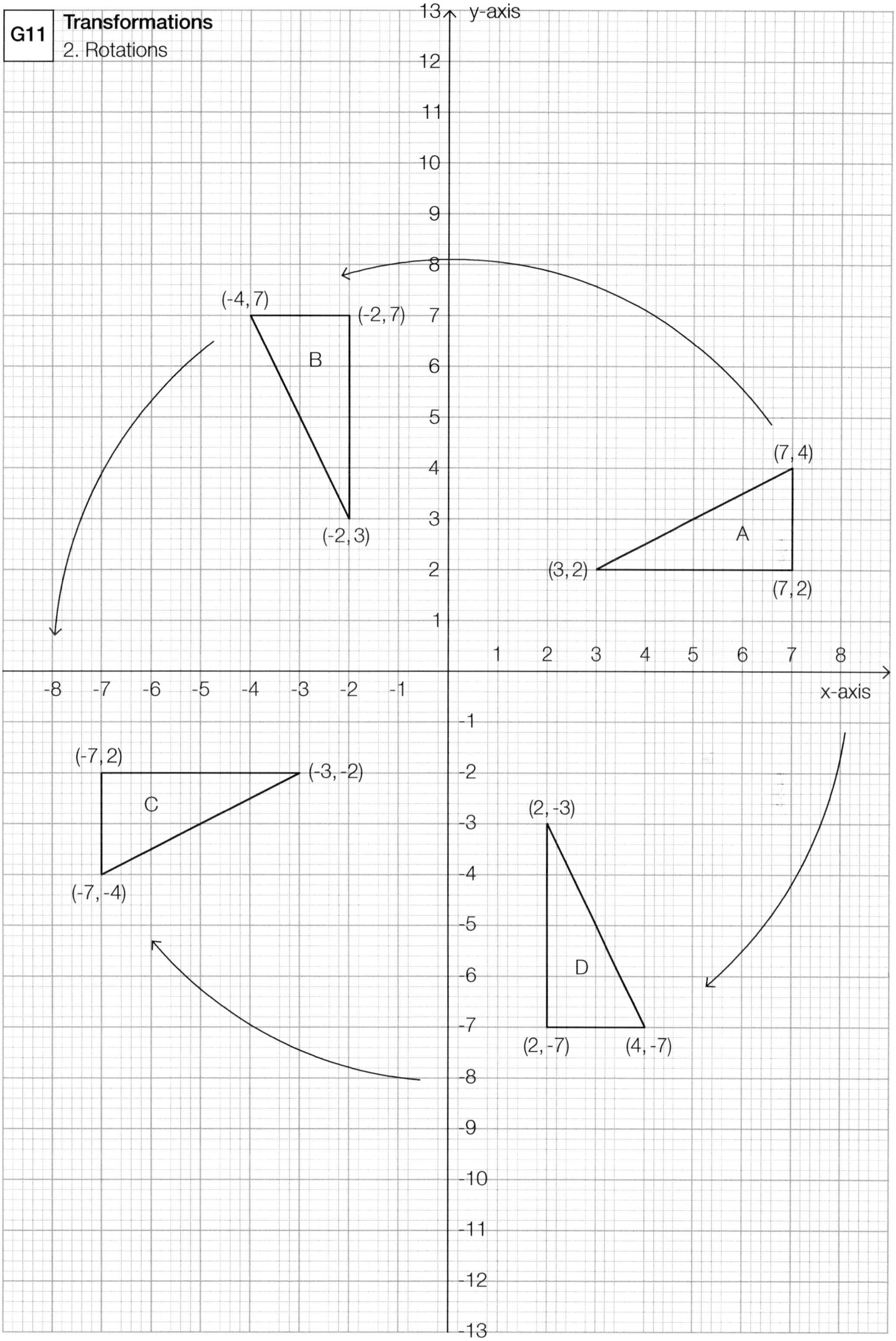

y-axis
x-axis
(-4, 7)
(-2, 7)
B
(-2, 3)
(7, 4)
A
(3, 2)
(7, 2)
(-7, 2)
(-3, -2)
C
(-7, -4)
(2, -3)
D
(2, -7)
(4, -7)

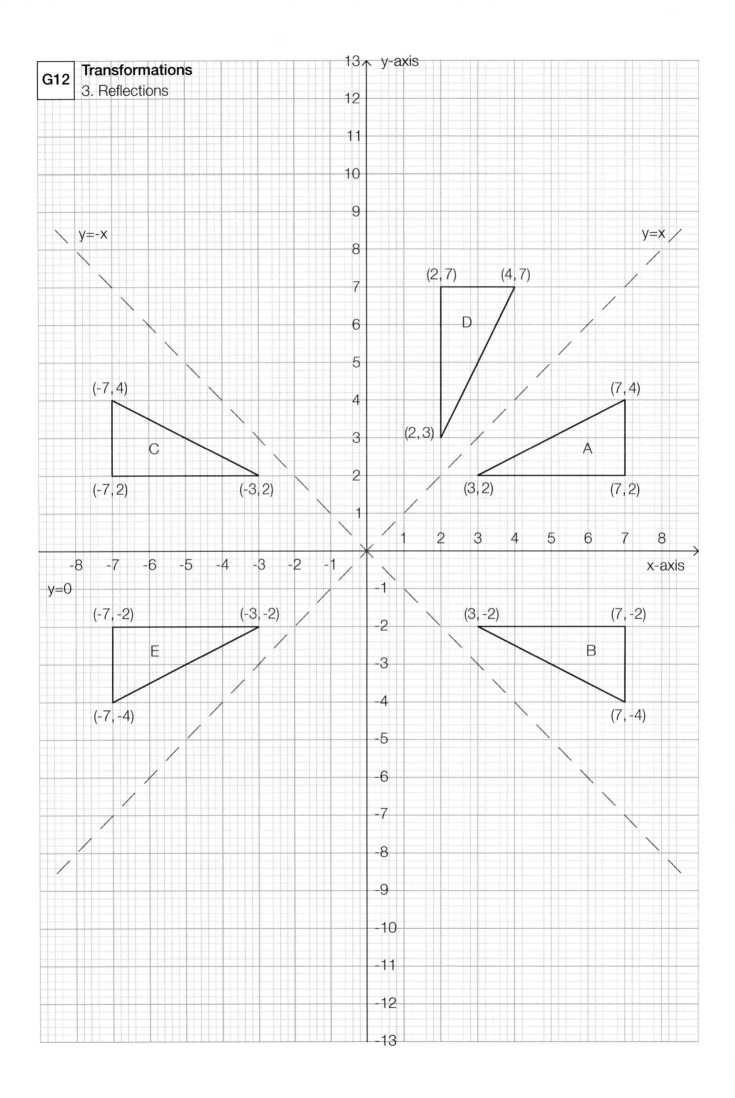

y-axis

y=-x

y=x

(2,7)   (4,7)

D

(-7,4)   (7,4)

(2,3)

C   A

(-7,2)   (-3,2)   (3,2)   (7,2)

x-axis

y=0

(-7,-2)   (-3,-2)   (3,-2)   (7,-2)

E   B

(-7,-4)   (7,-4)

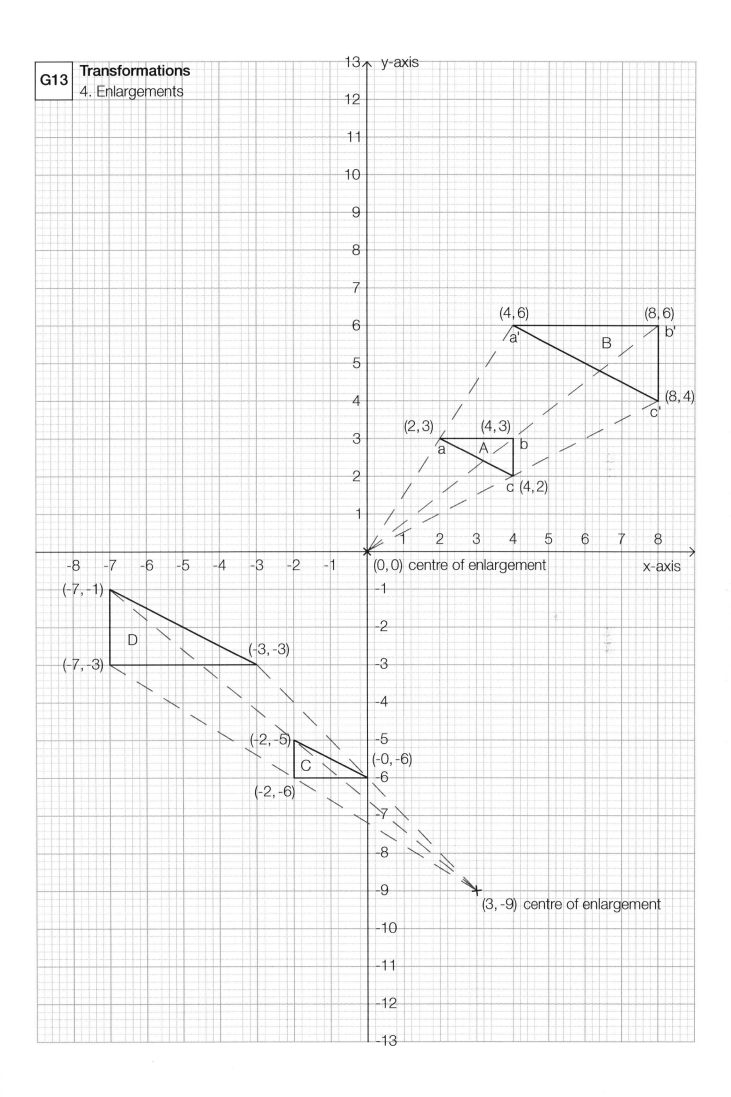

G13 **Transformations**
4. Enlargements

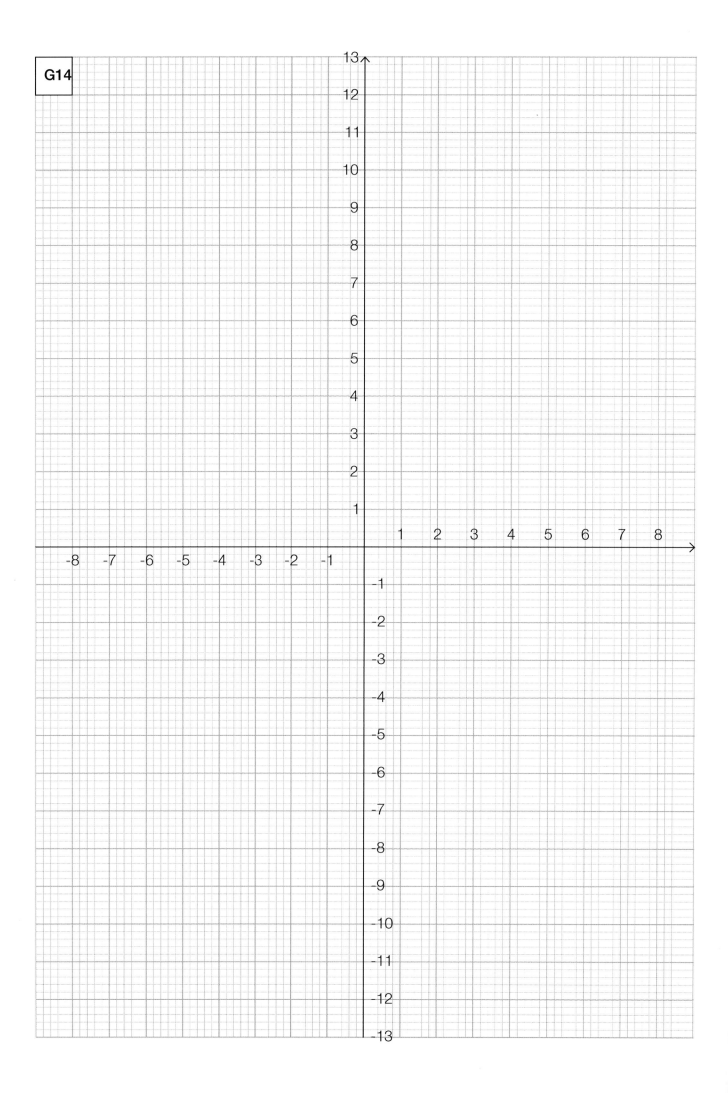

G14

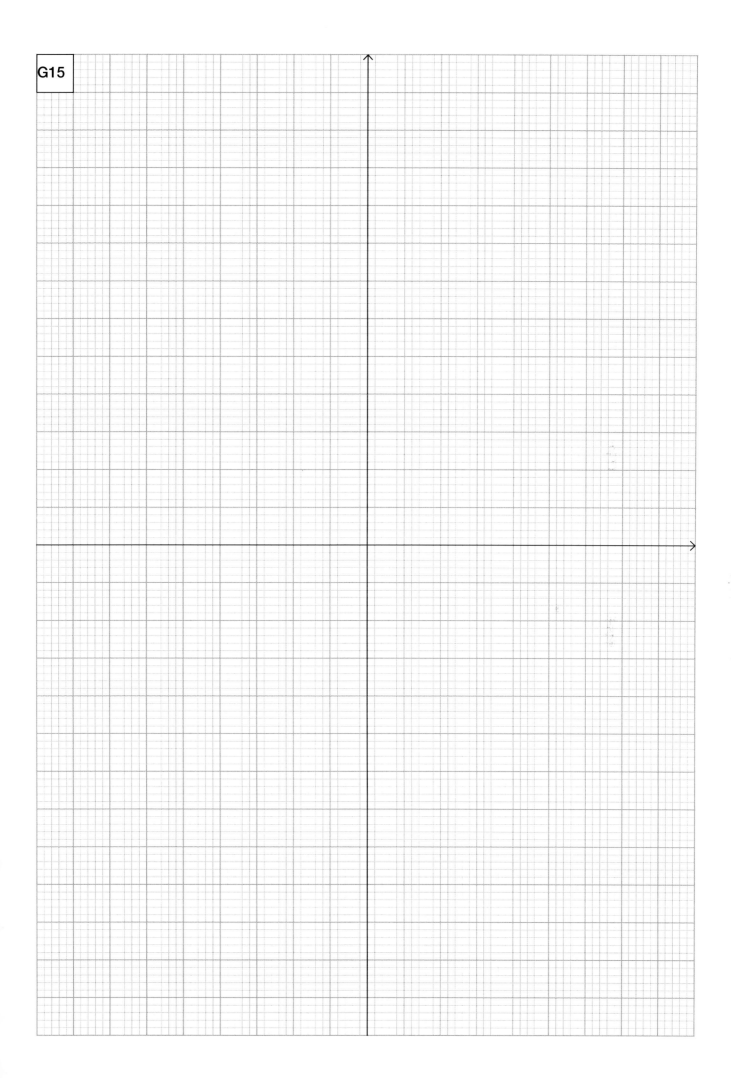

G15

G16

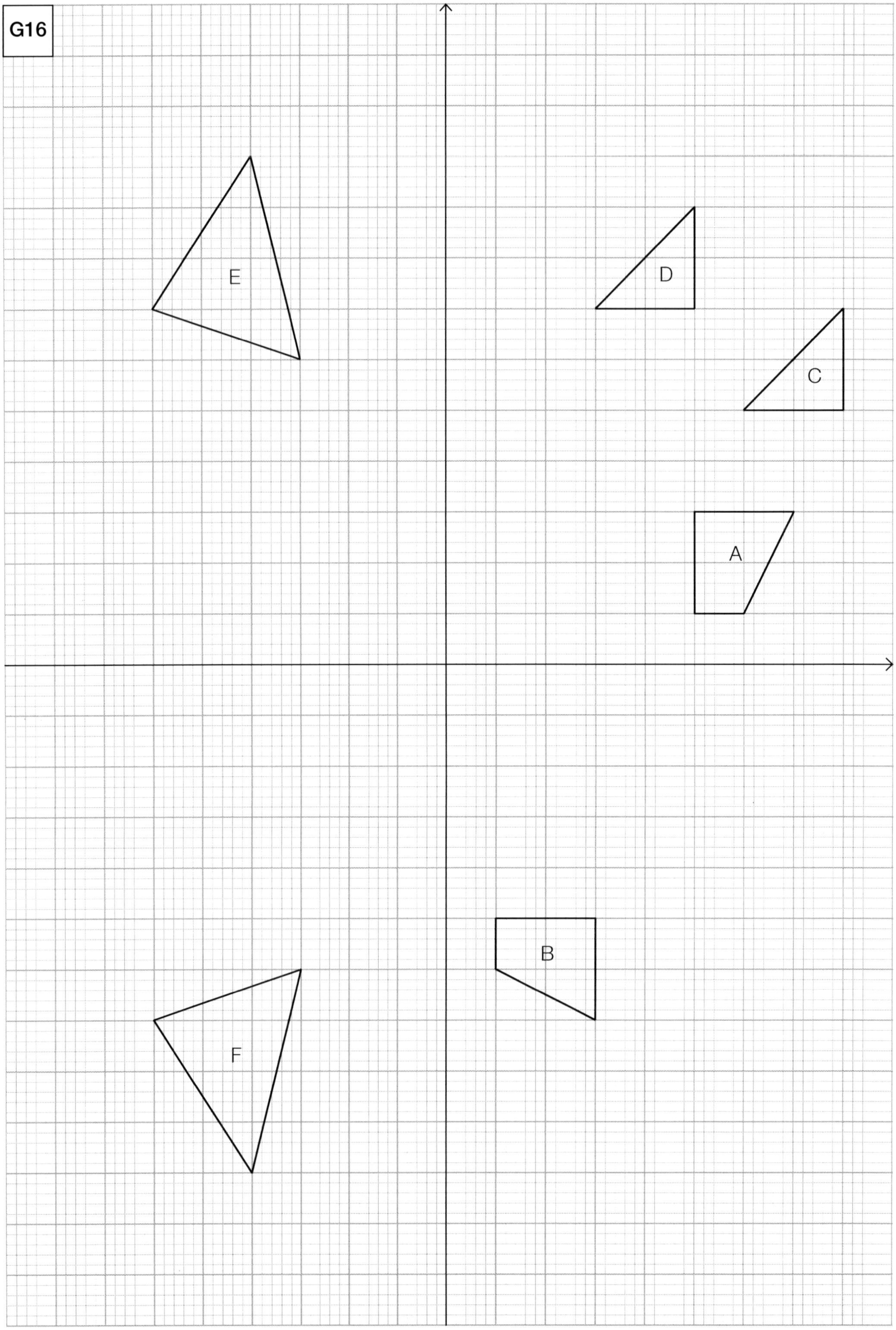
E
D
C
A
B
F

G17

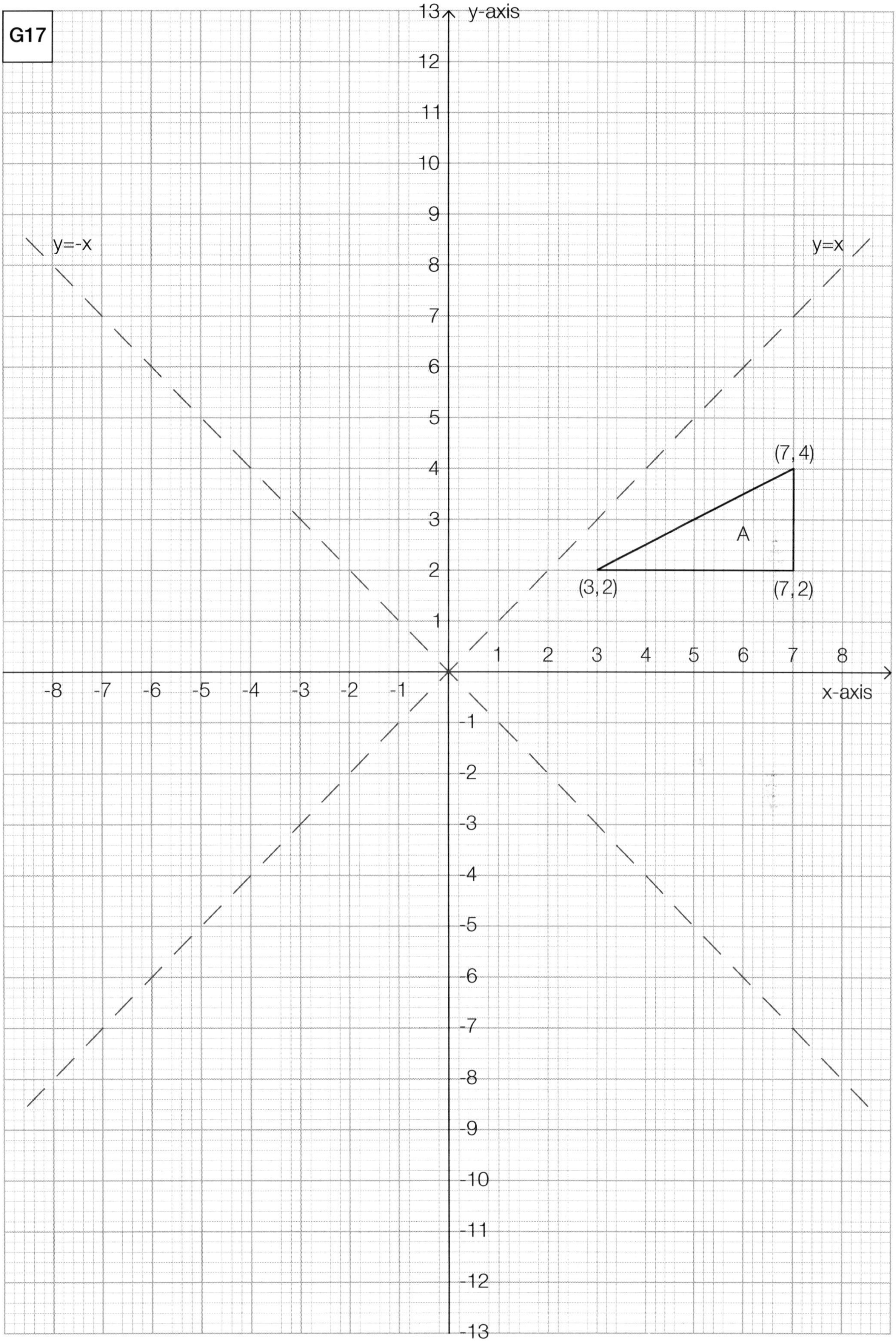
y-axis
x-axis
y=-x
y=x
(7, 4)
(3, 2)
(7, 2)
A
1 2 3 4 5 6 7 8
-8 -7 -6 -5 -4 -3 -2 -1
13 12 11 10 9 8 7 6 5 4 3 2 1
-1 -2 -3 -4 -5 -6 -7 -8 -9 -10 -11 -12 -13

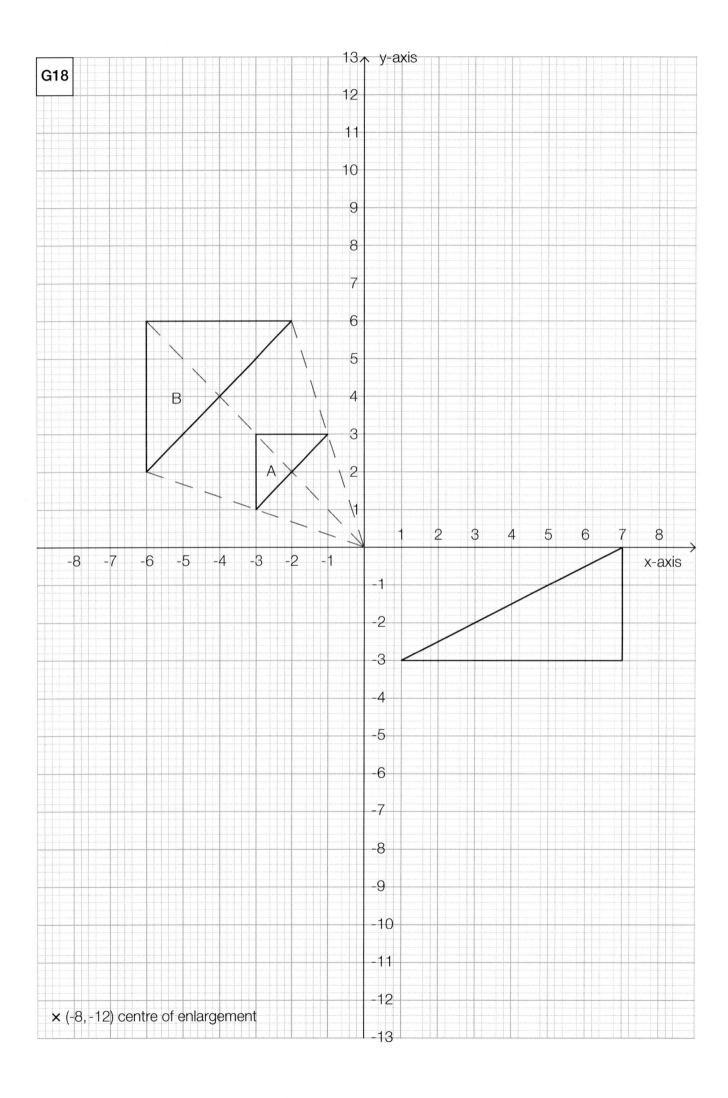

G18

y-axis

x-axis

B

A

× (-8, -12) centre of enlargement

Lines of symmetry and order of rotational symmetry

A **line of symmetry** is a 'mirror line' across a shape which allows both sides of the line to be folded together exactly. A shape can have one or more lines of symmetry, or none at all. For example, the following shapes have one, two, four and no lines of symmetry respectively:

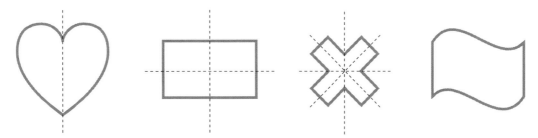

The **order of rotational symmetry** is the number of different positions that look exactly the same when a shape is rotated 360° about its centre. Every shape has at least a rotational symmetry of order 1. In other words, if any shape is rotated 360°, it will map back onto its original position. In the above examples, the shapes have rotational symmetry of order 1, 2, 4 and 1 respectively.

Questions on lines of symmetry and order of rotational symmetry

Q1.   Draw in the lines of symmetry on the following shapes and state the order of rotational symmetry for each one:

a Regular pentagon   b Equilateral triangle   c

rotational symmetry   rotational symmetry   rotational symmetry
of order =   of order =   of order =

d   e   f

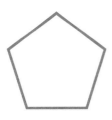

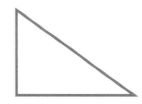

rotational symmetry   rotational symmetry   rotational symmetry
of order =   of order =   of order =

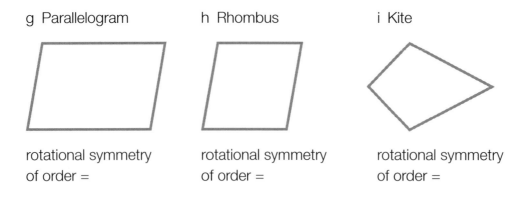

g Parallelogram

rotational symmetry
of order =

h Rhombus

rotational symmetry
of order =

i Kite

rotational symmetry
of order =

Vectors

As stated earlier (under translations), vectors represent a movement of a given size in a given direction. The vectors shown were column vectors, e.g. $\begin{pmatrix} 6 \\ 4 \end{pmatrix}$ represents a movement of 6 places across to the right on the x-axis and 4 places up on the y-axis. Column vectors can be added or subtracted. For example:

$$\begin{pmatrix} 5 \\ 2 \end{pmatrix} + \begin{pmatrix} 3 \\ -4 \end{pmatrix} = \begin{pmatrix} 8 \\ -2 \end{pmatrix} \quad \text{and} \quad \begin{pmatrix} 7 \\ 6 \end{pmatrix} - \begin{pmatrix} 4 \\ 3 \end{pmatrix} = \begin{pmatrix} 3 \\ 3 \end{pmatrix}$$

However, vectors can also be represented by an arrow. The following example represents the vector from point A to point B ($\overrightarrow{AB}$ = **a**):

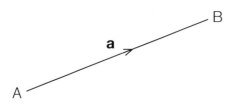

If the direction of the vector is reversed, then it will have a negative value ($\overrightarrow{AB}$ = **-a**):

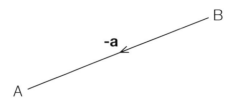

If a vector is multiplied by a positive number, its size changes, but not its direction:

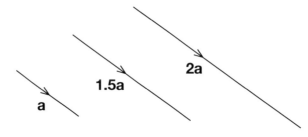

Vectors of a known size and direction can also be added and subtracted.
In this example, the vector $\overrightarrow{DE}$ is along a and b. So, $\overrightarrow{DE}$ = **a** + **b**

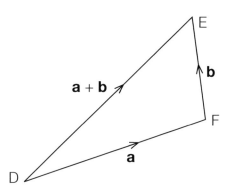

In this example, the vector $\overrightarrow{PQ}$ is along **a**
and then in the reverse direction to **b**
So, $\overrightarrow{PQ}$ = **a** - **b**

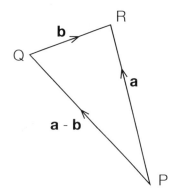

Questions on vectors

Q1.   Add the following 2 column vectors: $\begin{pmatrix} -2 \\ 4 \end{pmatrix} + \begin{pmatrix} -3 \\ -2 \end{pmatrix}$

Q2.   Subtract the following 2 column vectors: $\begin{pmatrix} 5 \\ 7 \end{pmatrix} - \begin{pmatrix} 3 \\ -3 \end{pmatrix}$

Q3.   Find $\overrightarrow{AB}$ in the following:

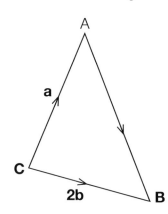

Q4.   Find $\overrightarrow{LM}$ in the following:

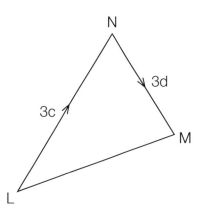

Questions on SOH [Sine = Opposite]
                      Hypotenuse

CAH [Cosine = Adjacent]
                Hypotenuse

TOA [Tangent = Opposite] and Pythagoras
              Adjacent

Q1.   Find x to one decimal place in each of the following right-angled triangles
      (which are not to scale):

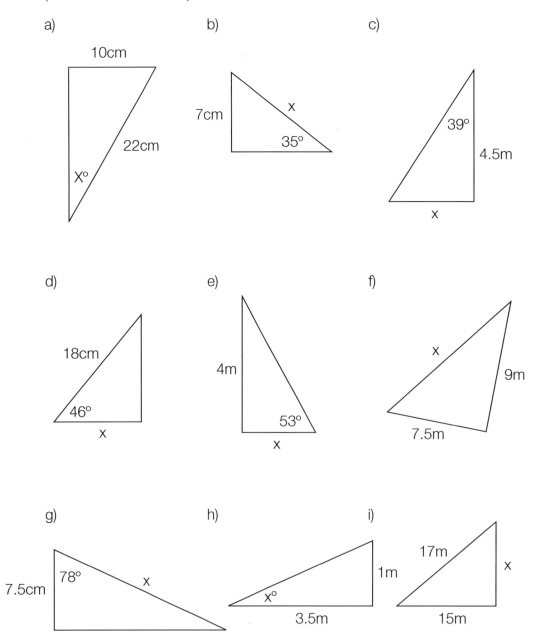

a)

10cm

22cm

X°

b)

7cm

X

35°

c)

39°

4.5m

X

d)

18cm

46°

X

e)

4m

53°

X

f)

X

9m

7.5m

g)

7.5cm

78°

X

h)

x°

3.5m

i)

17m

1m

X

15m

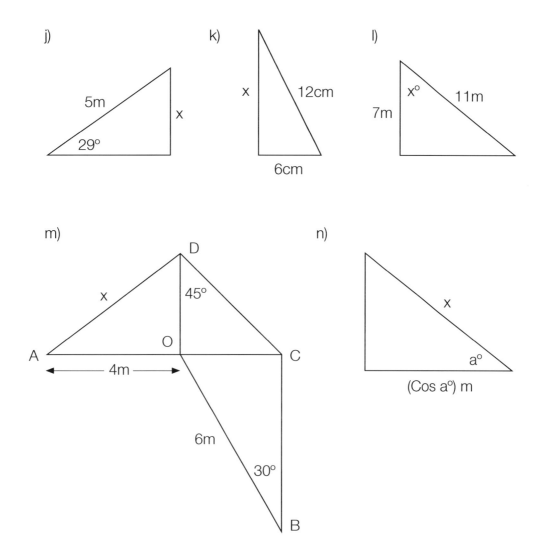

Questions on ratios

Q1). If £96 was shared between two people in a ratio of 1 : 5 how much did the person with the largest share receive?

Q2). If the ratio of an internal angle of a regular polygon to its exterior angle is 4 : 1 then which polygon is it?

Q3). £88,000 is shared between John, Stephen and Olivier. If the ratio of John's share to Stephen's share is 1 : 3 and Stephen's share is £16,000 more than John's share, then calculate Olivier's share.

Q4. The ratio of the areas of two rectangular fields is 2 : 3. If the width of both fields is 6m and the perimeter of the larger field is 42m, then calculate the length of the smaller field.

Q5. A solid cone and a solid cylinder have the same length and radius, then calculate the ratio of the volume of the cone to the volume of the cylinder.

Q6 a) John and Teresa both do a day's casual labour. If John earns £90 for the day and Teresa earns 20% more, then what is the ratio of the amounts they earn in the day?

b) If John worked for 8 hours in the day and Teresa 12.5% more, then calculate the ratio of the hourly rates of the two.

c) An investigation into the manufacturing of England's £160 2018 football World Cup kit, found that workers in a factory in Bangladesh were paid 24p an hour. Calculate the ratio of these workers' hourly rate to Teresa's hourly rate.

d) Another investigation found that workers in factories in Bangladeshi were involved in producing 'Gay Pride' merchandise for major retailers in the UK. Being Gay is illegal in Bangladesh, punishable by life imprisonment, so work that one out!

Q7. A teacher has £60 to spend on pens and pencils, and needs to buy an equal amount of each for the pupils in his class. If the pens cost £1.40 and the pencils £1.15 then calculate:

a) The ratio of the cost of the cost of pens to the cost of the pencils.

b) The change he will receive from the £60

Q8.   A party organiser wanted to buy 3 packets of crisps and 2 packets of peanuts for every guest at a party. If 3 packets of crisps weighed 120g and 2 packets of peanuts weighed 90g then:

a) Calculate the ratio of the weight of 1 packet of crisps to 1 packet of peanuts.

b) Calculate how many guests could be provided for if the organiser decided on a limit of 10kg of crisps and peanuts.

Q9.   A group of adults took part in a survey in regard to gender, in which they were asked to identify as male, female or transgender. The ratio was found to be 16 : 18 : 1 with 8 people choosing 'prefer not to say'. If 54 people in the survey identified as female, then calculate how many people took part in the survey.

Q10. In another survey in regard to sexual orientation, a group of 190 men were asked to identify as heterosexual, bisexual or gay. Ten people chose 'prefer not to say', and out of the rest 90% identified as heterosexual or bisexual, and the number of men identifying as bisexual was equal to the number of men identifying as gay. What was the ratio of those identifying as heterosexual to bisexual to gay?

Volumes of cylinders, triangular prisms, cones, frustums and square-based pyramids

The volume of a cylinder is the area of its base ($\pi r2$) multiplied by its height (or length). Volume = $\pi r2h$

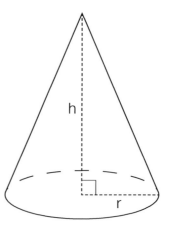

The volume of a triangular prism = cross-sectional area of prism (the area of the triangle) multiplied by its length.
In the example below, the area = ½ b x h and the volume of the prism =

½ b x h x l = $\dfrac{b.h.l}{2}$

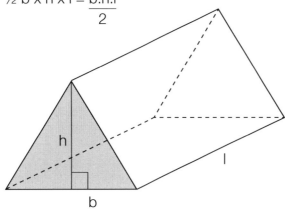

The volume of a cone is the area of its base ($\pi r2$) multiplied by a third of its height = $\frac{1}{3}\pi r^2h$

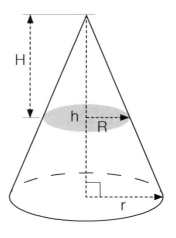

If the top part of a cone is cut off, parallel to its base, then the remainder of the cone is called a frustum. Its volume can be calculated by subtracting the volume of the removed cone from the volume of the original cone.

So, volume of frustum = $\frac{1}{3}\pi r^2h$ - $\frac{1}{3}\pi R^2H$

The volume of a square-based pyramid is the area of its base multiplied by a third of its height = ⅓Bh where B is the area of the base and h is the pyramid's height.

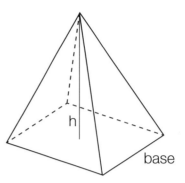

base

Questions on volumes of cylinders, triangular prisms, cones, frustums and square-based pyramids. Take π = 3.142

Q1. Calculate the amount of water (in litres) that can be held in a cylinder that is 1.5m long, with a diameter of 60cm. Give your answer to the nearest Litre. 1m3 = 1,000L

Q2. A triangular prism has a volume of 1,200cm³. If its base is 15cm and length is 20cm, then calculate the prism's height.

Q3. A volume of 540L of water is poured into a Perspex tank measuring 1.5m long by 80cm wide by 80cm tall. When a solid cone is placed in the water, it sinks and the water rises by 20%.
Calculate the volume of the cone.

Q4. A square-based pyramid with a height of 6m has a volume of 32m³
Calculate the length of a side of its base.

Q5. A cone of height 80cm and base diameter of 40cm is cut parallel to its base a quarter of the way down from its apex. Calculate the volume of the remaining frustum.

Density

The density of a substance can be found by dividing its mass by its volume. The unit for density is g/cm^3

Density = Mass ÷ Volume = $\dfrac{Mass}{Volume}$

Also, Mass = Volume x Density, and Volume = $\dfrac{Mass}{Density}$

Worked example

Calculate the density of a 2kg block of steel of length 10cm, width 5cm and height 5cm

Density = $\dfrac{Mass}{Volume}$ = $\dfrac{2,000}{10 \times 5 \times 5}$ = $\dfrac{2,000}{250}$ = **8g/cm³**

Questions on density

Q1.   In Q2 on volumes (above), the volume of the triangular prism is 1,200cm³. If its mass is 3.24kg calculate the density of the prism.

Q2.   If the density of gold is 19.32g/cm³ calculate the volume of 5 x 10³g of the metal (to the nearest cubic centimetre).

Q3.   If one litre of water weighs 1kg, calculate its density.

Q4.   Mercury has a density of 13.56g/cm³. Calculate the mass (in kilogram) of a quarter of a litre of the liquid metal.

Q5.   Calculate the density (to two decimal places) of a metal sphere of radius 3cm that weighs 1.009kg

Distance-Time graphs

Distance-time graphs are used to represent the details of a given journey, with the vertical axis (y) representing the distance from the starting point and the horizontal axis (x) representing the time taken from the start of the journey.

In the following distance-time graph for example, the first line represents the first part of the journey. The gradient of the line (Distance/Time or y/x) represents the speed of the journey. As it is a straight line, its gradient (hence the speed) is constant. The steeper the line, the higher is the gradient (distance increases whilst the time decreases), hence the faster is the speed.

The second line, which is horizontal, shows the time increasing, but no change in the distance from the starting point. In other words, it is a stationary part of the journey.

The third line then represents the return part of the journey, back to the starting point. As the line is straight, it again represents a constant speed.

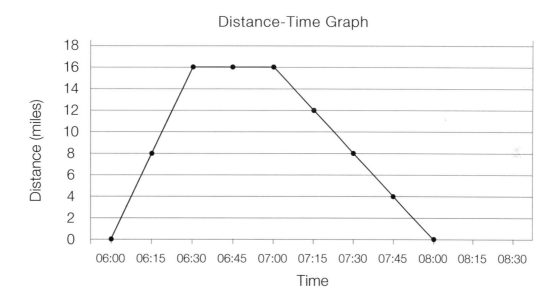

So, in the first part of the journey,

Speed = $\dfrac{\text{Distance}}{\text{Time}}$ = $\dfrac{16 \text{ miles}}{30\text{mins}}$ = $\dfrac{32 \text{ miles}}{60\text{mins}}$ = 32 miles/hour

In the third part of the journey,

Speed = $\dfrac{\text{Distance}}{\text{Time}}$ = $\dfrac{16 \text{ miles}}{1 \text{ hour}}$ = 16 miles/hour

The break in the journey is 30 minutes and the total time for the journey is 2 hours

Questions on Distance-Time graph

Q1.   The journey of a group of walkers is recorded on the distance-time graph below:

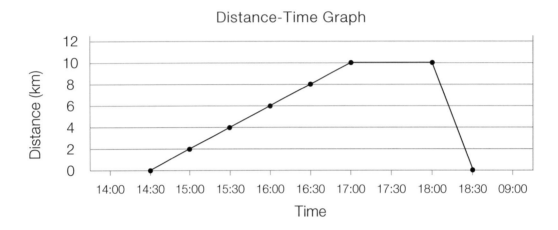

a)   From the graph, calculate the average walking speed of the walkers during the first part of the journey.

b)   Following a tea break, the walkers decide to take a bus back to the starting point of the walk. If the bus was driven at a steady speed, then calculate the average speed of the bus during the walkers' journey back.

Q2.   A cyclist leaves home at 10:15 and cycles at a steady speed of 12mph for 75 minutes. She then takes a break of 15 minutes then continues her journey at the same speed for a further 45 minutes. She then takes a further break for 15 minutes before heading back home at a speed of one third faster than her previous speed.
Complete the following distance-time graph for the cyclist's journey, and state the time that the cyclist arrives back home.

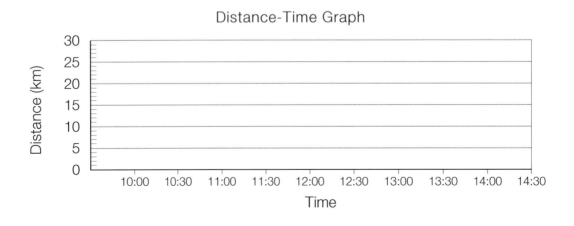

Constructing a triangle using a pair of compasses

A triangle of given lengths can be constructed accurately using a pair of compasses. For example, to construct a triangle AB = 7cm, AC = 6cm and BC = 5cm, we can start by drawing one of the lines (AB) with a ruler:

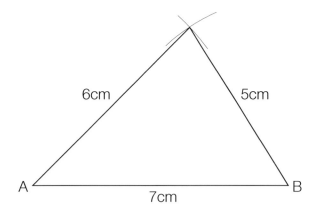

Placing the point of the compass on point A, an arc of radius 6cm is drawn. Then, placing the point of the compass on point B, an arc of radius 5cm is drawn to intersect with the previous arc (point C). Lines are then drawn linking points A and B to the point of intersection to form the triangle with AC = 6cm and BC = 5cm.

Constructing an angle bisector

A pair of compasses can be used to accurately bisect an angle between two given lines. In the example below, the compass point is placed at point 0. Keeping the compass setting the same, arcs are drawn to intersect the two given lines. Then, placing the compass point on the two intersections (and still keeping the compass setting the same), further arcs are drawn between the two given lines. The line joining the point of intersection of the two arcs and point 0 is the angle bisector. This can be checked by measuring the angles with a protractor.

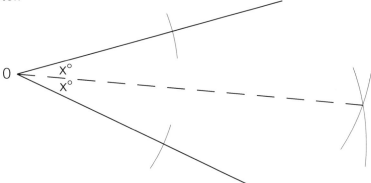

The angle bisector is referred to as a locus, which is a line that shows all the points which fit a given rule, in this case, points that are equidistant from two lines.

Constructing the perpendicular bisector of a line joining two points

A pair of compasses can be used to accurately construct a perpendicular bisector of a line joining two points. In the example below, the compass point is placed on one of the points (A) and two arcs are drawn opposite each other between points A and B. Keeping the compass setting the same, the compass point is then placed on point B and 2 arcs are drawn between A and B to intersect the two arcs from point A. A line is then drawn between the two points where the arcs intersect. This is then the perpendicular bisector of the line joining points A and B. This is also referred to as a locus, the given rule being that all points on the line are the same distance from A as they are from B.

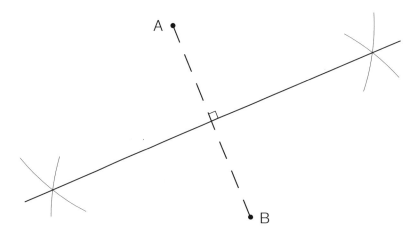

Constructing the locus of points which are a fixed distance from a given line

In this example, in order to construct a locus which is a fixed distance from the line AB, the pair of compasses is set to the fixed distance (a radius of 2cm in the example below), the point of the pair of compasses is placed on point A and a semi-circle is drawn to the left of A. The point of the compass is then placed on point B and a semi-circle is drawn to the right of B. Lines parallel to AB (above and below) at the fixed distance of 2cm can then be drawn by joining the ends of the two semi-circles together i.e. from the points 2cm directly above and below A and B:

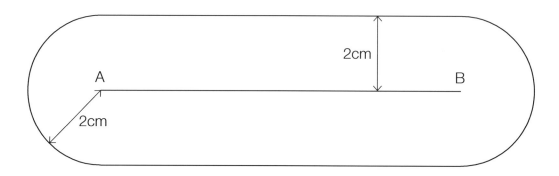

Constructing the locus of points which are a fixed distance from a given shape

In this example, in order to construct a locus which is a fixed distance from the rectangle ABCD, the pair of compasses is again set to a fixed distance (a radius of 3cm in the example below), the point of the pair of compasses is placed on points A, B, C and D in turn and a quarter of a circle is drawn from each point. Then, in a similar way to above, a line parallel to AB (above), CD (below), AC(to the left) and BD (to the right) at the fixed distance of 3cm can then be drawn by joining the ends of the quarter-circles together:

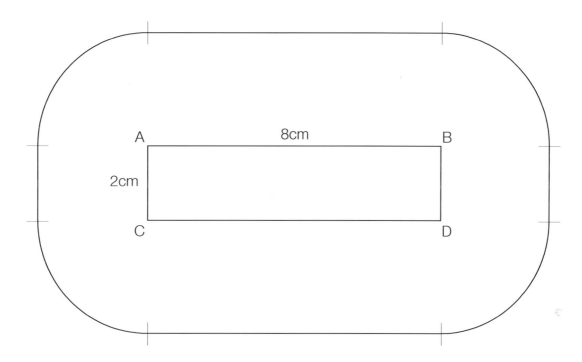

Questions on constructing triangles and angle bisectors

Q1.   Using a ruler and a pair of compasses, construct a triangle of dimensions
      AB = 8cm, BC = 6cm and AC = 4cm

Q2. Construct an angle bisector of the two given lines below:

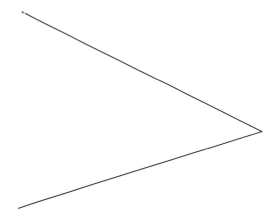

Q3. Construct the perpendicular bisector of the two points P and Q

P •

Q •

Q4 a) Construct the locus of points that is 3.5cm from the line PQ

P ————————————————————— Q

b) Calculate the enclosed area of the shape. Take π = 3.14

Q5. The diagram below is a scale drawing of a plot of land, drawn to a scale of 1cm : 4m. A fence is to be built all the way around the plot of land at a constant distance of 10m from it.

a) Draw in the fence around the plot of land.

b) Calculate the enclosed area between the fence and the plot of land.

Answers to L1 Numeracy Learning Assessment

Part A

Q1 Busiest day – Friday (56)   Quietest day – Tuesday (33)   56
                                                               − 33
                                                               23

Q2 June (425)   January (250) $^3\!4^1\!2\,5$
                                  −   2 5 0
                                  1 7 5

Q3 **201,926**

Q4 **Twenty three thousand and sixty four**

Q5 **miles per hour**

Q6 jackal (35 miles per hour)   pig (10 miles per hour)   35
                                                          − 10
                                                          25 miles per hour

Q7 **A key (or legend)** is missing

Q8 **95kg**

Q9 **24°C**

Q10 **85,000**

Q11   38
      − 25
      13 minutes

Q12 8.25 + 25mins = 8.50 + 10mins = 9.00 + 10 mins = **9.10**

Part B
Q13

	Fraction	Percentage	Decimal
	1/2 (a half)	50%	0.5
	1/4 (a quarter)	25%	0.25
	3/4 (three quarters)	75%	0.75
	1/5 (a fifth)	20%	0.2
	2/5 (two fifths)	40%	0.4
	3/5 (three fifths)	60%	0.6
	4/5 (four fifths)	80%	0.8
	1/3 (a third)	33%	0.33

Q14 $\frac{1}{4}$ of 220 = $4\overline{)22\,^2 0}$ **55** were women

(quotient: 0 5 5)

Q15 $\frac{1}{3}$ of £180.00 = $3\overline{)180.00}$ $\frac{2}{3}$ = 60 x 2 = **£120**

(quotient: 060.00)

Q16 Average = 132 ÷ 6 = $6\overline{)13^1 2}$ = **22** minutes

(quotient: 022)

Q17 Range = highest number – lowest number = 29 – 16 = **13** minutes

Q18 10% of £78$\overset{\frown}{2}$.00 = **£78.20**

Q19 10% of 7$\overset{\frown}{0}$0. = 70   20% = 2 x 70 = **140**

Q20 10% of £11$\overset{\frown}{0}$.00 = £11.00   30% = 3 x £11.00 = £33.00
Therefore, cost of membership = £110.00 - £33.00 = **£77.00**

Q21 6 out of 30 = $\dfrac{6\,^1}{30\,_5}$ = $\dfrac{1}{5}$ = **20%**

Q22
£1.15		£1.80		£4.60	
x	4	+	£1.80	+	£3.60
£4.60		£3.60		£8.20	Total = **£8.20**
2		1		1	

Q23
       1.5
   x   7
   10.5 m²   Area = **10.5m²**
      3

Q24 40 x 10 = 400   400 x 30 = 400 x 10 x 3 = 4,000 x 3 = **12,000 cm³**

Q25 £6.15 x 30 = £6.15 x 10 x 3 = £61.50 x 3 = £   61.50

x _____3

£ $\overline{184.50}$ = **£184.50**

1

Q26 **11.1** seconds

Q27 **29m**

Q28 4 x 70g = **280g**

Q29 7 x 3 = **21km**

Q30 400g = 0.4kg   0.4kg x 40 = 0.4 x 10 x 4 = 4 x 4 = **16kg**

Answers to L1 Practice Questions

Q1a
$$\begin{array}{r} £8.65 \\ \times \quad 3 \\ \hline £25.95 \\ \hline {\scriptstyle 1\ 1} \end{array} \quad = \quad £\mathbf{25.95}$$

Q1b
$$£25.95 \div 3 \ = \ \frac{25.95}{3} \ = \ 3\overline{)25.^19^15}^{\,8.65} \ = \ £\mathbf{8.65}$$

Q1c
$$\begin{array}{r} {}^{4}5^{9}0.^{9}0^{1}0 \\ -\ 2\,5.9\,5 \\ \hline 2\,4.0\,5 \end{array} \quad = \quad £\mathbf{24.05}$$

Q2
$$£44.61 \div 3 \ = \ \frac{44.61}{3} \ = \ 3\overline{)4^14.^26^21}^{\,14.87} \ = \ £\mathbf{14.87}$$

Q3 A quarter of $36 = ¼ \times 36 = \frac{36}{4} = \frac{\cancel{36}^{9}}{\cancel{4}^{1}} = 9$ Therefore $\frac{3}{4}$ of $36 = 3 \times 9 = \mathbf{27}$

Q4
$$£85.00 \div 5 \ = \ \frac{85.00}{5} \ = \ 5\overline{)8^35.0\,0}^{\,17.00} \ = \ £\mathbf{17.00}$$

Q5a
$$\begin{array}{r} 2.30 \\ 1.70 \\ 1.85 \\ 2.25 \\ 1.85 \\ 2.60 \\ +\ 2.15 \\ \hline 14.70 \\ \hline {\scriptstyle 3\ 2} \end{array} \qquad 14.70 \div 7 \ = \ 7\overline{)14.70}^{\,2.10} \ = \ £\mathbf{2.10}$$

Q5b Range = highest number minus the lowest number
= £2.60 − £1.70 = £**0.90**

Q6a

One fifth of 820 = $\frac{1}{5}$ × 820 = $5\overline{)8^3 2^2 0}$ = 1 6 4

Therefore, two fifths of 820 = 2 × 164 = 164
$$\begin{array}{r} 164 \\ \times\ \ \ 2 \\ \hline \mathbf{328} \\ {\scriptstyle 1} \end{array}$$

Q6b

2/5 as a percentage = 40%
10% of 820 = 82
40% of 820 = 82 × 4 =
$$\begin{array}{r} 82 \\ \times\ \ \ 4 \\ \hline \mathbf{328} \end{array}$$

Q7

10% of 600 = 60
30% of 600 = 60
$$\begin{array}{r} 60 \\ \times\ \ \ 3 \\ \hline \mathbf{180} \end{array}$$

Q8a **60%**   b **0.6**

Q9a **0.1**   b **1/10**

Q10

108.9p × 30 = 108.9 × 10 × 3 =
$$\begin{array}{r} 1089 \\ \times\ \ \ \ 3 \\ \hline 3267 \\ {\scriptstyle 2\ 2} \end{array}$$
= 3267p = **£32.67**

Q11

Area = length × width = 2.2 × 0.5 = 2.2 × ½ = 2.2 ÷ 2 = $2\overline{)2.2}$ = **1.1**m² (quotient 1.1)

Q12

Area = 42m² length = 7m width = ?
Area = length × width 42 = 7 × ?   So, ? = $\frac{42}{7}$ = 42 ÷ 7 = **6**m

Q13

Volume = length × width × height = 8m × 6m × 2.5m

$$\begin{array}{r} 2.5 \\ \times\ \ \ 8 \\ \hline 20.0 \\ {\scriptstyle 4} \end{array}\qquad \begin{array}{r} 20 \\ \times\ \ \ 6 \\ \hline 120 \end{array} = \mathbf{120m^3}$$

Q14

$$\begin{array}{r} 150 \\ \times\ \ \ 6 \\ \hline 900 \\ {\scriptstyle 3} \end{array}\qquad \begin{array}{r} 900 \\ \times\ \ \ 6 \\ \hline 5400 \end{array} = \mathbf{£5,400.00}$$

Q15   £6.20 x 20 = £6.20 x 10 x 2 = £62.00 x 2 = £124.00 per week

In 4 weeks, he will earn 124

$$\begin{array}{r} \text{x} \quad 4 \\ \hline 496 \\ \hline 1 \end{array}$$ =   **£496.00**

Q16   14 out of 42 $= \dfrac{14}{42} = \dfrac{\overset{1}{7}}{\underset{3}{21}} = \dfrac{1}{3}$ =   **33%**

Q17   3 out of 15 $= \dfrac{3}{15} = \dfrac{31}{\underset{5}{15}} = \dfrac{1}{5}$ =   **20%**

Q18   Two hundredths of a second = 0.02 seconds

$$\begin{array}{r} 19.30 \\ + \; 0.02 \\ \hline 19.32 \end{array}$$ previous world record   =   **19.32** seconds

Q19 $2^{1}0^{9}.^{1}0$

$$\begin{array}{r} - \quad 3 . 4 \\ \hline 1 6 . 6 \end{array}$$ The tailor has **16.6**m of cloth left

Q20 $5^{4}0^{9}.0^{9}{}^{1}0$

$$\begin{array}{r} - \; 2 2 . 3 \; 8 \\ \hline 2 7 . 6 \; 2 \end{array}$$ He has £**27.62** left

Q21 $36^{5},0^{9}{}^{1}00$

$$\begin{array}{r} - 2 3 , 3 \; 5 \; 0 \\ \hline 1 2 , 6 \; 5 \; 0 \end{array}$$ They need £**12,650**

Q22a   11.58

$$\begin{array}{r} - 1 1 . 5 2 \\ \hline 0 . 0 6 \end{array}$$ million   =   60,000

So, there are **60,000** more pensioners than under-16s living in the UK

b   60,000 = **sixty thousand**

Q23   3 children : 1 carer
       18 children : 6 carers

Q24   The car emits 300g of carbon dioxide per kilometre = 0.3kg/km
       So, in 30km, it will emit 30 x 0.3 kg of carbon dioxide

0.3 x 30 = 0.3 x 10 x 3 = 3 x 3 = **9**kg

Q25 400g = 0.4kg
0.4 x 30 = 0.4 x 10 x 3 = 4 x 3 = **12**kg

Q26 1km = 1,000m   4km = 4,000m
0.5km = 500m 0.05km = 50m
Therefore, 4.05km = 4,000m + 50m = **4,050**m

Q27 100cm = 1m   50cm = 0.5m = ½ m
So, how many 0.5m are there in a 7.5m roll? **15**

Q28 1km = 1,000m   3.5km = 3,500m
So, how many 50m lengths are there in 3,500m?

$$3{,}500 \div 50 \quad = \quad 50\overline{)3{,}500}^{\,0070} \quad = \quad 70 \text{ lengths}$$

Q29 **65**kg

Q30 **50.3**m

Answers to L2 Numeracy Learning Guide

Forming and Simplifying Fractions

Q1 Total number of visitors = 43 + 28 +33 +36 = 140
The proportion of visitors who played table tennis = 28 out of 140 = $\frac{28}{140}$

$$\frac{28}{140} = \frac{14}{70} = \frac{7}{35} = \frac{1}{5}$$

Q2 Total number of children = 41 + 17 + 20 + 41 +34 = 153
The proportion of children who chose indoor sports = 17 out of 153 = $\frac{17}{153}$

$$\frac{17}{153} = \frac{1}{9}$$

Calculating Percentages - Conversion Table

	Fraction	Percentage	Decimal
	1/8 (an eighth)	12.5%	0.125
	1/4 (a quarter)	25%	0.25
	3/8 (three eighths)	37.5%	0.375
	5/8 (five eighths)	62.5%	0.625

	Fraction	Percentage	Decimal
	7/8 (seven eighths)	87.5%	0.875
	1/6 (one sixth)	16.7%	0.167
	1/7 (one seventh)	14.3%	0.143
	2/7 (two sevenths)	28.6%	0.286
	3/7 (three sevenths)	42.9%	0.429
	4/7 (four sevenths)	57.1%	0.571
	1/9 (one ninth)	11.1%	0.111
	2/9 (two ninths)	22.2%	0.222
	4/9 (four ninths)	44.4%	0.444

	Fraction	Percentage	Decimal
	1/10 (one tenth)	10%	0.1
	3/10 (three tenths)	30%	0.3

Calculating Percentages

Q1 57% of the people are men, therefore 43% of the people are women.
To find 43% of 900
10% of 900 = 90   40% of 900 = 90 x 4 = 360
1% of 900 = 9   3% of 900 = 9 x 3 = 27
Therefore 43% of 900 = 360 + 27 = **387**

Q2 To find 17.5% of £16,500.00
10% of £16,500.00 = £1,650.00
1% of £16,500.00 = £165.00   7% of £16,500 = 165

$$\begin{array}{r} \times \quad 7 \\ \hline 1{,}155 \\ \hline \scriptstyle 4\,3 \end{array} = £1{,}155$$

0.5% of £16,500.00 = 165.00 ÷ 2

$$165.00 \div 2 = 2\overline{)165\overset{1}{.}00} \quad \begin{array}{c} 82.50 \end{array}$$

17.5% = 10% + 7% + 0.5%   =   1,650.00
                                             1,155.00
                                       +   82.50
                                          ─────────
                                           2,887.50   =   £2,887.50
                                          ─────────
                                               1

Therefore, the cost of the car =   16,500.00
                                       + 2,887.50
                                       ──────────
                                        19,387.50   =   **£19,387.50**
                                       ──────────
                                            1

Q3 To find 26% of 23,600

10% of 23,600 = 2,360   1% = 236

$$\begin{array}{r} 20\% \;=\; 2,360 \\ \times\quad 2 \\ \hline 4,720 \\ \tiny{1} \end{array} \qquad \begin{array}{r} 6\% \;=\; 236 \\ \times\quad 6 \\ \hline 1,416 \\ \tiny{2\ 3} \end{array}$$

So, 26% = 20% + 6% $= \begin{array}{r} 4,720 \\ +1,416 \\ \hline \mathbf{6,136} \\ \tiny{1} \end{array}$

Q4 16% of 350 chose Turkish as their preferred cuisine

10% of 350 = 35   1% of 350 = 3.5 $\begin{array}{r} 6\% \text{ of } 350 = 3.5 \\ \times\quad 6 \\ \hline 21.0 \\ \tiny{3} \end{array}$

Total number = 35 + 21 = **56**

Calculating percentage increase (or decrease)

Q1a Percentage increase in the house price of House 1 =

$$\frac{\text{actual increase}}{\text{original amount}} \times 100\%$$

$$= \frac{24,000}{120,000} \times 100\% = \frac{24}{120} \times 100\% = \frac{2}{10} \times 100\% = \frac{1}{5} \times 100\% = \mathbf{20\%}$$

Q1b Percentage decrease in the house price of House 2 =

$$\frac{\text{actual decrease}}{\text{original amount}} \times 100\%$$

$$= \frac{12,000}{120,000} \times 100\% = \frac{12}{120} \times 100\% = \frac{1}{10} \times 100\% = \mathbf{10\%}$$

Q2 Percentage increase in the party's vote $= \dfrac{\text{actual increase}}{\text{original amount}} \times 100\%$

actual increase = $16^{5,1}250$ original amount = 12,500
                  $-12,500$
                  $\overline{3,750}$

Percentage increase =

$$\frac{3,750}{12,500} \times 100\% \;=\; \frac{3750 \,(\div 5)}{125 \,(\div 5)} \;=\; \frac{750 \,(\div 5)}{25 \,(\div 5)} \;=\; \frac{150}{5} \;=\; \mathbf{30}\%$$

Q3 Percentage increase in temperature $\;=\; \dfrac{\text{actual increase}}{\text{original amount}} \times 100\%$

actual increase = 37.8°C - 36°C = 1.8°C   original amount = 36 °C

$$\text{Percentage increase} \;=\; \frac{1.8 \times 100\%}{36} \;=\; \frac{180\,(\div 9)}{36\,(\div 9)} \;=\; \frac{20}{4} \;=\; \mathbf{5\%}$$

Calculations involving Multiplication

Q1 £5.85 x 36 hours
(36 = 30 + 6)

£5.85 x 30 = £58.50   £5.85 x 6 = £5.85
            $\times\quad 3$ $\times\quad 6$
            $\overline{\text{£175.50}}$ $\overline{\text{£35.10}}$
            $\;{\scriptstyle 2\;1}$ $\;{\scriptstyle 5\;\;3}$

So, £5.85 x 36 = 175.50
              $+\;\;$ 35.10
              $\overline{\textbf{£210.60}}$
              $\;{\scriptstyle 1\;1}$

Q2 8 hours overtime at time and a half = 8 + 4 = 12 hours

£5.85 x 12 = £5.85
            $\times\quad 12$
            $\overline{\textbf{£70.20}}$
            $\;{\scriptstyle 10\;\;6}$

Q3a £6.00 x 42.5 hours
    (42.5 = 40 + 2 + 0.5)

£6.00 x 40 = £60.00   £6.00 x 2 = £12.00   £6.00 x 0.5 = £3.00

$$\begin{array}{r} \text{x} \quad 4 \\ \hline £240.00 \end{array}$$

So, £6.00 x 42.5 = 240.00

$$\begin{array}{r} 12.00 \\ + \quad 3.00 \\ \hline \mathbf{£255.00} \end{array} \quad \text{per week}$$

Q3b   255

$$\begin{array}{r} \text{x} \quad 4 \\ \hline \mathbf{£1,020} \\ {\scriptstyle 2\ 2} \end{array} \quad \text{in 4 weeks}$$

Q4a £6.30 x 175 hours
£6.30 x 175
(175 = 100 + 70 + 5)

£6.30 x 100 = £630.00   £6.30 x 70 = £63.00

$$\begin{array}{r} \text{x} \quad 7 \\ \hline £441.00 \\ {\scriptstyle 2} \end{array} \qquad \begin{array}{r} £6.30 \\ \text{x} \quad 5 \\ \hline £31.50 \\ {\scriptstyle 1} \end{array}$$

So, £6.30 x 175   =   630.00

$$\begin{array}{r} 441.00 \\ + \quad 31.50 \\ \hline \mathbf{£1,102.50} \\ {\scriptstyle 1} \end{array}$$

Q4b   1,102.50

$$\begin{array}{r} \text{x} \quad 12 \\ \hline \mathbf{£13,230.00} \\ {\scriptstyle 1 \quad 3\ 6} \end{array}$$

Q5 Area of lawn A = length x width = 16m x 11m   =   16

$$\begin{array}{r} \text{x 11} \\ \hline 176m^2 \\ {\scriptstyle 6} \end{array}$$

Area of lawn B = length x width = 13m x 7m   =   13

$$\begin{array}{r} \text{x 7} \\ \hline 91m^2 \\ {\scriptstyle 2} \end{array}$$

Combined area of A and B   =   176
$$+ \underline{91}$$
267m²
$$\overline{1}$$

Q6 Area of warehouse = length x width = 63m x 22.4m

(63 = 60 + 3)

22.4 x 60   =   224   22.4 x 3   =   22.4
$$ \text{x} \quad \underline{6} \text{x} \quad \underline{3}$$
$$ 1,344\text{m}^2 67.2\text{m}^2$$
$$ \overline{1\ 2} \overline{1}$$

Therefore, area   =   1,344.0
$$+ \quad \underline{67.2}$$
1,411.2 m²
$$\overline{1\ 1}$$

Q7 Volume of topsoil = length x width x height
Length = 22m   Width = 15m   Height (or Depth) = 20cm = 0.2m = 1/5m
Volume = 22 x 15 x 1/5

$$15 \text{ x } 1/5 = \frac{15}{5} = 3 \qquad 22 \text{ x } 3 = \mathbf{66}\text{m}^3$$

Q8 450g x 33
450g = 0.45kg
(33 = 30 + 3)

0.45kg x 30 = 4.5   0.45 x 3 = 0.45
$$ \text{x} \quad \underline{3} \text{x} \quad \underline{3}$$
$$ 13.5\text{kg} 1.35\text{kg}$$
$$ \overline{1} \overline{1\ 1}$$

Weight of soup = 13.50
$$+ \quad \underline{1.35}$$
14.85 kg

Mean, Range, Median and Mode

Q1a Average cost of the flights $=$ $\dfrac{\text{Total cost}}{\text{Number of flights}}$

Total cost $=$ Number of flights $=$ 13

$$
\begin{array}{r}
43 \\
47 \\
43 \\
47 \\
43 \\
47 \\
43 \\
53 \\
46 \\
56 \\
46 \\
61 \\
+\ 49 \\
\hline
624 \\
{\scriptstyle 6}
\end{array}
$$

Therefore, average cost $= £624.00 \div 13 = 13\overline{)62^{10}4.00}$ $4\ 8.00 = £\mathbf{48.00}$

Q1b Range of flight costs over the week =
highest cost – lowest cost = £61.00 - £43.00 = £**18.00**

Q1c Median cost =
43 43 43 43 46 46 **47** 47 47 49 53 56 61
= £**47.00**

Q1d The mode = £**43.00**
(i.e. the number which occurs most frequently).

Ratios

Q1 Ratio of hospitality : retail : sport : leisure : engineering =
36 : 18 : 24 : 12 (÷ 6) = **6 : 3 : 4 : 2**

Q2 Ratio of apprenticeship trainees across the 4 NVQs =
Food and drink service : Food processing : Customer service :
Front of house
15 : 9 : 6 : 6 (÷ 3) = **5 : 3 : 2 : 2**

Q3 Ratio of 'boxes of strawberries' to 'boxes of blueberries' sold in one day

   13 : 2
208 : ?

208 is 16 times 13 so number of boxes of blueberries = 16 x 2 = **32**

Q4a Ratio of ascents on highest mountain to ascents on second highest
mountain

= 145 : 45 (÷5) = **29 : 9**

Q4b Ratio of ascents on 2nd highest mountain to ascents on 5th highest
mountain

= 45 : 45 = **1 : 1**

Answers to questions on 'Priming learners for L2 Functional Skills maths'

Q1

1 year = 12 months = 52 weeks

$\qquad$ 3 months = 52 weeks ÷ 4 = 13 weeks

For 1 car, 8 weeks @£199/week = £199 x 8 = £1,592

There are 13 – 8 = 5 additional weeks, each with a 15% discount

Discount for 1 car = £199 x 0.15 = £29.85
Cost for 1 car = £199 - £29.85 = £169.15

5 weeks @ £169.15/week = £169.15 x 5 = £845.75

Therefore, cost of 1 car for 13 weeks = £1,592 + £845.75 = £2,437.75

And, cost of 5 cars for 13 weeks = £2,437.75 x 5 = **£12,188.75**

Check: £845.75 ÷ 5 = £169.15 (or any other suitable reverse calculation)

Q2

Choice 1: John   Reason: Because he had the highest mean score.

Choice 2 Afshah   Reason: He has the joint (equal) second highest mean score, along with Sarah, but has a lower range than Sarah, meaning that his scores were more consistent (varied less) than Sarah's.

Q3

Area of floor = 6.5m x 4m = 26 m^2

Area of tile = 0.5m x 0.5m = 0.25 m^2

Therefore, number of tiles = 26 m^2 ÷ 0.25m^2 = **104 tiles**

Or, consider how many tiles (0.5m x 0.5m) there are in 1m^2 (1m x 1m)

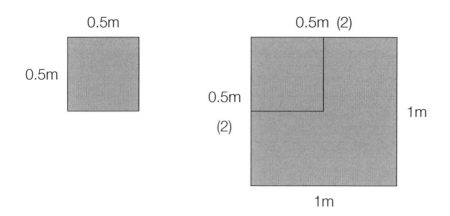

2 x 2 = 4 tiles in 1m²   So, in 26 m² there are 26 x 4 = **104 tiles**

Or, calculate how many tiles will fit along (6.5m) and across (4m) the floor.

6.5m ÷ 0.5m = 13   4m ÷ 0.5m = 8

Then, 13 x 8 = **104 tiles** (each of the methods above reinforces the others).

Q4

a) Range = £10,000 - £0 = **£10,000**

b) Mean = Total = £23, 205 ÷ 7 = **£3,315**
   Median = £0, £87, £500, **£718**, £5,000, £6,900, £10,000

c) £3,315 x 7 = £23,205

d) Either, I chose the mean so that all values would be taken into account.
   Or, I chose the median so that no one value could distort the average.

e) £915 - £320 = **£595**

f) The results in the first group varied more (were less consistent) than the results in the second group.
   Or, the results in the second group were more consistent (varied less) than the results in the first group.

Q5

2 out of 3 or ⅔

Q6

Q7

a) 10% of £225,000 = 225,000 x ¹⁄₁₀ = £22,500

£225,000 + £22,500 = **£247,500**

b) Tim : Bill : Sarah

2 : 3 : 5 2 + 3 + 5 = 10 parts = £247,500

£49,500 : £74,250 : £123,750 So, 1 part = £24,750

Q8

a) 2hrs ÷ 4 = 30 mins 2 mins ÷ 4 = ½ min = 30 secs

57 seconds ÷ 4 = 14.25 secs

So, time taken at a quarter of the way around the course =

30 mins 44.25 secs

= **30 mins 44 seconds** (to the nearest second)

b) 41.92 km ÷ 4 = **10.48 km**

c) 41.92 ÷ 1.6 = **26.2 miles**

Q9

a) Mean weight $= \dfrac{\text{Total}}{\text{Number}} = \dfrac{240}{20} = $ **12kg**

b) Range = 20.1 − 7.4 = **12.7kg**

c) Mode = **11kg**

d) Median = 7.4, 7.8, 8.0, 8.5, 9.0, 9.3, 9.8, 10.1, 10.5, **11, 11**, …

11kg

e) 12.7kg + 7.4kg = 20.1kg (or any other suitable reverse calculation).

f) Mean weight = 12kg

Number of suitcases with a weight higher than the mean = 7

So, probability = **⁷⁄₂₀**

Q10

The range of results shows that the students' marks were consistent.

Or, the range of results shows that the students' marks did not vary much.

Q11

a) £2,000,0̶0̶0̶ x ¹⁄₁̶₀̶ = £200,000
£2,000,000 - £200,000 = **£1,800,000**

b) £2,000,0̶0̶0̶ x ¹⁵⁄₁̶₀̶₀̶ = **£300,000** (money needed to be added to the original value)
£2,000,000 + £300,000 = **£2,300,000** (new value)

Q12

a) Area of wall = 3m x 2.5m = 7.5m²
Area of 1 tile = 0.25m x 0.25m = 0.0625 m²
(or, ¼m x ¼m = ¹⁄₁₆ m² = 0.0625 m²)
7.5m² ÷ 0.0625m² = **120** tiles

Or, consider how many tiles (0.25m x 0.25m) there are in 1m² (1m x 1m)

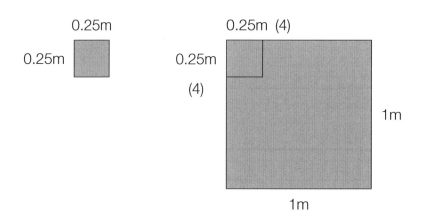

4 x 4 = 16 tiles in 1m²   So, in 7.5 m² there are 7.5 x 16 = **120** tiles

Or, consider how many tiles will fit along (3m) and down (2.5m) the wall.

3m ÷ 0.25m = 12   2.5m ÷ 0.25m = 10

Then, 12 x 10 = **120** tiles (again, each method reinforces the other).

b) Three boxes are required (3 x 50 = 150)

One box costs £79.50 + VAT @ 20%

20% of £79.50 = £79.50 x 0.2 = £15.90

So, one box costs £79.50 + £15.90 = £95.40

and 3 boxes cost £95.40 x 3 = **£286.20**

c) $120 \times 0.0625m^2 = 7.5m^2$ (or any other suitable reverse calculation).

Q13

The ratio is 2 : 3 : 4 So, there are 9 parts

1 part = £72,122 ÷ 9 = £8,013.55' = £8,013.56

Peter	:	Sam	:	Vivian
2	:	3	:	4
£16,027.11	:	**£24,040.67**	:	**£32,054.22**

Q14

Johnny	Rash
flour = ~~200~~ x $^{15}/_{~~100~~}$ = 30g	flour = ⅕ x ~~180~~^{36} = 36g
oil = 200g	oil = 190g
sugar = 75g	sugar = 80g
salt = 5g	salt = 5g
colouring = 1g	colouring = 0.5g
Total = 311g	**Total = 311.5g**

So, **Rash** will use the highest weight of ingredients, by **0.5g**

Q15

a) 600cm ÷ 150cm = 4 table tops (across) 350cm ÷ 80cm = 4.375 (down)

= 4 whole table tops.

So, number of table tops from one sheet of wood = 4 x 4 = 16

60 ÷ 16 = 3.75   So, **4** sheets of wood are required.

b) 250ml = 0.25L   For 60 table tops, 60 x 0.25L = 6 x 10 x 0.25L

= 6 x 2.5L = 15L

Two coats, so 2 x 15L = 30L are required

Each tin = 5L, so 30L ÷ 5L = **6 tins** of varnish are needed.

Q16

Circumference of a sphere = $2\pi r$ = 20cm

$r = \frac{20}{2\pi}$ cm = $\frac{10}{\pi}$ cm = $\frac{10}{3.14}$ = 3.18cm

Volume of a sphere = $\frac{4}{3}\pi r3$ = $\frac{4}{3}$ x 3.14 x $(3.18)^3$ = $\frac{4}{3}$ x 3.14 x 3.18 x 3.18 x 3.18 = **134.63cm³**

Q17

If the exchange rate between the Euro and the pound is: **1 Euro** = £**0.91** then calculate how many Euros (to the nearest cent) you would get from £**70.00**

1 Euro = £0.91   or   £0.91 = 1 Euro

If we divide both sides by 0.91, then $\frac{£0.91}{0.91}$ = $\frac{1}{0.91}$ Euro

So, £1 = $\frac{1}{0.91}$ Euro

Then, if we multiply both sides by 70,   70 x £1 = 70 x $\frac{1}{0.91}$ Euro

So, £70 = $\frac{70}{0.91}$ Euro

This, naturally, would not be easy to solve since it would involve carrying out the following tricky division:

$0.91\overline{)70.00}$

However, to get rid of the decimal point in the 0.91 we can multiply the top and bottom by 100

i.e. $\frac{70}{0.91}$ = $\frac{70 \times 100}{0.91 \times 100}$ = $\frac{7,000}{91}$

This, however, would still involve dividing 7,000 by 91 which is not too easy either. To make it a little simpler, we could factorise it since 7 will go into 91 13 times.

So, $\dfrac{{}^{1}7{,}000}{9\!\!\!\!\;/\,{}^{13}} = \dfrac{1{,}000}{13}$

This at least then is a little easier to solve:

$$\dfrac{7\,6\,.\,9\,2\,3}{13\overline{)100{}^{9}0.{}^{12}0{}^{3}0{}^{4}0{}^{1}0}} = \mathbf{76.92}\text{ Euros (to the nearest cent)}$$

When explaining this problem to students, we can put across the idea that with any equation we can do the same to both sides of that equation or the same to the top (nominator) and bottom (denominator) of either side of an equation, and still keep it balanced.

   To help clarify and reinforce the above methods, we can compare them with something more familiar, for example:

8 x 3 = 24   and $\dfrac{8\text{ x }3}{4} = \dfrac{24}{4} = 6$

4 x 2 = 8   and   4 x 2 x 100 = 8 x 100 = 800

The above methods can also be used in the context of introducing algebra, and/or manipulating and simplifying equations, for example:

2.5a = 4b   2 x 2.5a = 2 x 4b   5a = 8b $a = \dfrac{8b}{5} = 1.6b$

Alternatively:

2.5a = 4b $\dfrac{5a}{2} = 4b$ $a = 4b\text{ x }\dfrac{2}{5}$ $a = \dfrac{8b}{5} = 1.6b$

Q18

The thickness of the ten pence piece was increased in January 2011 from 1.7mm to 1.9mm. Calculate the percentage increase in the thickness of the coin (to the nearest whole number).

Percentage increase   = $\dfrac{\text{actual increase}}{\text{original amount}}$ x   100%

actual increase = 1.9mm – 1.7mm = 0.2mm   original amount   =   1.7mm

So, % increase = $\dfrac{0.2}{1.7}$ x 100% = $\dfrac{20}{1.7}$ = $\dfrac{200}{17}$ = $\dfrac{1\,1.\,7}{17\overline{)20{}^{3}0.{}^{13}0}}$ (r 11)

= 12% (to the nearest whole number)

Q19

Jamal

$$94\text{kg} \times \tfrac{1}{8} = 8\overline{)9^14.^60^40} = 11.75\text{kg} \quad 94 - 11.75 = 82.25\text{kg}$$

(working shown: 11.75)

Byron

1kg = 2.2lbs   198lbs ÷ 2.2lbs = 90kg

8% of 90kg = 90 × $\tfrac{8}{100}$ = $\tfrac{72}{10}$ = 7.2kg   90 − 7.2 = 82.8kg

$$
\begin{array}{r}
8\,2\,.\,{}^78\,{}^10 \\
-\,8\,2\,.\,2\,5 \\
\hline
0\,.\,5\,5
\end{array}
= \textbf{0.55kg}
$$

Q20

42 tests were taken, and the overall pass rate was approximately 93%

Let the number of test passes = n

$$\frac{n}{42} \times 100\% \approx 93\%$$

$$n \approx \frac{93 \times 42}{100} = \frac{3{,}906}{100} = 39.06 = 39 \text{ test passes}$$

So, the number of students who passed the L2 test = 39 − 21 = **18**

Q21

a)

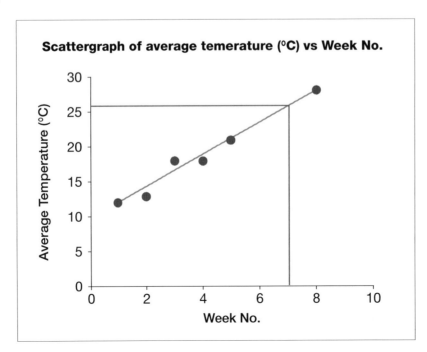

Scattergraph of average temerature (°C) vs Week No.

b) **25°C** (or **25.5°C** or **26°C**)

c) Over the period of 8 weeks, the average temperature in the UK increased.
Or, there was a positive correlation between the average temperature in the UK and the period of 8 weeks.

Q22

a)

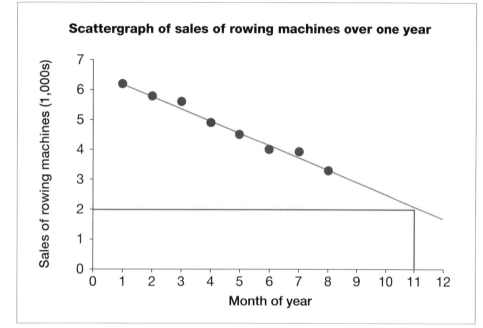

b) 20,000

c) Over the course of the year, the sales of rowing machines decreased.
Or, there was a negative correlation between the sales of rowing machines and the number of the month of the year.

Q23

a) Total waiting time = 14hrs + 1hr (45mins + 15mins) + 1hr (25mins + 35mins) + 1hr (30mins + 30mins) + 2hrs (45mins + 45mins + 20mins + 10mins) + 12mins

= 19hrs and 12 mins   12 mins = $^{12}\!/_{60}$ hrs = $\frac{1}{5}$ hr = 0.2hrs

So, total waiting time = 19.2 hrs

Mean waiting time = $\dfrac{\text{Total waiting time}}{\text{Number}}$ = $\dfrac{19.2}{12}$ = $12\overline{)19.2}$ = 1.6 hrs

1.6hrs (1hr 36 mins) > 1.5hrs (1hr 30 mins), so the airport has not met its target.

b) 8 out of 12 $= {}^8\!/_{12} = {}^2\!/_3 =$ **66.6'%**

   $=$ **66.7%** (to one decimal place) or **67%** (to nearest whole number).

c) 2hrs 10 mins – 1hr 12mins $=$ **58 mins**

d) 1hr 12 mins + 1hr 6mins $=$ **2hrs 18 mins**

Q24

a) The line graph shows that percentage obesity levels increased between 1993 and 2004.

b) The percentage obesity levels of women are higher than for men.

c) The percentage obesity levels of men and women of social class 1 are higher than the percentage obesity levels of men and women of social class V.

Q25

a) Life expectancy in the UK increased between 1972 and 2005.

b) The life expectancy of non-manual workers is higher than that for manual workers (in both men and women).

c) The life expectancy of women is higher than that for men (in both manual and non-manual occupations).

Q26

a) £4,500,000 ÷ 130 = £34,615.38 = **£34,615** (to the nearest pound)

b) £4,500,000 ÷ £28,000 = 160.7 = **161 years** (to the nearest year)

Q27

½ hour = 30 mins   £100 in 20secs = £300 in 1min

So, in 30 mins, a gambler could lose 30 x £300 = **£9,000**

Q28

a) $\dfrac{46,000,000}{7,500,000,000} \times 100\% = 0.6\%$

$0.6\% = \dfrac{0.6}{100} = \dfrac{0.6 \times 10}{100 \times 10} = \dfrac{6}{1,000}$ (six out of a thousand)

Q29

500,000 x £2,000 = £1,000,000,000   500,000 x £3,000 = £1,500,000,000

So, money lost by disabled people falls between £1,000,000,000 and £1,500,000,000

Q30

Chad (44%)

Egypt (14%)

Q31

$£125 \times \dfrac{160}{100} = £125 \times 1.6 = £200$

So, total cost of barbecue = £200 + £160 = £360

Answers to questions on Scale Drawing

Scale drawing 1

Area of hall = 9m x 6m = 54m^2 Area of stage = 4m x 2.5m = 10 m^2

So, area of floor = 54 – 10 = 44 m^2

Area of 1 carpet tile = 0.5m x 0.5m = 0.25 m^2

So, number of tiles = 44 ÷ 0,25 = **176** tiles

Or, consider how many tiles (0.5m x 0.5m) there are in 1m^2 (1m x 1m)

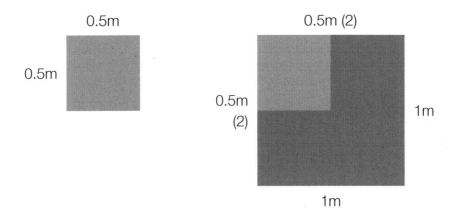

2 x 2 = 4 tiles in 1m^2 So, in 44 m2 there are 44 x 4 = **176** tiles

Scale drawing 2

- Scale = 1cm : 1m

- Perimeter of field = (16m x 2) + (13m x 2) = 32m + 26m = 58m

- Area of field = (13m x 9m) + (7m x 6m) = 117m^2 + 42 m^2 = 159m^2
  Or, (16m x 6m) + (9m x 7m) = 96m^2 + 63m^2 = 159m^2
  Or, (16m x 13m) – (7m x 7m) = 208m^2 - 49m^2 = 159m^2

- Area of 1 wigwam = πr2
  r = 1m, so area = 3.14 x 1m x 1m = 3.14 m^2
  So, area of 11 wigwams = 11 x 3.14 = 34.54 m^2

- Area of remaining grass = area of field – area of wigwams
  = 159 m^2 – 34.54 m^2 = 124.46 m^2

- 34.54 m^2 ÷ 11 = 3.14 (or any similar reverse calculation)

Scale drawing 3

a) Area of classroom = 6.5m x 4m = 26 m²
    Area of tile = 0.5m x 0.5m = 0.25 m²

    So, number of tiles classroom floor needs = 26 ÷ 0.25 = **104** tiles

b) To check the distance of 4m:

    Scale 4cm : 1m
           (x 4)   (x 4)
        16cm : 4m

    The distance for the line of 16cm was checked through using the above
    scale and measuring with a ruler.

Scale drawing 4

24m – 3.2m = 20.8m

20.8 ÷ 2.6m = 8 car park spaces on each side of the car park.

8 x 2 = **16** spaces in total

Scale drawing 5

a) 1 foot = 0.3m   So, 5 feet = 5 x 0.3m = 1.5m

    So, size of blocks = 1.5m by 1.5m

    The stage needs to be at least (a minimum of) 6m by 10m

    6m ÷ 1.5m = 4 blocks   10m ÷ 1.5m = 6.66' blocks

                              So, at least 7 blocks are needed

                              7 x 1.5m = 10.5m

    So, number of blocks needed to build the stage = 4 x 7 = **28** blocks

Scale drawing 6

Length of study = 2.5m = 250cm   width of cabinet = 45cm

$\frac{250}{45} = \frac{50}{9} = \frac{55}{9} = 5$.   So, 5 filing cabinets can fit along the wall

But, the filing cabinets can be stacked two high, so 5 x 2 = 10 filing cabinets
can fit along the wall.

1. Scale drawing of a hall with stage, doors and tables

Scale 2cm : 1m

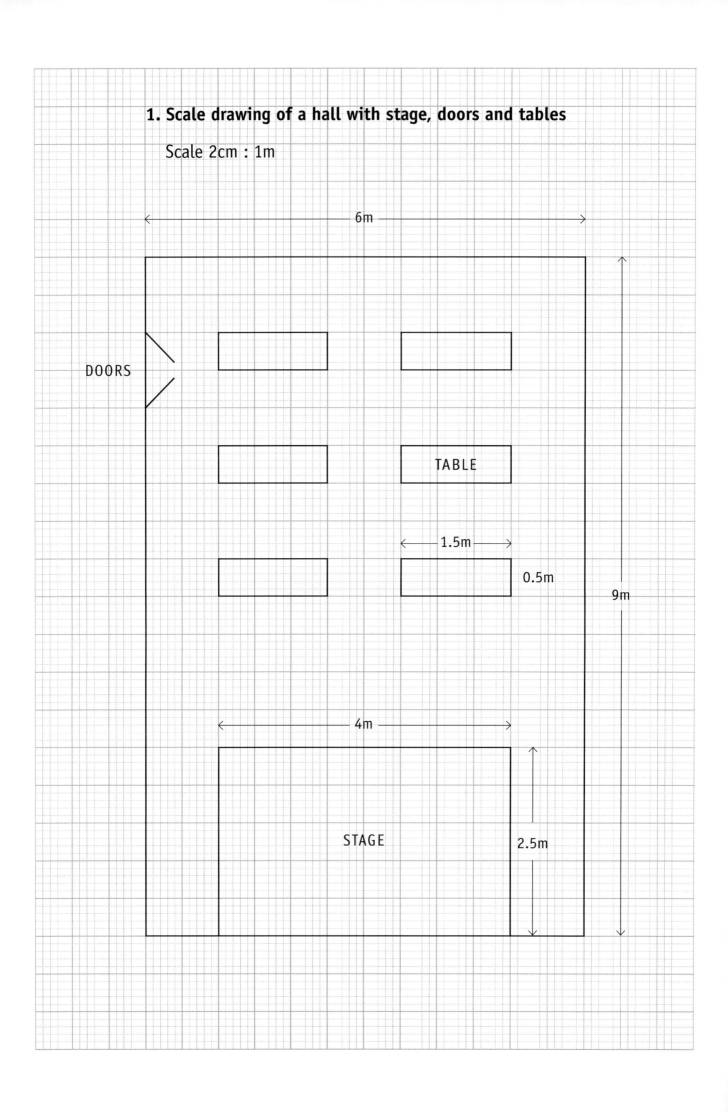

2. Scale drawing of an L-shaped field and Wigwams

Scale 1cm : 1m

1m

7m

7m

16m

9m

13m

3. Scale drawing of a classroom and carpet tiles   Scale 4cm : 1m

6.5m

4m

4. Scale drawing of a car park

Scale 1cm : 1m

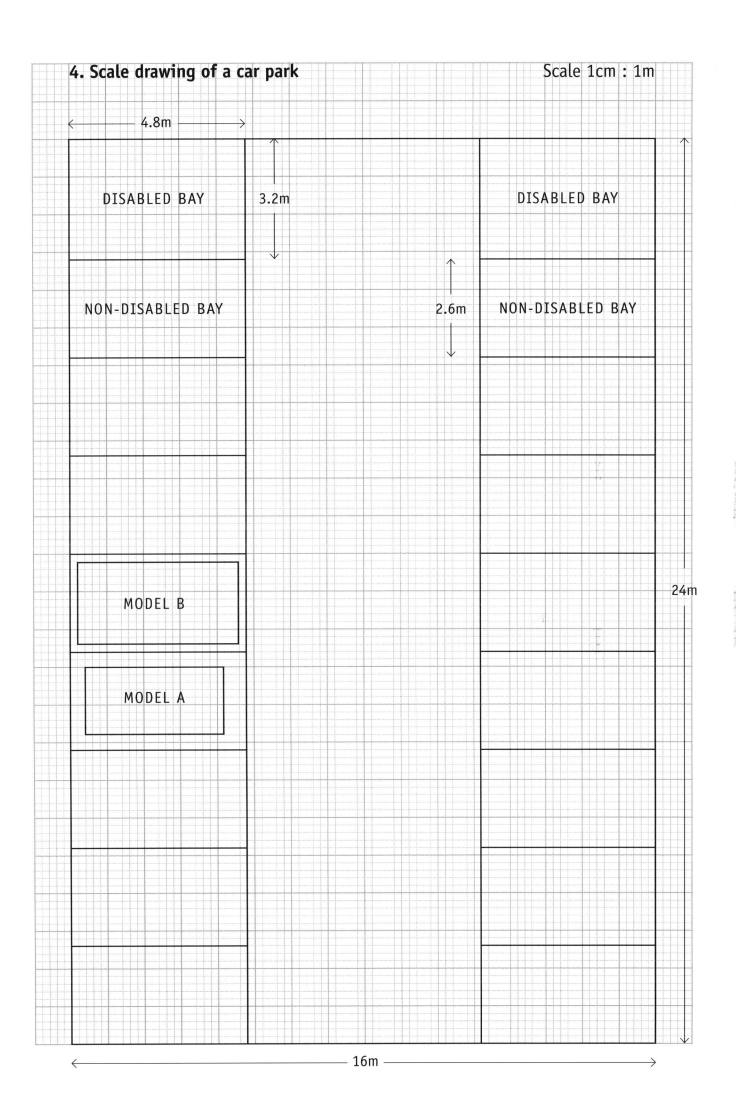

4.8m

DISABLED BAY

3.2m

DISABLED BAY

NON-DISABLED BAY

2.6m

NON-DISABLED BAY

MODEL B

MODEL A

24m

16m

5. Scale drawing of a stage with square blocks

Scale 2cm : 1m

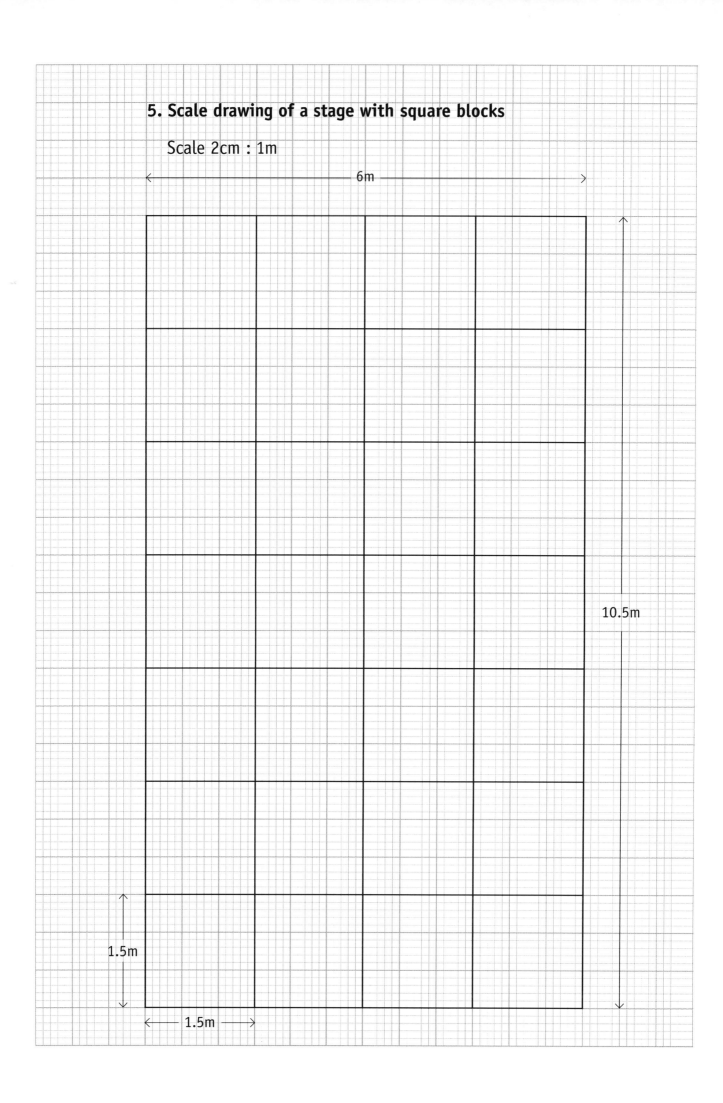

6. Scale drawing of a chest of drawers   Scale 10cm : 1m

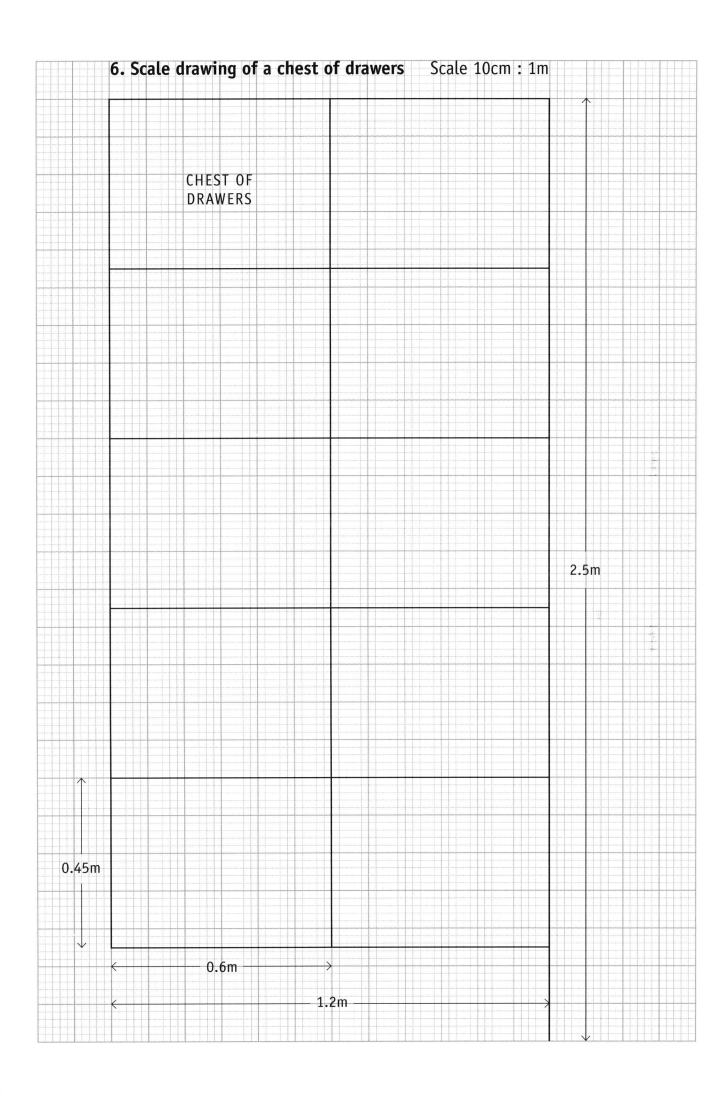

CHEST OF
DRAWERS

2.5m

0.45m

0.6m

1.2m

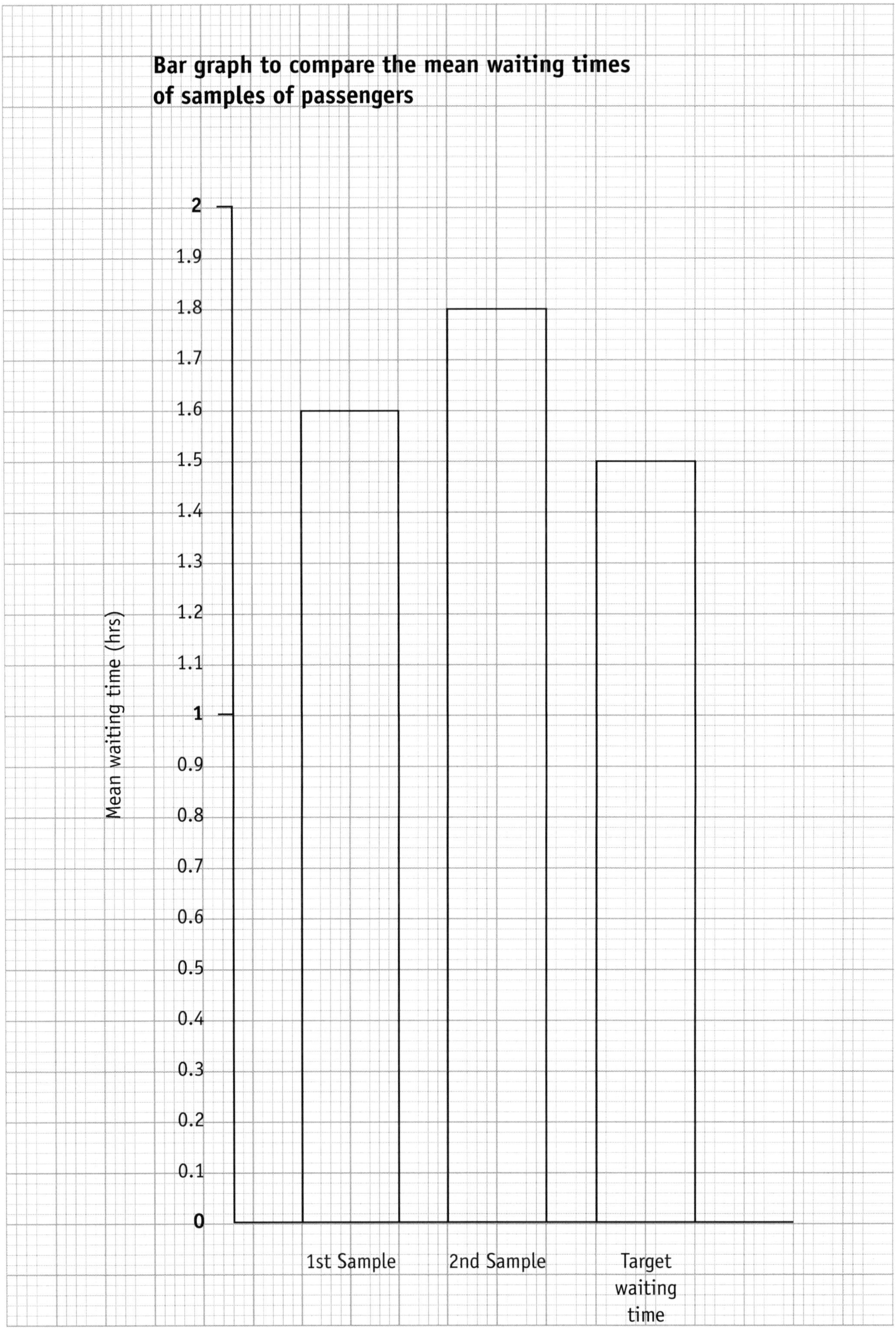
Bar graph to compare the mean waiting times
of samples of passengers
Mean waiting time (hrs)
2
1.9
1.8
1.7
1.6
1.5
1.4
1.3
1.2
1.1
1
0.9
0.8
0.7
0.6
0.5
0.4
0.3
0.2
0.1
0
1st Sample
2nd Sample
Target waiting time

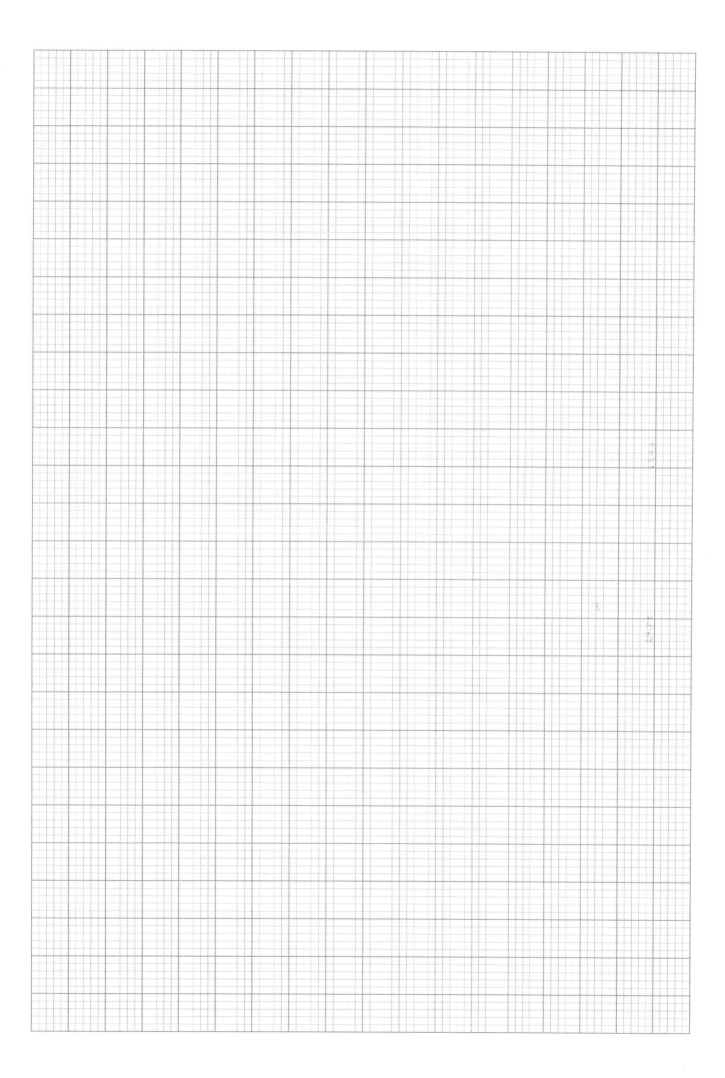

Scale drawing 7

1cm : 1m   4cm : 100cm   10cm : 1m

1cm : 100cm   4cm : 100cm   10cm : 100cm

1 : 100   4 : 100   10 : 100

1 : 25   1 : 10

Scale drawing 8

A → B = 3.5cm   B → C = 7cm   C → D = 5.5cm   D → E = 7cm

Total = 23cm

Scale 1 : 25,000

    1cm : 25,000cm

    1cm : 250m

    4cm : 1,000m

    4cm : 1km

   23cm : $\underline{23}$km = **5¾ km**   or $4\overline{)23.^30^20}$ = **5.75km**

       4

Scale drawing 9

Scale 1 : 500,000

    1cm : 500,000cm

    1cm : 5,000m

    1cm : 5km

     ? : 80km   (80 ÷ 5 = 16)

  16cm : 80km

Scale drawing 10

Scale 10cm : 25km

     10cm : 25,000m

     10cm : 2,500,000cm

     1cm : 250,000cm

    1 : 250,000

Answers to questions on conversion integration methodology

Q1

$$400g = 0.4kg = \frac{2}{5} kg \qquad \frac{2}{5} kg \times 40 = \frac{80}{5} = 5\overline{)8^30} \,\, ^{1\,6} = \textbf{16kg}$$

$$400g = 0.4kg \quad 0.4kg \times 40 = 0.4 \times 10 \times 4 = 4 \times 4 = \textbf{16kg}$$

In the above example, we are converting from grams to kilograms (by dividing by 1,000), from a decimal to a fraction, multiplying a fraction by a whole number, division and multiplying decimals, again with a view to manipulating numbers, through conversions, in order to create a more straightforward sum to solve.

Q2

$$80cm = 0.8m = \frac{4}{5}m \quad \frac{4}{5} \times 12 = \frac{48}{5} = 5\overline{)48^30} \,\, ^{09.\,6} = \textbf{9.6m}$$

$$12 \times 80cm = 120$$
$$\frac{\times \; 8}{960} \quad = \quad 960cm \quad = \quad \textbf{9.6m}$$
$$\scriptstyle 1$$

$$80cm = 0.8m \quad 0.8 \times 12 = (0.8 \times 10) + (0.8 \times 2) = 8 + 1.6 = \textbf{9.6m}$$

In the above example, we are converting from cm to m (by dividing by 100), converting a decimal into a fraction, multiplying a fraction by a whole number, dividing a decimal, and multiplying whole numbers and decimals.

I believe it would be good practice to work through each of the above methods with learners (even if they have a preferred method), on the basis that they help to reinforce each other, and give learners a wider range of methods upon which to draw in solving numeracy problems in general. The rationale behind the methods is that learners become used to the idea of being able to manipulate numbers, through conversions, in order to be able to create for themselves a more straightforward sum to solve.

Q3

1 pack = 4 x 5 = 20 bottles   4 packs = 4 x 20 = 80 bottles

$300ml = 0.3L = \dfrac{3}{10}$ L $\dfrac{3}{10}$ x 80 = **24L**

Or, 0.3 x 80 = 0.3 x 10 x 8 = 3 x 8 = **24L**

Q4

1 large loaf of bread weighs 800g = 0.8kg = $\dfrac{8}{10}$ kg

$\dfrac{8}{1\theta}$ x 6θ = **48kg**

Or, 0.8 x 60 = 0.8 x 10 x 6 = 8 x 6 = **48kg**

Q5

$0.25L = \dfrac{1}{4}$ L $\dfrac{1}{4}$ x $\cancel{12}^{30}0$ = **30L**

Or, 0.25 x 120 = 0.25 x 10 x 12 = 2.5 x 12 = (12 x 2) + (12 x ½) = 24 + 6 = **30L**

Q6

1 pack = 48 jars   5 packs = 48 x 5 = 240 jars

1 jar weighs 200g = 0.2kg = $\dfrac{2}{10}$ kg   240 x $\dfrac{2}{10}$ = **48kg**

Or, 0.2 x 240 = 0.2 x 10 x 24 = 2 x 24 = **48kg**

Q7

2.5kg = 2½kg = $\dfrac{5}{2}$ kg $\dfrac{5}{2}$ x 30 = **75kg**

Or, 2.5 x 30 = 2.5 x 10 x 3 = 25 x 3 = **75kg**

Q8

Length = 25m   Width = 12m   Depth = 300mm

Depth = 300mm = 30cm = 0.3m = $\dfrac{3}{10}$ m

Volume = Length x Width x Depth

= 12 x 255 x $\dfrac{3}{\cancel{10}^{2}}$ = $\dfrac{180}{2}$ = **90m³** of concrete

Alternatively (although slightly more long winded):

$$\begin{array}{r} 25 \\ \times\ 12 \\ \hline 300 \\ \end{array}$$

$\underset{6}{300}$ 300 x 0.3 = 3 x 100 x 0.3 = 3 x 30 = **90m³** of concrete

In the above example, we are converting from mm to cm to m, from a decimal to fraction, multiplying a fraction by two whole numbers, and multiplying whole numbers and decimals, again with a view to manipulating numbers, through conversions, in order to create a more straightforward sum to solve.

Q9

80cm = 0.8m = $\dfrac{4}{5}$ m   25cm = 0.25m = $\dfrac{1}{4}$ m

Volume = Length x Width x Depth = $\dfrac{4}{5}$ x $\dfrac{\cancel{4}^{1}}{5}$ x $\dfrac{1}{\cancel{4}^{1}}$ = $\dfrac{4}{25}$ m³ x $\dfrac{4}{\times 4}$ = $\dfrac{16}{100}$ = **0.16 m³**

In the above example, we are converting from cm to m, from a decimal to a fraction, multiplying, and simplifying, three fractions, expanding the result to a proportion of a hundred, then converting to a decimal for a final answer. Here, the concept of performing the same multiplication task to both numerator and denominator, without changing the sum, is introduced, again as a means of manipulating numbers in order to create a more manageable sum to solve.

By the way, as the more observant amongst you will have noticed, the actual answer is zero!

Q10

75cm = 0.75m = $\dfrac{3}{4}$ m   Volume of water = 3 x 4 x $\dfrac{3}{4}$ = 9m³

1m³ = 1,000L   9m³ = **9,000L**

Answers to Level 2 Functional Skills Numeracy

1a

40g x 18 = 180

$$\begin{array}{r} 180 \\ \times\ \ 4 \\ \hline 720g \\ \end{array} = \textbf{0.72kg}$$

3

b

18 x 200 calories = 3,600 calories

240 calories = 1 kilojoule

Therefore, 3,600 calories $= \dfrac{3,600}{240} = \dfrac{360^{30}}{24^{2}} = \textbf{15 kilojoules}$

c

$$\dfrac{9.2g}{40} \times 100\% = \dfrac{920}{40} = 4\overline{)9^{1}2}^{\,23} = \textbf{23\%}$$

d

6% = 0.3g   Therefore, 1% $= \dfrac{0.3g}{6} = 6\overline{)0.30}^{\,0.05g}$

1% = 0.05g   Therefore, 100% = **5g**

e

$$\dfrac{0.5g}{30g} \times 100\% = \dfrac{50}{30} = \textbf{1.67\%} \text{ (to 2 d.p.)} < 2\%$$

Therefore, the claim is true.

f

12 : 8 : 2 : 3 : 4 : 4

60g : ? : 10g : ? : 20g : 20g

The 2 parts of parmesan weigh 10g   Therefore, 1 part would weigh 5g

There are 8 parts gorgonzola and 3 parts walnuts

The weight of the of gorgonzola = 8 x 5g = **40g**

The weight of the walnuts = 3 x 5g = **15g**

g

7% = 133 calories   Therefore, 1% = $\frac{133}{7}$ calories = $7\overline{)13^63}$ 1 9 calories

1% = 19 calories   100% = **1,900 calories**

h

6% = 114 calories   Therefore, 1% = 114 calories = $6\overline{)11^54}$ calories   1 9

1% = 19 calories   100% = **1,900 calories**

Therefore, the guidelines are the same.

2a

33,^{3}4^{1}34
-33,092
342 kWh

b

342 x 5.296

300 x 5.296 = 529.6
x   3
1,588.8
  2 1

40 x 5.296 = 52.96
x   4
211.84
  1 3 2

$$2 \times 5.296 = \begin{array}{r} 5.296 \\ \times \quad 2 \\ \hline 10.592 \\ \hline {}^{1}{}^{1} \end{array}$$

$$\begin{array}{r} 1588.8 \\ 211.84 \\ + \quad 10.592 \\ \hline 1811.232\text{p} \\ \hline {}_{1}\,{}_{1}\,{}_{2}\,{}_{1} \end{array} = \textbf{£18.11} \text{ (to the nearest penny)}$$

c

$$\begin{array}{r} 1\,{}^{7}8\,{}^{9}0\,{}^{1}2\,4 \\ -1\,7\,5\,3\,1 \\ \hline \textbf{4\,9\,3}\ \textbf{kWh} \end{array}$$

d

493 x 12.472

$$400 \times 12.472 = \begin{array}{r} 1247.2 \\ \times \quad 4 \\ \hline 4988.8 \\ \hline {}_{1}\,{}_{2} \end{array}$$

$$90 \times 12.472 = \begin{array}{r} 124.72 \\ \times \quad 9 \\ \hline 1122.48 \\ \hline {}_{2}\,{}_{4}\,{}_{6}\,{}_{1} \end{array}$$

$$3 \times 12.472 = \begin{array}{r} 12.472 \\ \times \quad 3 \\ \hline 37.416 \\ \hline {}_{1}\,{}_{2} \end{array}$$

$$\begin{array}{r} 4988.8 \\ 1122.48 \\ + \quad 37.416 \\ \hline 6148.696\text{p} \\ \hline {}_{1}\,{}_{1}\,{}_{1}\,{}_{1} \end{array} = \textbf{£61.49} \text{ (to the nearest penny)}$$

e

$$\begin{array}{r} £18.11 \\ + \ £61.49 \\ \hline \textbf{£79.60} \end{array}$$

f

$$\frac{£79.60}{40} = \frac{7.96}{4} = 4\overline{\smash{)}7.^39^36} \;\; = \;\textbf{£1.99}$$

g

24% of £537.60

10% = £53.76

$$\begin{array}{r} 20\% = 53.76 \\ + 53.76 \\ \hline £107.52 \\ {\scriptstyle 1\;\;1} \end{array}$$

1% = 5.376

$$\begin{array}{r} 4\% = 5.376 \\ \times 4 \\ \hline £21.504 \\ {\scriptstyle 1\;\;32} \end{array}$$

$$\text{Therefore, } 24\% = \begin{array}{r} 107.52 \\ + 21.50 \\ \hline \textbf{£129.02} \end{array}$$

h

37% - 27% = 10%

10% of £537.60 = **£53.76**

i

10% of £537.60 = £53.76

$$5\% \text{ of } £537.60 = \frac{£53.76}{2} = 2\overline{\smash{)}5^13^1.7^16} \;=\; 26.88$$

$$\text{Therefore, } 15\% \text{ of } £537.60 = \begin{array}{r} 53.76 \\ + 26.88 \\ \hline 80.64 \\ {\scriptstyle 1\;1\;\;1} \end{array}$$

However £80.64 < £85.00 so the student would not make a saving.

j

$$\frac{6.5}{34} = \frac{\cancel{65}^{13}}{\cancel{340}^{68}} = \frac{13}{68} \approx \mathbf{\frac{1}{5}}$$

K

6.5 kg per 1,000 hours

Number of hours per leap year = 366 x 24 = 366 x 12 x 2

$$
\begin{array}{r}
366 \\
\times \quad 12 \\
\hline
4,392 \\
{\scriptstyle 7\,7}
\end{array}
\qquad
\begin{array}{r}
4,392 \\
+ \; 4,392 \\
\hline
8,784 \quad \text{hours} \\
{\scriptstyle 1}
\end{array}
$$

For every 1,000 hours, 6.5kg of Carbon Dioxide is produced

Therefore, for 8,784 hours, 8.784 x 6.5kg of Carbon Dioxide is produced

$$
\begin{array}{r}
8.784 \\
\times \quad 6 \\
\hline
52.704 \\
{\scriptstyle 4\;5\,2}
\end{array}
\qquad
8.784 \times \tfrac{1}{2} = 2\overline{\smash{)}8.7^{1}8\,4}^{\;4.392}
$$

$$
\begin{array}{r}
52.704 \\
+ \quad 4.392 \\
\hline
\mathbf{57.096}\ \mathbf{kg} \\
{\scriptstyle 1}
\end{array}
$$

3a

Student A's car: $\dfrac{42\cancel{0}\ \text{miles}}{4\cancel{0}\ \text{litres}} = 4\overline{\smash{)}42.0}^{\;10.5\ \text{miles/litre}}$

Student B's car: 16km/litre = 10 miles/litre

Therefore, **Student A** has the more fuel efficient car

b

12½ % of 40L

10% = 4L   1% = 0.4L   2% = 0.8L   0.5% = 0.2L

Therefore, 12½ % of 40L = 4 + 0.8 + 0.2 = 5L

Student B's car therefore takes 45L

4.5L ≈ 1 gallon, so 45L ≈ **10 gallons**

c

1cm : 2,000,000 cm = 1cm : 20,000 m = 1cm : 20 km

33cm : ?

Estimated distance = 20 km x 33 = 660 km

1 mile ≈ 1.6 km $\frac{1}{1.6}$ mile = 1 km

Therefore, 660 km = $\frac{660}{1.6}$ miles = $\frac{66^{33}00}{16^{8}}$ = $8\overline{)3\,3^{1}0^{2}0.^{4}0}$ $\overset{4\ 1\ 2.5}{}$ miles

Therefore, the difference between the estimation (412.5 miles) and the Sat-Nav reading (420 miles) is **7.5 miles**

d

The distance to Edinburgh and back is 840 miles
Student A's car does 10.5 miles/litre

So, the amount of fuel used = $\frac{840}{10.5}$ = $\frac{8400}{105}$ = $105\overline{)8400}$ $\overset{80}{}$ Litres

If the cost of the fuel is shared equally, each student will pay for 20 litres

20L x 133.9p/litre = £13.39

$$\begin{array}{r} 13.39 \\ \times\ \ \ \ \ 2 \\ \hline 26.78 \\ \tiny{1} \end{array}$$

Therefore, each student should pay **£26.80** (to the nearest ten pence)

e

Highest temperature: London, 20°C
Lowest temperature: Edinburgh, 8 °C
Therefore, temperature range across the five capital cities = **12°C**

f

1.4mm
0.7mm
0.1mm
0.9mm
0.0mm
——
3.1mm   Average rainfall $= 3.1 \div 5 = 5\overline{)3.1^10} =$ **0.62mm**
2

g

Aberdeen, with a temperature range of 10°C

h

Leuchars

i

16 hours and 12 minutes

j

$\dfrac{97\cancel{0,000}}{1,\cancel{000,000}} \times 1\cancel{00}\% =$ **97%**

K

```
  1,900,000
- 1,200,000
  ─────────
    700,000   x 5 = 3,500,000
```

3,500,000 x £75 = 245,000,000
+   17,500,000
= £**262,500,000**
1

4

Product	Supermarket	
	Safeburies	**Morose**
1 Litre of skimmed milk	£0.83	£0.86
2 x 1 litre cartons of orange juice	£1.75 per carton **£2.50**	£1.95 per carton **£1.95**
Broccoli (335g)	£1.27	£1.35
Organic spinach	£1.00	£1.10
Large wholemeal loaf of Bread (800g)	£1.36	£1.38
600g bag of apples	£1.67	£1.70
2 kg of bananas	35p/lb **£1.54**	35p/lb **£1.54**
1 kg of carrots	30p/lb **£0.66**	35p/lb **£0.77**
Peppered steak (435g)	£4.00	£4.00)
Pork loin steaks (0.66kg)	£4.00	£4.00) **£10.00**
Chicken (1.45kg)	£4.00	£4.00)
Original coffee granules (200g)	£4.00	£3.85
Pure vegetable oil (1L)	£1.10	£1.25
Salted butter (750g)	£0.98	£0.94
12 free range medium eggs	£2.73	£2.80
Milk chocolate digestives	£1.00	£1.10
Easy cook rice	£1.06	£1.06
3 in 1 Shampoo	£2.20	£2.45
TOTAL	**£35.90**	**£34.10**

a

Student A's car does 10.5 miles/litre

Therefore, 16 miles (10½ + 5½) requires approximately 1½ litres

At 133.9p/litre, cost of petrol used to drive to Morose ≈ £1.34 + £0.67 = £2.01

Therefore, cost of shopping trip to Morose = £34.10 + £2.01 = £36.11

Therefore, it would be more economical for Student A to shop at Safeburies, since:

£35.90 < £36.11

b

The statement should read '10 items or fewer', since the items are countable. For example, there was less crime in the town centre last year (you can't count crime); there were fewer crimes committed in the town centre last year (you can count the number of crimes).

c

10% of £35.90 = £3.59   40% = 3.59

$$35.\overset{8}{9}\overset{1}{0}$$

$$\begin{array}{r} 3.59 \\ \times \quad 4 \\ \hline 14.36 \\ 2\ 3 \end{array}$$

$$\begin{array}{r} 35.\overset{8}{9}\overset{1}{0} \\ -\ 14.36 \\ \hline 21.54 \end{array} = \textbf{£21.54}$$

d

Safeburies: 10% of £35.90 = £3.59   Therefore, on-line cost = $3\,5.\overset{8}{9}\overset{1}{0}$

$$\begin{array}{r} -\quad 3.5\,9 \\ \hline £\,3\,2.3\,1 \end{array}$$

Morose: 5% of £34.10 = £3.41 ÷ 2 = £1.71

Therefore, on-line cost = $3^{3}4.^{10}\overset{1}{1}0$

$$\begin{array}{r} -\quad 1.7\,1 \\ \hline £\,3\,2.3\,9 \end{array} = \textbf{£32.39}$$

Therefore, **Safeburies** would be cheaper on-line for Student A's shopping (by 8p).

e

Model A does not have unlimited texts

Model D: 1st year cost = £20 x 12 = £240
2nd year cost = £10 x 12 = £120

Total cost = £360 which is above student A's maximum price.

Model C: cost over 2 years =
(£15 x 24) - £50 = £360 - £50 = £310 < £350

Model B: Cost over 2 years = £15 x 21 = £315 < £350

Model C has more memory and minutes than Model B, so Student A should choose **Model C**

5a

Total number of students = 19

Total number of students who have competed all the requirements
of the Functional Skills L2 English = 13

Therefore, fraction of students who have competed = $\frac{\textbf{13}}{\textbf{19}}$

b

For group 1, 5 out of 8 passed =

$$\frac{5}{8} \times 100\% = \frac{500}{8} = \frac{250}{4} = \frac{125}{2} = 62.5\%$$

For group 2, 7 out of 11 passed =

$$\frac{7}{11} \times 100\% = \frac{700}{11} = 11\overline{)70^40.^70^40} \quad 63.63 \text{ r7} = 63.6\%$$

Therefore, the difference between the percentage pass rates =
$$\begin{array}{r} 63.6 \\ -\ 62.5 \\ \hline \textbf{1.1\%} \end{array}$$

c

Total number of students = 19

Number of students who passed L2 maths = 12

Therefore, the overall percentage pass rate in maths = $\frac{12}{19} \times 100\% = \frac{1200}{19}$

$$= 19\overline{)120^60.^30^{11}0} \quad 63.1\ 5 \text{ r}15 = \textbf{63.2\%}$$

d

The new overall percentage pass rate = $\frac{14}{19} \times 100\% = \frac{1400}{19}$

$$= 19\overline{)140^70.^{13}0^{16}0} \quad 73.6\ 8 \text{ r8} = \textbf{73.7\%}$$

UK Unemployment

		Short-term (Less than a year)	Long-term (More than a year)
18 – 24 years	**Male**	299,000	135,000
	Female	226,000	85,000
25 – 49 years	**M**	332,000	281,000
	F	328,000	155,000
50+ years	**M**	136,000	134,000
	F	79,000	50,000
Total	**M**	767,000	550,000
	F	633,000	290,000
		1,400,000	**840,000**

f

Total number of short-term unemployed people   =   1,400,000

Total number of long-term unemployed people   =   840,000

Ratio of short-term unemployed to long-term unemployed =

1,40̶0̶,0̶0̶0̶ : 84̶0̶,0̶0̶0̶ = 140 : 84 = 70 : 42 = 35 : 21 = **5 : 3**

g

Number of short-term unemployed people (50+) = 136,000

                                                                        +   79,000

                                                                          215,000
                                                                            ₁ ₁

Number of long-term unemployed people (50+) = 134,000

                                                                        +   50,000

                                                                          184,000

Therefore, there are 215,000 – 184,000 = **31,000 more short-term unemployed adults.**

h

In the 18 – 24 years old age range, how many more male unemployed adults are there than female unemployed adults?

Number of male unemployed adults (18 - 24) = 299,000

                                                                    +   135,000

                                                                      434,000
                                                                        ₁ ₁

Number of male unemployed adults (18 - 24) $=$ 226,000

$+$ ⟨85,000⟩

311,000

1 1

Therefore, there are 434,000 – 311,000 $=$ **123,000 more male unemployed adults.**

i

0.5 million $=$ **Five hundred thousand**

6

	Mon	Tues	Weds	Thurs	Fri	Sat	Sun	Total
9 – 10	1	0	4	3	1	5		**14**
10 – 11	4	5	7	5	3	5	3	**32**
11 – 12	4	6	7	8	5	4	4	**38**
12 – 1	6	9	10	6	3	7	4	**45**
1 – 2	5	8	9	9	8	9	8	**56**
2 – 3	7	6	10	10	8	9	6	**56**
3 - 4	8	3	8	9	8	6	4	**46**
4 - 5	4	5	5	4	4	5		**27**
5 - 6	6	5	9	8	7	6		**41**
6 - 7				6	5	2		**13**
7 - 8				4	3	3		**10**
Total	**45**	**47**	**69**	**72**	**55**	**61**	**29**	**378**

a

$\dfrac{45}{9} =$ **5 books per hour**

b

$$\dfrac{378}{7} = 7\overline{)37^28}$$ with quotient **5 4**

c

$\dfrac{56}{7} =$ **8**

d

$$10 - 0 = \mathbf{10}$$

e

29 (Sun), 45 (Mon), 47 (Tues), 55 (Fri), 61 (Sat), 69 (Wed), 72 (Thurs)
The median occurred on **Friday** (55)

f

$$\frac{55}{11} = \mathbf{5}$$

g

Percentage increase $= \dfrac{\text{actual increase}}{\text{original amount}} \times 100\% = \dfrac{(420 - 378)}{378} \times 100\%$

$$= \frac{{}^{14}\cancel{42}}{{}^{126}\cancel{378}} \times 100\% = \frac{7}{63} \times 100\% =$$

$$\frac{1}{9} \times 100\% = \frac{100}{9} = 9\overline{)10^{1}0.^{1}0}$$

$$1\,1.\,1' = \mathbf{11.1\%} \text{ (to 1d.p.)}$$

h

140 cm	125 cm	160 cm
$\updownarrow 4$	$\updownarrow 5$	$\updownarrow 8$
35cm	25cm	20cm

Number of boxes that can fit in the space $= 4 \times 5 \times 8 = 160$

There are 6 books per box, so maximum number of books $= \begin{array}{r} 160 \\ \times \quad 6 \\ \hline \mathbf{960} \textbf{ books} \\ {}_{3} \end{array}$

i

$$\frac{72}{378} \times 360° = \frac{24}{126} \times 360 = \frac{12}{{}^{21}\cancel{63}} \times {}^{120}\cancel{360} = \frac{4}{7} \times 120 = \frac{480}{7} = 7\overline{)48^{6}0.^{4}0}$$

$$6\,8.5$$

$$= \mathbf{69°} \text{ (to the nearest whole number).}$$

j

$$\frac{45}{378} \times 100\% = \frac{15}{126} \times 100\% = \frac{5}{42} \times 100\% = \frac{500}{42} = \frac{250}{21} = 21)\overline{2\,5^4 0.^{19}0}^{\,1\,1.\,9\,r1}$$

= **12%** (to the nearest whole number)

k

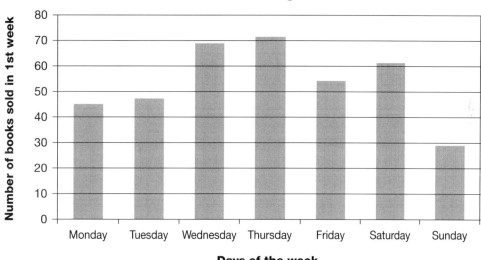

Bar chart showing book sales

l

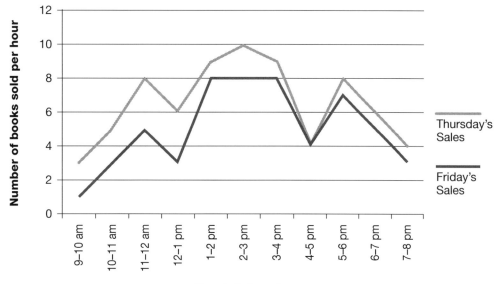

Line graph comparing hourly book sales on Thursday and Friday

7

Site A, cost/m² $= \dfrac{£420}{48} = \dfrac{210}{24} = \dfrac{105}{12} = \dfrac{35}{4} = 4\overline{)35.^30^20}$ $\dfrac{8.75}{} = £8.75/m²$

Site B, cost/m² $= \dfrac{£360}{42} = \dfrac{180}{21} = \dfrac{60}{7} = 7\overline{)60.^40^50^10}$ $8.571\ r3 = £8.57/m²$

Site C, cost/m² $= \dfrac{£468}{54} = \dfrac{234}{27} = \dfrac{78}{9} = \dfrac{26}{3} = 3\overline{)26.^20^20^20}$ $8.666' = £8.67/m²$

Therefore, **Site B @ £8.57/ m²** offers the best value for money.

6 people per day use the facilities and pay £20 each.

6 x £20 = £120 per day = £600 per week

Annual rent = £360
            x   12
            £4,320
              7

£600 x 7 = £4,200   £600 x 8 = £4,800

Therefore, 8 weeks are required for the woman to cover the cost of the annual rent.

b

Area = length x width
So, b = 42m² = 7m x **6m**

c

Scale = 1 : 25
          c : 7m

Therefore, c = $\dfrac{7\ m}{25}$ = $\dfrac{700\ cm}{25}$ = **28 cm**

d

$$d = \frac{6}{25}\,m = \frac{600}{25}\,cm = \textbf{24 cm}$$

e

Scale = 1 : 25

   11 cm : e

Therefore, e = 11cm x 25 = 275 cm = **2.75m**

f

f = 9cm x 25 = 225cm = **2.25m**

g

Desk area = 4m x 1.5m = **6m²**

h

$$h = \frac{4}{25}\,m = \frac{400}{25}\,cm = \textbf{16 cm}$$

i

$$i = \frac{1.5}{25}\,m = \frac{150}{25}\,cm = \textbf{6 cm}$$

j

j = 7cm x 25 = 175cm = **1.75m**

k

k = 5cm x 25 = 125cm = **1.25m**

l

Area (7m²) = 2 x l

Therefore, l = **3.5m**

m

$$m = \frac{3.5}{25} m = \frac{350}{25} cm = \textbf{14 cm}$$

n

$$n = \frac{2}{25} m = \frac{200}{25} cm = \textbf{8 cm}$$

8a

32% of 19,200,000

10% = 1,920,000   30% = 1,920,000

                                        x   3

                                       5,760,000
                                         ₂

1% = 192,000   2% = 192,000

                                 x   2

                                384,000
                                ₁

Therefore, 32% = 5,760,000
+   384,000

                     6,144,000 = **6,100,000**
                     ₁ ₁
                                 (to the nearest one hundred thousand).

b

68% of 19,200,000

60% = 1,920,000
        x   6
       11,520,000
         ₅ ₁

8% = 192,000
      x   8
    1,536,000
       ₇ ₁

Therefore, 68% = 11,520,000

$+ \underline{\ \ 1,536,000}$

$\underline{13,056,000}$ = **13,100,000**

$\qquad\qquad 1$

(to the nearest one hundred thousand)

c

19,200,000 = 42%

$$\frac{19,200,000}{42} \times 100\% = \frac{9,6\overset{32}{0}0,000}{2\overset{7}{1}} \times 100\% = \frac{3,200,000}{7} \times 100\%$$

$$= \frac{320,000,000}{7} = 7\overline{)3\ 2\ {}^40\ {}^50\ {}^10\ {}^30\ {}^20\ {}^60\ {}^40\ {}^50}\ \overset{4\ 5,7\ 1\ 4,2\ 8\ 5.}{}$$

= **45,700,000** (to the nearest one hundred thousand).

d

Percentage increase $= \dfrac{\text{actual increase}}{\text{original amount}} \times\ 100\%$

$= \dfrac{11\text{m}}{60\text{m}} \times\ 100\% = \dfrac{1,10\theta}{6\theta} = \dfrac{55}{3} = 3\overline{)5\ {}^25.\ {}^10\ {}^10}\ \overset{1\ 8.3\ 3'}{}$

= **18.3 %** (to one decimal place).

e

$6^0\overset{.}{+}{}^{10}\overset{.}{+}{}^11\ 3,{}^1\overset{2}{9}\overset{9}{\theta}{}^15$

$-\ 6\ 0,\ 4\ 3\ 2,0\ 9\ 8$

$\underline{\qquad\qquad \bf 6\ 8\ 1,1\ 0\ 7}$

f

10% of 30 million = 3,000,000 people

100,000 people per month x 12 = 1,200,000 people in one year

= 2,400,000 people in two years

= 3,600,000 people in three years

Therefore, it would take two and a half years for the number of Facebook accounts to reduce by 10% which would take us to **the end of October, 2013.**

g

1% of 65,640,000 = 656,400 = 660,000 (to the nearest 10,000)

h

10% of 50,760,000 = 5,076,000   80% = 5,076,000

$$\begin{array}{r} x \quad\quad 8 \\ \hline 40,608,000 \\ \hline {\scriptstyle 6\,4} \end{array}$$

1% = 507,600   9% = 507,600

$$\begin{array}{r} x \quad\quad 9 \\ \hline 4,568,400 \\ \hline {\scriptstyle 6\,5} \end{array}$$

Therefore, 89% = 40,608,000

$$\begin{array}{r} + \quad 4,568,400 \\ \hline 45,176,400 \\ \hline {\scriptstyle 1 \quad 1} \end{array}$$

Therefore, non BME population of England $\approx$ **45,200,000**
(to the nearest 100,000)

i

$$\frac{10,000}{80,000} \times 100\% = \frac{1}{8} \times 100\% = \textbf{12.5\%} > \textbf{11\%}$$

Therefore, Bedford has a higher than average BME population within England.

j

We need to calculate 14.3% of 382,000

10% = 38,200

1% = 3,820   4% = 3,820

$$\begin{array}{r} x \quad\quad 4 \\ \hline 15,280 \\ \hline {\scriptstyle 3} \end{array}$$

0.1% = 382   0.3% = 382
                      x   3
                     ———
                     1,146
                       2

Therefore, 14.3% = 38,200
                 15,280
            +   1,146
               ————
               54,626
                1 1

k

Comparison of work-related incidents of ill health and injury – 2009/10

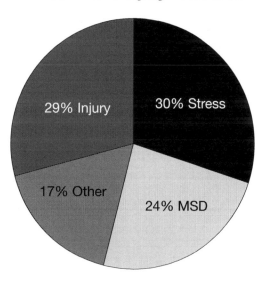

Comparison of days lost due to work-related ill health and injury – 2009/10

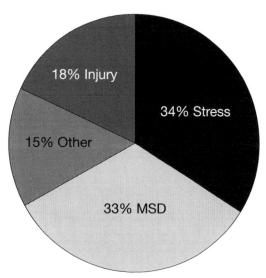

m

Actual decrease = 1,500 – 1,350 = 150

Percentage decrease = $\underline{\text{actual decrease}}$ x 100% = $\underline{150}$ x 1~~00~~% = **10%**
original amount   1,5~~00~~

9a
26/11/2010

b

862 x £0.40

800 x 0.4 = 40 x 8 = 320

60 x 0.4 = 4 x 6 = 24

2 x 0.4 = 0.8

Therefore, employee's travel allowance = **£344.80**

C

6.4% of £2,345.00

1% = £23.45   6% = 23.45
                          x   6
                        140.70
                          2 2 3

0.1% = £2.35   (to the nearest penny)   0.4% = 2.35
                                           x   4
                                          9.40
                                          1 2

Therefore, employee's pension contribution = 140.70
                                             +   9.40
                                             £150.10
                                                 1 1

d

Gross pay = Salary + Project Allowance + Travel Expenses

```
    2,345.00
       90.00
+    344.80
£2,779.80
      1
```

e

```
  349.00
  183.27
+ 150.10
 £682.37
   1 1
```

f

```
 £ 2,⁶7̶¹7 9.⁷8̶¹0
- £   6 8 2.3 7
 £  2,0 9 7.4 3
```

g

```
 £  2,345
 x      12
£28,140
     4  5 6
```

10a

The student's BMI falls within the '**Obese**' category i.e. with a value > 30 (where the horizontal line at 1.7m crosses the vertical line at 90kg

b

Body Mass Index $= \dfrac{90}{(1.7)^2} = \dfrac{90}{1.7 \times 1.7} = \dfrac{90}{2.89} = \dfrac{9{,}000}{289} = 289\overline{)9{,}0\,0\,0^{33}0^{41}0}$ $\quad 3\ 1.\ 1\,r121$

Therefore, **BMI = 31** (to the nearest whole number), which places it in the same category (obese) as indicated on the Body Mass Index chart.

C

1 stone = 14 lbs

So, 11 stone and 6 pounds = (11 x 14) + 6 = 154 + 6 = 160 lbs
160 lbs crosses 5' 9" just within the Normal Range (18.5 – 25) of the Body Mass Index.

g

The first number shows your distance from an eye chart in feet.
The second number refers to the size of letter you can read

h

120 mm Hg
────
80

The top number refers to Systolic Blood Pressure (the force exerted by the blood on the walls of the arteries as the heart muscle contracts to pump blood around the body).

The bottom number refers to Diastolic Blood Pressure (the force exerted by the blood on the walls of the arteries as the heart muscle relaxes between beats).

j

32 for an adult including: 8 incisors, 4 canines, 8 premolars and 12 molars (which include the 4 wisdom teeth).

20 for young children below the age of six:

k

38 inches for a man and **35 inches** for a woman

l

30 minutes a day

m

635 litres per second

n

Decibels on a scale from 0 to 140

o

24,902 miles   40,075 km

p

238,857miles   384,403 km

q

25 million miles   40.5 million km

r

93 million miles   150 million km

s

330 metres per second (330m/s)

t

670,616,629 mph   299,792,458 m/s

u

Trick question, but do follow events at the Hadron Collider in Zurich!

Answers to L3 Numeracy Learning Guide

Q1a £337,104,120,000 in standard form = **3.3710412 x 10^{11}**

Q1b Value of painting = £23,500,000
The value of the painting as a percentage of the country's assets =

$$\frac{23,500,000}{337,104,120,000} \times 100\% = \frac{235,000}{33,710,412}\% = \mathbf{6.9711 \times 10^{-3}}$$

Q2 Diameter of one atom = 10^{-8} cm = 10^{-10}m
150,000 atoms = 1.5 x 10^5
So, length of atoms = 1.5 x 10^5 x 10^{-10}m = 1.5 x **10^{-5}**m

Q3a To calculate distance CB,
Speed = 42 miles per hour Time = 42 minutes = $\frac{42}{60} = \frac{21}{30} = \frac{7}{10}$ = 0.7hours

Speed = $\frac{\text{Distance}}{\text{Time}}$

and Distance (CB) = Speed x Time = 42 x 0.7 = 29.4 miles

AB can be calculated by using pythagorus theorem
$AC^2 = CB^2 + AB^2$
$(63)^2 = (29.4)^2 + (AB)^2$
$(AB)^2 = (63)^2 - (29.4)^2 = 3969 - 864.36 = 3,104.64$

Therefore, AB = $\sqrt{3,104.64}$ = 55.719 miles (to 3 decimal places)
0.621 miles = 1km

1 mile = $\frac{1}{0.621}$ km = 1.61km

55.719 miles = 55.719 x 1.61km = 89.708km (to 3d.p.)
The car emits 0.27kg per kilometre = 89.708 x 0.27 = **24.221**kg (to 3d.p.)

Q3b To calculate angle BAC:

$$\text{Sine (BAC)} = \frac{\text{Opposite}}{\text{Hypotenuse}} = \frac{BC}{AC} = \frac{29.4}{63} = 0.467 \text{ (to 3 dp)}$$

Therefore, angle BAC = **27.8°** (to 1 dp)

$$\text{Cosine (BAC)} = \frac{\text{Adjacent}}{\text{Hypotenuse}} = \frac{AB}{AC} = \frac{55.719}{63} = 0.884 \text{ (to 3 dp)}$$

Therefore, angle BAC = **27.8°** (to 1 dp)

Q4a Area of field = 0.18 Hectares = 0.18 x 10,000m² = 1,800m²
So, area of field = length of field x width of field = 1,800m²
Length of field = 2 x width of field
If we say the width of the field is Y, then the length of the field is 2Y

Area of field then = 2Y x Y = 2Y²

$$2Y^2 = 1,800m^2 \qquad Y^2 = \frac{1,800}{2} = 900m^2$$

$$Y^2 = 900m^2 \quad Y = \sqrt{900} = 30m$$

Therefore, length of field = 2 x 30m = **60m** and width of field = **30m**

Q4b Scale = 1 : 200
1cm : 200cm
1cm : 2m
(x 15) (x 15)
15cm : 30m

Therefore, on the scale drawing, the width of field = **15**cm and the length of field = **30**cm

Q5a Let the number of flights to France sold = A and the number of flights to Germany sold = B

Then, **A + B = 380** (Equation 1)

and, **£33.50A + £37.00B = £13,629.50** (Equation 2)

Q5b If A + B = 380 then A = 380 − B
We can now substitute A = 380 − B into equation 2:
So, 33.50(380 − B) + 37B = 13,629.50

Next, we expand the brackets:

$33.50 \times 380 - 33.5B + 37B = 13{,}629.50$

$12{,}730 + 3.5B = 13{,}629.50$

Therefore, $3.5B = 13{,}629.50 - 12{,}730 = 899.5$

$3.5B = 899.5 \quad B = \dfrac{899.5}{3.5} = \mathbf{257} =$ number of flights to Germany sold

We can now substitute $B = 257$ into equation 1

$A + 257 = 380$ so $A = 380 - 257$

$= \mathbf{123} =$ number of flights to France sold

Answers to GCSE Learning Guide

Questions on factor trees

Q1

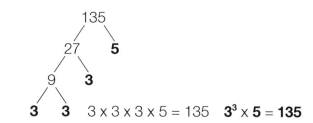

$3 \times 3 \times 3 \times 5 = 135$ $\mathbf{3^3 \times 5 = 135}$

Q2

235

5   47 $\mathbf{5 \times 47 = 235}$

Find the factors of algebraic expressions:

1) **2(3n + 1)**   2) **3(3y + 2)**   3) **7(p + 3)**   4) **2(9a + 2)**   5) **7(8y + 2)**
6) **8(8b + 3)**

Expand the factors of algebraic expressions:

1) **12x + 6**   2) **-10x − 6**   3) **-4x + 8**   4) **24x + 36**

Questions on factors of quadratic expressions

Q1a) **(3x + 1) (x + 1)**   b) **(2x − 3) ((x − 2)**   c) **(2x − 7) (2x + 2)**
   d) **(2x + 6) (2x − 2)**   e) **(3x + 2) (x − 2)**   f) **(5x − 2) (x + 1)**

Q2a)
$(2x + 3)(4x + 1) = 2x(4x + 1) + 3(4x + 1) = 8x^2 + 2x + 12x + 3 = \mathbf{8x^2 + 14x + 3}$

b) $(2x + 2)(x + 1) = 2x(x + 1) + 2(x + 1) = 2x^2 + 2x + 2x + 2 = \mathbf{2x^2 + 4x + 2}$

c) $(5x − 3)(x − 1) = 5x(x − 1) − 3(x − 1) = 5x^2 − 5x − 3x + 3 = \mathbf{5x^2 − 8x + 3}$

d) $(3x + 3)(2x − 2) = 3x(2x − 2) + 3(2x − 2) = 6x^2 -6x + 6x − 6 = \mathbf{6x^2 − 6}$

e) $(2x + 3)^2 = (2x + 3)(2x + 3) = 2x(2x + 3) + 3(2x + 3) = 4x^2 + 6x + 6x + 9$
   $= \mathbf{4x^2 + 12x + 9}$

f) $(x -2)(5x + 3) = x(5x + 3) − 2(5x + 3) = 5x^2 + 3x − 10x − 6 = \mathbf{5x^2 -7x − 6}$

g) $(3x − 4)(2x − 2) = 3x(2x − 2) − 4(2x − 2) = 6x^2 − 6x − 8x + 8 = \mathbf{6x^2 − 14x + 8}$

h) $(x + 1)(6x − 5) = x(6x − 5) +1(6x − 5) = 6x^2 − 5x + 6x − 5 = \mathbf{6x^2 + x − 5}$

Solve the following quadratic equations:

Q1 $(x + 4)(x + 3) = 0$ $x =$ **-4** and **-3**

Q2 $(3x + 3)(x + 3) = 0$ $x =$ **-3** and $3x + 3 = 0$ so, $3x = -3$ $x = -3/3 =$ **-1**

Q3 $(4x + 1)(x + 1) = 0$ $x =$ **-1** and $4x + 1 = 0$ so, $4x = -1$ $x =$ **-1/4**

Q4 $(2x - 4)(2x - 1) = 0$ $2x - 4 = 0$ so, $2x = 4$ $x = 4/2 =$ **2** and $2x - 1 = 0$
   $2x = 1$ $x = ½$

Q5 $(5x - 2)(x + 1) = 0$ $5x - 2 = 0$ so, $5x = 2$ $x =$ **2/5** and $x + 1 = 0$ $x =$ **-1**

Q6 $6(x^2 - 1) = 0$ $x^2 - 1 = 0$ so, $x^2 = 1$ and $x = \pm 1$

Questions on inequalities

1a) $5p + 2 \leq 17$ $5p \leq 15$ **p ≤ 3**
 b) $2.5m - 1.5 > 6$ $2.5m > 7.5$ **m > 3**
 c) $7x + 6 < 13$ $7x < 7$ **x < 1**
 d) $y + 10 \geq 3$ **y ≥ -7**

2) **p ≤ 3**

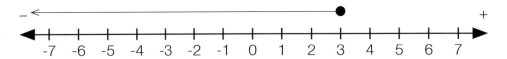

   m > 3

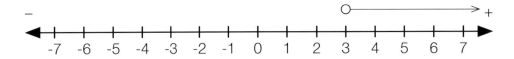

   x < 1

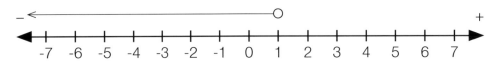

   y ≥ -7

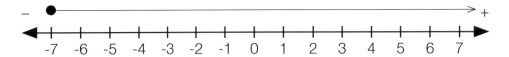

3) **-5 ≤ y ≤ 4**

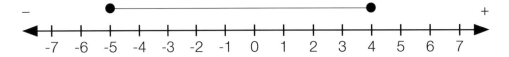

4) **-1 < x < 4**

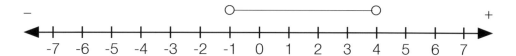

5) **5 < x ≤ 7**

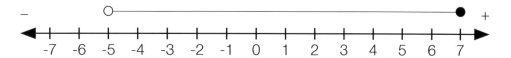

6) **y ≥ -2**

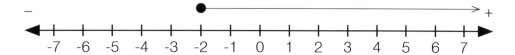

7) **p < -1**

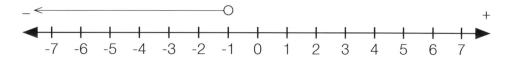

8) t = 2, 3, 4, 5, 6

9) r = -6, -5, -4, -3, -2

10) x = -3, -2, -1, 0, 1, 2, 3, 4, 5

Questions on adding and subtracting fractions

1) $\dfrac{1}{8} + \dfrac{7}{12} = \dfrac{3 + 14}{24} = \mathbf{\dfrac{17}{24}}$ 2) $\dfrac{7}{9} + \dfrac{2}{3} = \dfrac{7 + 6}{9} = \dfrac{13}{9} = \mathbf{1\frac{4}{9}}$

3) $3\frac{3}{4} + 5\frac{1}{3} = 8 + \dfrac{9 + 4}{12} = 8\frac{13}{12} = \mathbf{9\frac{1}{12}}$

4) $\dfrac{3}{7} - \dfrac{3}{8} = \dfrac{24 - 21}{56} = \mathbf{\dfrac{3}{56}}$ 5) $\dfrac{2}{3} - \dfrac{3}{8} = \dfrac{16 - 9}{24} = \mathbf{\dfrac{7}{24}}$

6) $5\frac{1}{8} - 2\frac{1}{5} = \dfrac{41}{8} - \dfrac{11}{5} = \dfrac{205 - 88}{40} = \dfrac{117}{40} = \mathbf{2\frac{37}{40}}$

Questions on multiplying and dividing questions

Q1. $\dfrac{4^1}{5} \times \dfrac{3}{4^1} = \mathbf{\dfrac{3}{5}}$ Q2. $\dfrac{7}{8^2} \times \dfrac{4^1}{11} = \mathbf{\dfrac{7}{22}}$ Q3. $2\frac{1}{5} \times 4\frac{3}{8} = \dfrac{11}{5^1} \times \dfrac{\cancel{25}^5}{8} = \dfrac{55}{8} = \mathbf{6\frac{7}{8}}$

Q4. $\dfrac{2}{3} \div \dfrac{1}{6} = \dfrac{2}{\cancel{3}^1} \times \dfrac{\cancel{6}^2}{1} = \mathbf{4}$ Q5. $\dfrac{7}{8} \div \dfrac{4}{11} = \dfrac{7}{8} \times \dfrac{11}{4} = \dfrac{77}{32} = \mathbf{2^{13}\!/_{32}}$

Q6. $2\frac{1}{5} \div 4\frac{3}{8} = \dfrac{11}{5} \div \dfrac{25}{8} = \dfrac{11}{5} \times \dfrac{8}{25} = \dfrac{\mathbf{88}}{\mathbf{125}}$

Questions on solving simultaneous equations

1) $4x - 3y = 5$ and $2x + y = 15$

$4x = 5 + 3y$ and $4x + 2y = 30$ $4x = 30 - 2y$

So, $5 + 3y = 30 - 2y$ $3y + 2y = 30 - 5$ $5y = 25$ **y = 5**

Substitute in $2x + y = 15$ $2x + 5 = 15$ $2x = 15 - 5 = 10$ **x = 5**

2) $2x - y = 5$ and $2y - 3x = -6$

$2x - 5 = y$ and $2y = 3x - 6$

$4x - 10 = 2y$ So, $4x - 10 = 3x - 6$ $4x - 3x = -6 + 10$ **x = 4**

Subs. in $2x - y = 5$ $8 - y = 5$ **y = 3**

3) $4x - 3y = -1$ and $x - 2y = 1$

$x = 1 + 2y$ Subs. in $4x - 3y = -1$

$4(1 + 2y) - 3y = -1$ $4 + 8y - 3y = -1$ $5y = -5$ **y = -1**

Subs. in $x - 2y = 1$ $x + 2 = 1$ **x = -1**

4) $5x - 3y = 1$ and $3x + y = 2$

$5x - 1 = 3y$ and $9x + 3y = 6$ $3y = 6 - 9x$

So, $5x - 1 = 6 - 9x$ $14x = 7$ **x = ½**

Subs in $3x + y = 2$ $1\frac{1}{2} + y = 2$ **y = ½**

Questions on sequences

Q1.

   a) 6, 9, 12, 15, 18, 21, 24, **27, 30, 33   3n + 3**

   b) -2, 5, 12, 19, 26, **33, 40, 47   7n - 9**

   c) 6, 12, 18, 24, 30, **36, 42, 48   6n**

   d) 1, 5, 9, 13, 17, **21, 25, 29   4n - 3**

   e) 49, 46, 43, 40, 37, **34, 31, 28   52 - 3n**

f) 9, 8, 7, 6, 5, **4, 3, 2   10 - n**

g) 7, 1, -5, -11, -17, **-23, -29, -35   13 – 6n**

h) 0, -4, -8, -12, -16, **-20, -24, -28   4 – 4n = 4(1 – n)**

Q2) 5(7) – 8 = 35 – 8 = **27**

Q3) 9 – 3(11) = 9 – 33 = **-24**

Q4) 6^2 – 6 = 36 – 6 = **30**

Q5) 14 – 2(5)^2 = 14 – 50 = **-36**

Q6) 7n + 7 = 42   7n = 35   **n = 5**

Q7) 9n – 15 = 39   9n = 54   **n = 6**

Q8) 5 – 3n = -19   3n = 5 + 19 = 24   **n = 8**

Q9) -8 – 4n = -40   4n = 40 – 8 = 32   **n = 4**

Q10) n^2 + 7 = 43   n2 = 36   **n = ± 6**

Q11) Complete the next 2 terms of the following sequences:

a) 4, 12, 36, 108, **324, 972**

b) 2, 8, 32, 128, **512, 2048**

a) 12500, 2500, 500, 100, **20, 4**

b) 880, 440, 220, **110, 55**

Q12) 1, 3, 6, 10, 15, 21, **28, 36**

Q13) 1, 1, 2, 3, 5, 8, 13, 21, 34, 55, **89, 144**

Q14) 1, 4, 9, 16, 25, 36, 49, **64, 81**

Q15) 1, 8, 27, 64, 125, **216, 343**

Questions on stem and leaf diagrams

Stem	Leaf
0	5, 8, 9
1	0,1,2,2,5,5,6,7,9
2	0,1,1,4,5,5,7
3	1

Key: 2/4 = 24

Median: $\frac{16 + 17}{2}$ = **16.5 mins**   Range: 31 – 5 = **26 mins**

Questions on frequency tables

Q1 a)

$3 \times 4 = 12$
$4 \times 4 = 16$
$5 \times 3 = 15$
$6 \times 6 = 36$
$7 \times 3 = 21$
$\overline{100}$
$\;_2$

Mean $= \dfrac{\text{Total age}}{\text{Number}} = \dfrac{10\cancel{0}}{2\cancel{0}} = \mathbf{5}$

b) Median age = **5**

c) Modal age = **6**

d) Range – 7 – 3 = **4**

Q2 a)

$3 \times 5 \;\; = \;\; 15$
$3 \times 15 = \;\; 45$
$1 \times 25 = \;\; 25$
$3 \times 35 = 105$
$5 \times 45 = \overline{225}$
$\qquad\qquad\;\; \overline{415}$
$\qquad\qquad\;\;_{1\,2}$

Mean $= \dfrac{\text{Total Distance}}{\text{Number}} = \dfrac{415}{15} = 27.66' = \mathbf{28\ miles}$

b) The answer is an estimate because for each result, the distance (in miles) is taken as mid-way between the two extremities
e.g. 3 x **15** for $10 < d \leq 20$

c) $\mathbf{30 < d \leq 40}$

d) $\mathbf{40 < d \leq 50}$

Q3)

$2 \times £1.80 = \;\; £3.60$
$4 \times £2.00 = \;\; £8.00$
$3 \times £2.20 = \;\; £6.60$
$5 \times £2.40 = £12.00$
$2 \times £2.60 = \;\; £5.20$
$\qquad\qquad\;\;\; \overline{£35.40}$
$\qquad\qquad\;\;\;_{2\,1}$

Mean $= \dfrac{\text{Total cost}}{\text{Number}} = \dfrac{35.40}{16} = 2.2125 = £2.21$

a) The answer is an estimate because for each result, the cost of the coffee is taken as mid-way between the two extremities
e.g. 3 x £2.20 for $2.10 < c \leq 2.30$

b) **2.10 < c ≤ 2.30**

c) **2.10 < c ≤ 2.30**

Questions on venn diagrams

Q1. 25 x 0.12 = 3 use neither Snapchat nor Instagram.
Therefore, **22** use Snapchat and/or Instagram.

Number using Snapchat = 15, so number using Instagram only =
22 − 15 = 7 = number using Instagram only.

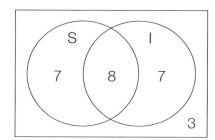 S = Snapchat   I = Instagram

Q2. 8 students had been to France and Spain. Ten had been to Spain,
so 10 − 8 = 2 had been to Spain only. Twenty had been to France,
so 20 − 8 = 12 had been to France only.
So, total number of students in survey = 8 + 2 + 12 = **22**

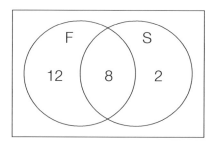 F = France   S = Spain

Q3. A tenth of the pupils played neither football nor cricket = 0.1

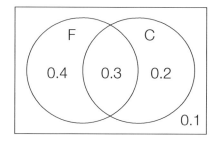 F = Football   C = Cricket

Probability of Football ∩ Cricket if one pupil is chosen at random =
0.3 or 3 out of 10 or 3/10

Questions on indices

Q1. **$2y^7$**

Q2. **2y**

Q3.   72 = **49**

Q4.   Calculate the following to 3 significant figures:

    a) $5^3 \times 5^2$ = 125 x 25 = 3,125 = **3,130** (to 3 significant figures)

    b) $4^{-4} \div 4^{-2}$ = 4-2 = 1/16 = **0.0625** (to 3 sig. figs.)

    c) $(2.1)^2 + (2.1)^3 = (2.1)^5$ = **40.8** (to 3 sig. figs.)

Questions on angle rules:

Q1.   a)   x = **250** Reason: Vertically opposed angles are equal

    b)   y = 180 – 25 = **1550**
         Reason: Angles in a straight line add up to 180°

Q2.

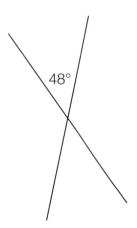

Q3.   x = **64°**

Q4.   AGF = 120° (Corresponding angles are equal)
       FGB = 180 – 120 = **60°** (angles in a straight line add up to 180°)
       Or, BGH = 120° (alternate angles are equal)
       FGB = 180 – 120 = **60°** (angles in a straight line add up to 180°)

Q5.   DBC = 180 – 37 = **143°** (allied angles add up to 180°)

Q6.   OAB = 26° (Vertically opposite angles are equal).
       OBA = 26° (Angles at the base of an isosceles triangle are equal)
       AOB = 180 – 52 = 128° (angles in a triangle add up to 180°)
       x = **128°** (Vertically opposite angles are equal)

Q7.   AEF = a (alternate angles are equal)
       GEB = c (alternate angles are equal)
       AEF + FEG + GEB = 180° (angles in a straight line add up to 180°)
       Therefore, **a + b + c = 180°**

Q8.   Exterior angle of octagon = 360 ÷ 8 = 45°
      (exterior angles of a polygon add up to 360°)
      interior angle of octagon = 180 − 45 = 135°
      (angles in a straight line add up to 180°)

$$x = \frac{180-135}{2} = \frac{45}{2} = \textbf{22.5°}$$

      (angles in a triangle add up to 180° and angles at the base of an
      isosceles are equal)

Q9.   Heptagon. x = 360 ÷ 7 = **51.4°** (to 1 decimal place).
      Exterior angles of a polygon add up to 180°

Q10. Exterior angle = 360 ÷ 11 = **32.7°** (to one decimal place)

Q11. CAB = 360 ÷ 6 = 60° and ABC = 360 ÷ 6 = 60°
      (exterior angles of a polygon add up to 360°)
      ACB = 180 − 120 = 600 (angles in a triangle add up to 1800)

As each of the 3 angles = 600 triangle ABC is an equilateral triangle.

Questions on straight line graphs

Q1.   **y = 4x + 3** See p.281

Q2.   y = 3x − 1 See p.282

x	-4	-3	-2	-1	0	1	2	3	4
y	-13	-10	-7	-4-	-1	2	5	8	11

Q3.   **y = -2x + 1**

x	-4	-3	-2	-1	0	1	2	3	4
y	9	7	5	3	1	-1	-3	-5	-7

Q4.   See p.283

Questions on solving simultaneous equations through the drawing of straight line graphs

Q1.   2x + y = 7   So, y = -2x + 7
      3x + 2y = 12   So, 2y = -3x + 12   y = -1.5x + 6

Point of intersection = **(2, 3)**   See p.284

Q2.   2x − y = 5   So, y = 2x - 5
      2y − 3x = -6   So, 2y = 3x − 6   y = 1.5x - 3

Point of intersection = **(4, 3)**   See p.284

Questions on quadratic graphs, cubic graphs and reciprocal graphs

Q1.   See graph of $y = 2x^2 - 2x - 2$ on p.285

x	-3	-2	-1	0	1	2	3	4
y	22	10	2	-2	-2	-2	10	22

Q2.   See graph of $y = -2x^2 + 4x + 5$ on p.316

x	-3	-2	-1	0	1	2	3	4
y	-25	-11	-1	5	7	5	-1	-11

Q3.   See graph of $y = -x^3 + 1$ on p.317

x	-3	-2	-1	0	1	2	3
y	28	9	2	1	0	-7	-26

Q4.

x	-4	-3	-2	-1	-0.5	-0.25	0	0.25	0.5	1	2	3	4
y	-0.25	-0.33'	-0.5	-1	-2	-4	infty	4	2	1	0.5	0.33'	0.25

infty = infinity

See graph of $y = 1/x$ on p.318 together with lines of symmetry ($y = x$ and $y = -x$)

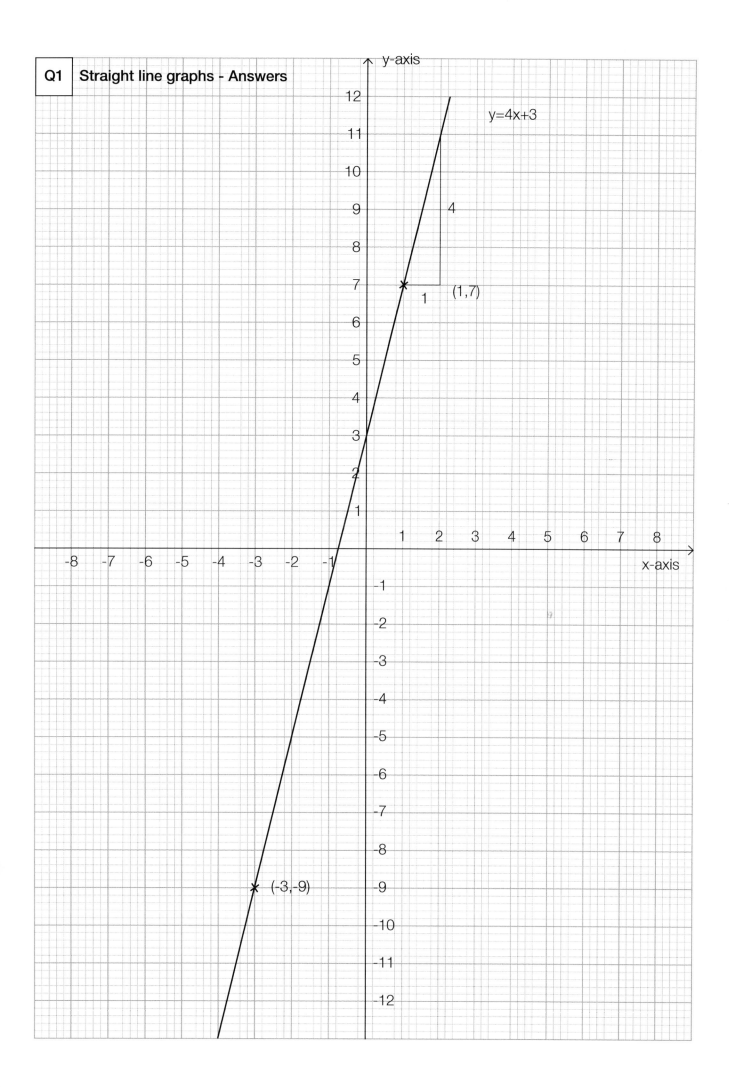

Q1 | Straight line graphs - Answers

y-axis

y=4x+3

(1,7)

(-3,-9)

x-axis

y=4x+3

Q2 **Straight line graphs - Answers**

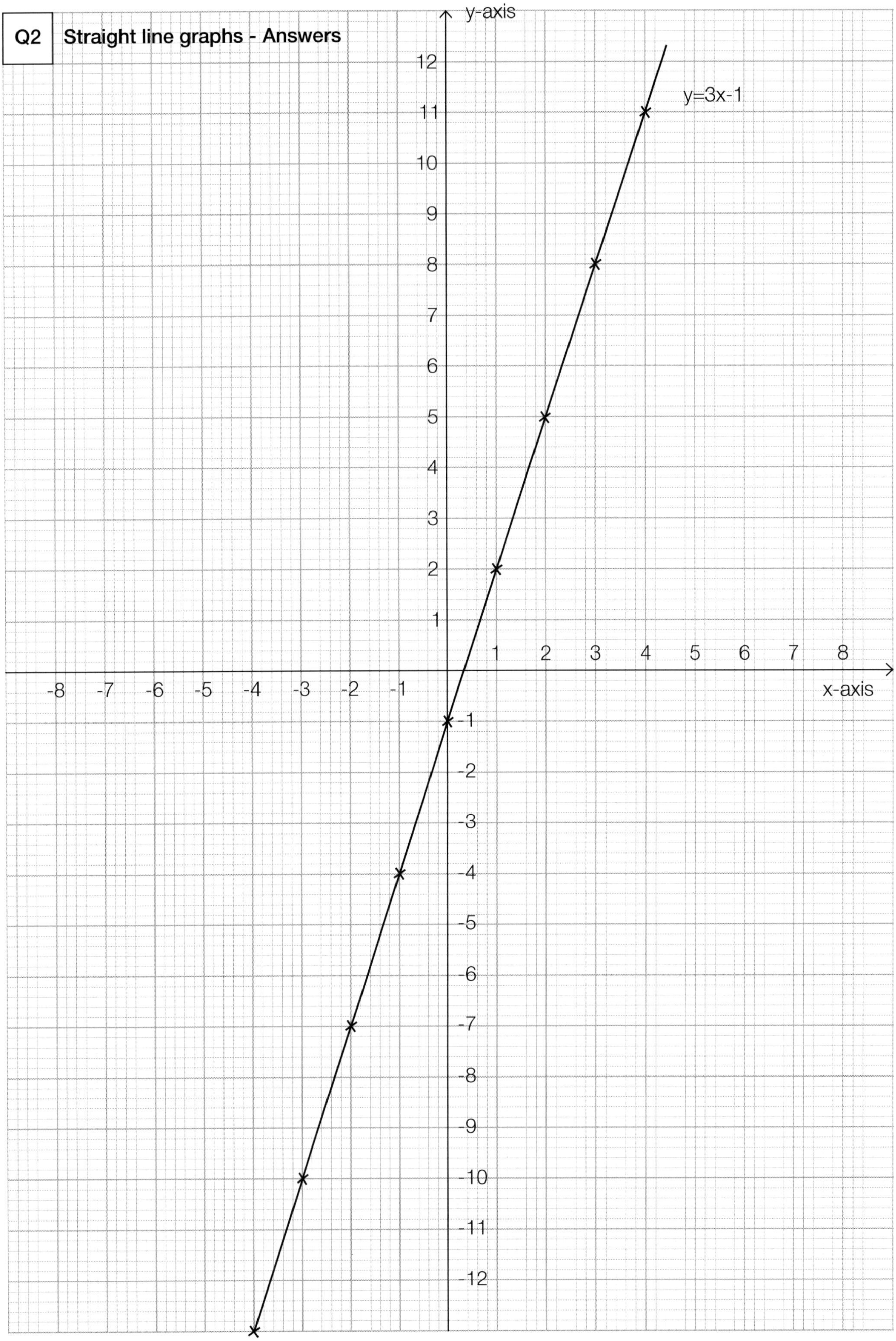

y-axis
x-axis
y=3x-1
12
11
10
9
8
7
6
5
4
3
2
1
-1
-2
-3
-4
-5
-6
-7
-8
-9
-10
-11
-12
-8
-7
-6
-5
-4
-3
-2
-1
1
2
3
4
5
6
7
8

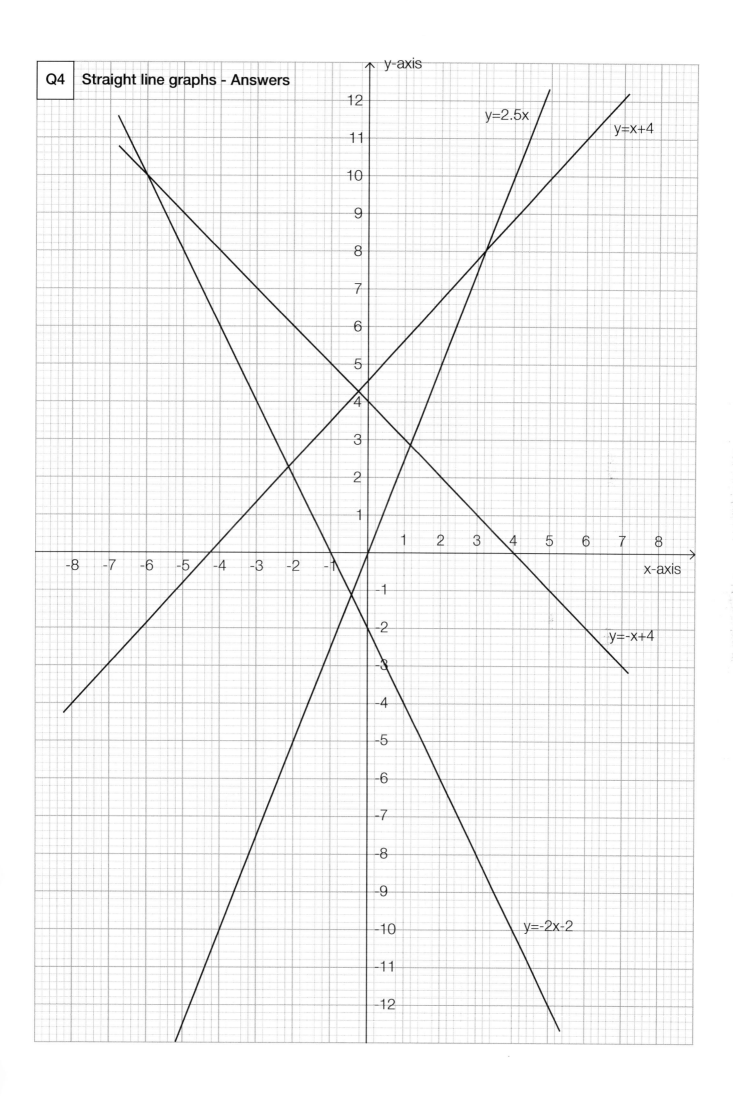

Q4 | Straight line graphs - Answers

y-axis

y=2.5x

y=x+4

y=-x+4

y=-2x-2

x-axis

Q1 & 2

Solving simultaneous equations through straight line graphs - Answers

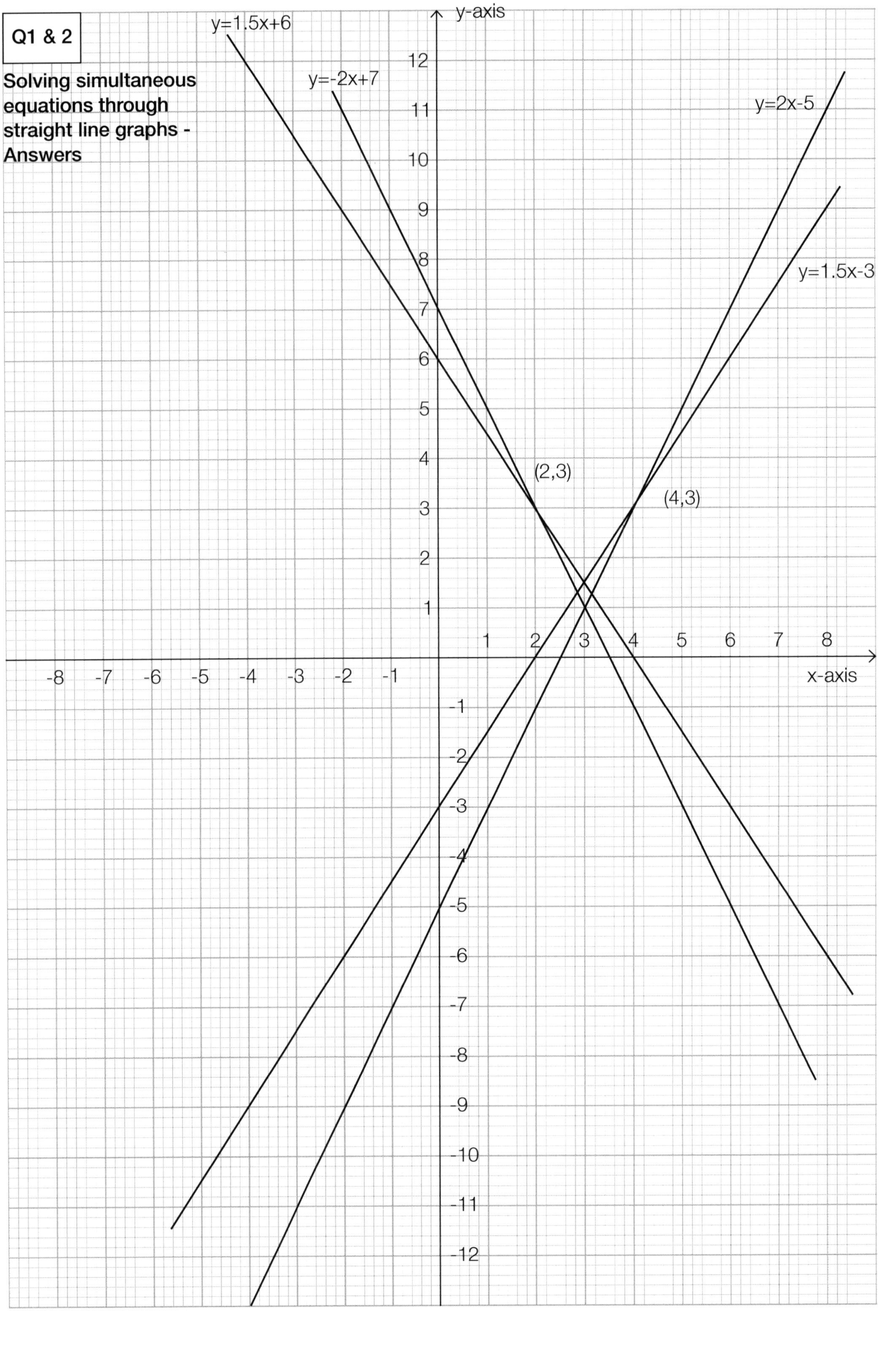

y-axis
x-axis
y=1.5x+6
y=-2x+7
y=2x-5
y=1.5x-3
(2,3)
(4,3)

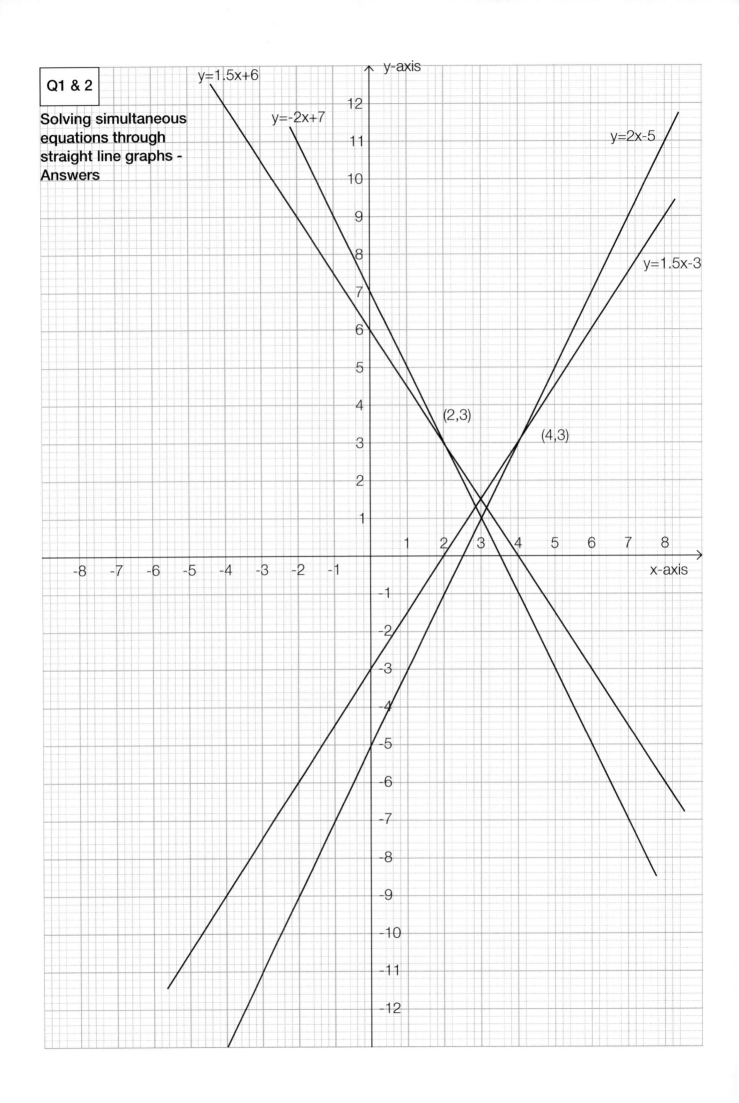

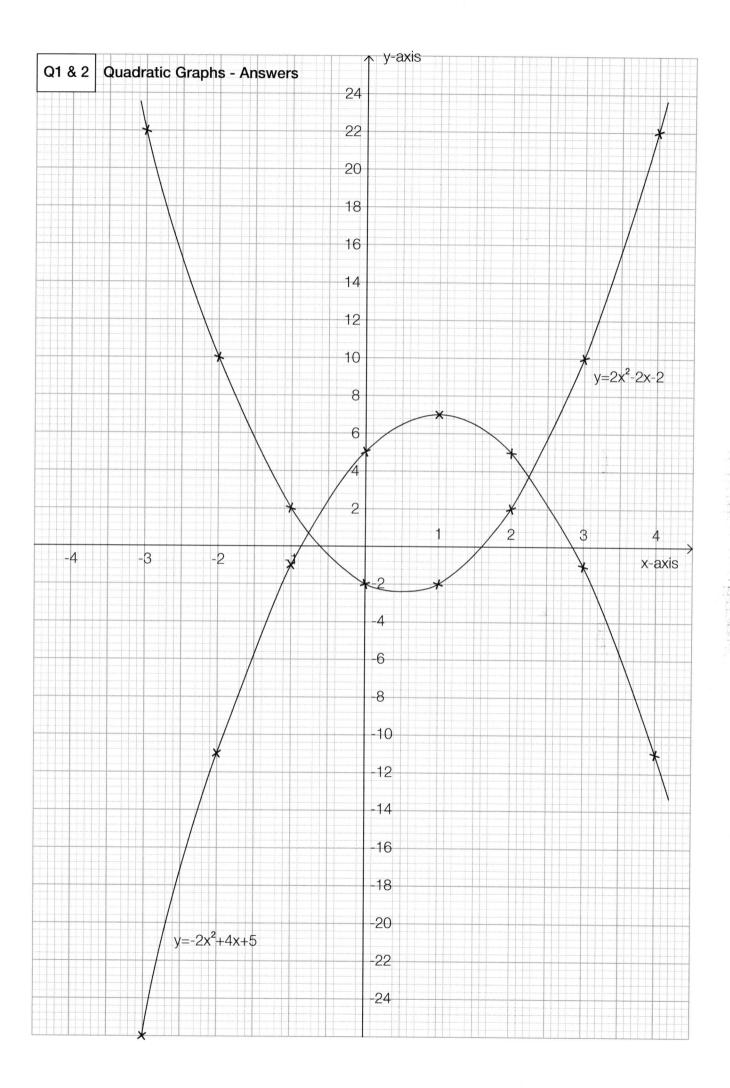

Q1 & 2 Quadratic Graphs - Answers

y-axis

$y=2x^2-2x-2$

$y=-2x^2+4x+5$

x-axis

Q3

Cubic graph - Answer

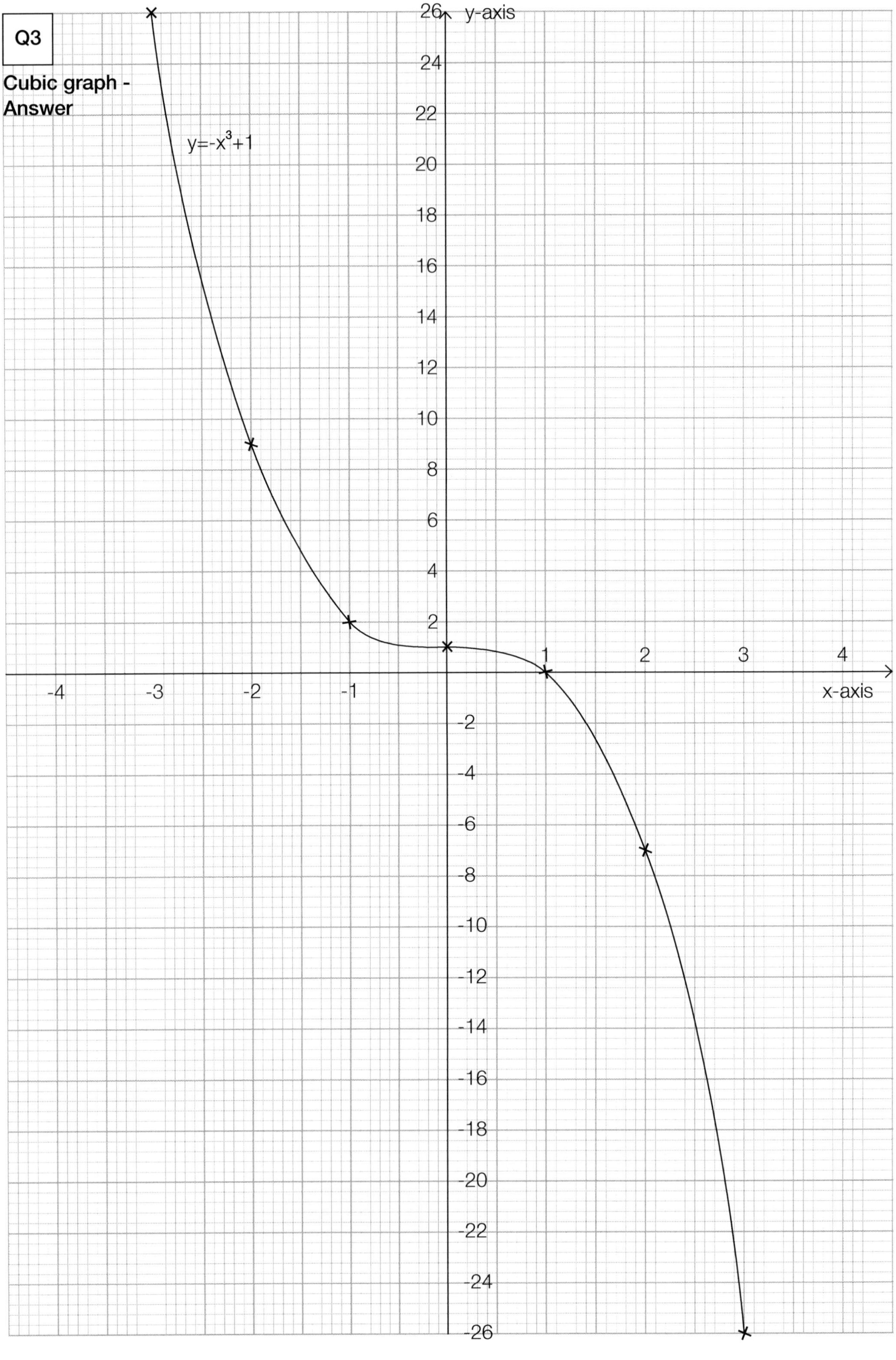

y-axis
x-axis
$y=-x^3+1$
26
24
22
20
18
16
14
12
10
8
6
4
2
-2
-4
-6
-8
-10
-12
-14
-16
-18
-20
-22
-24
-26
-4
-3
-2
-1
1
2
3
4

Q4 Reciprocal graph - Answer

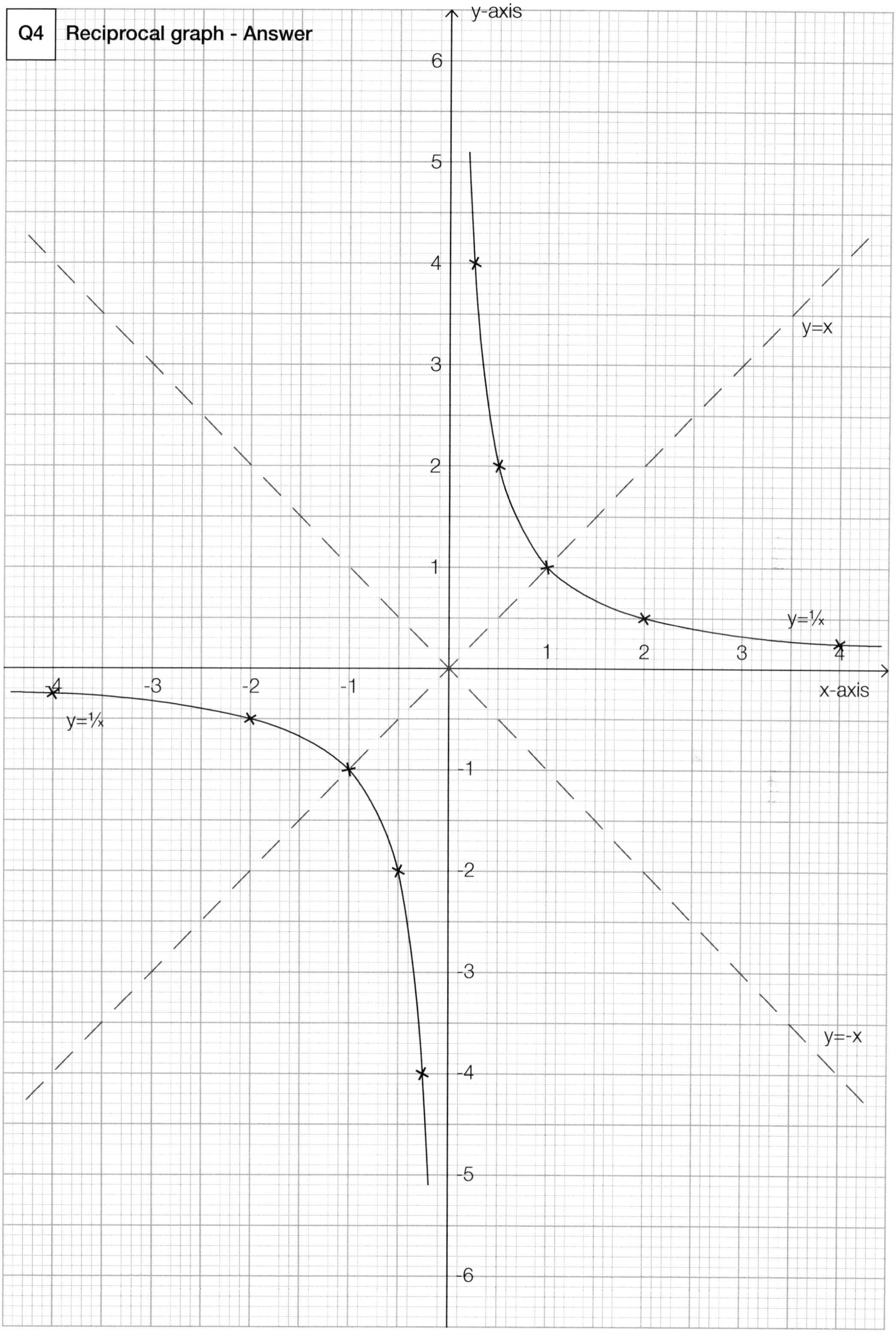

y-axis
6
5
4
3
2
1
-1
-2
-3
-4
-5
-6
x-axis
-4
-3
-2
-1
1
2
3
4
y=x
y=-x
y=1/x
y=1/x

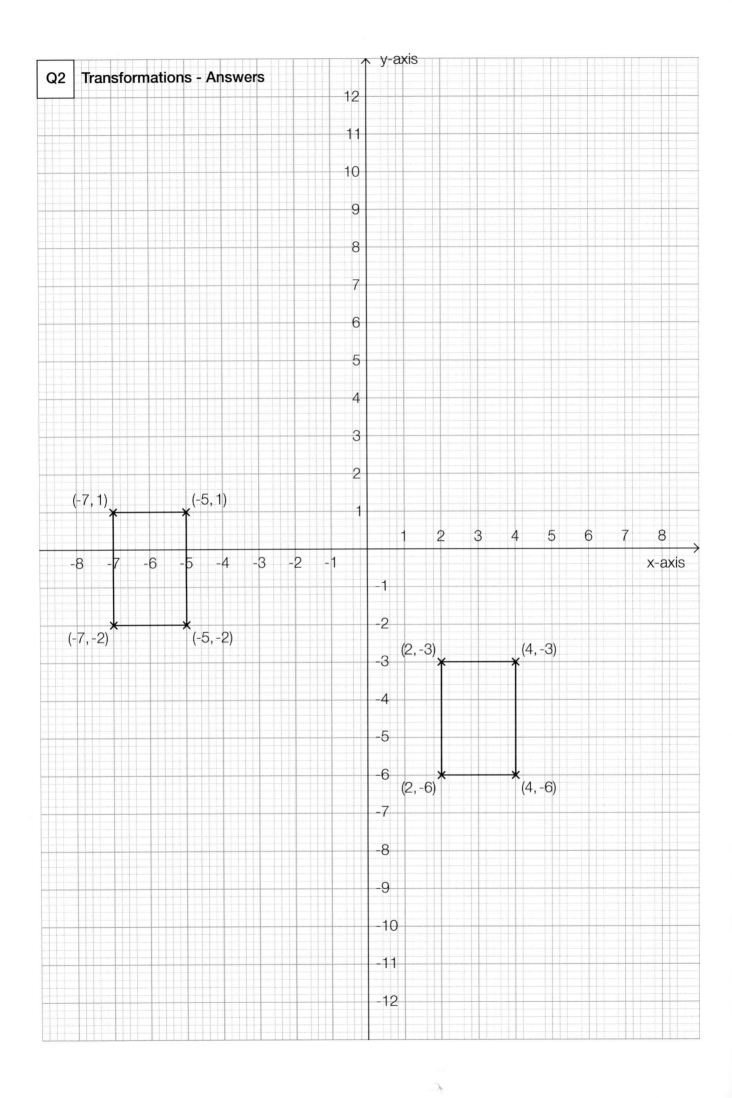

Q2 **Transformations - Answers**

y-axis

12

11

10

9

8

7

6

5

4

3

2

(-7, 1)   (-5, 1)

1

1   2   3   4   5   6   7   8

-8   -7   -6   -5   -4   -3   -2   -1   x-axis

-1

-2

(-7, -2)   (-5, -2)

(2, -3)   (4, -3)

-3

-4

-5

(2, -6)   (4, -6)

-6

-7

-8

-9

-10

-11

-12

Q2 **Transformations - Answers**

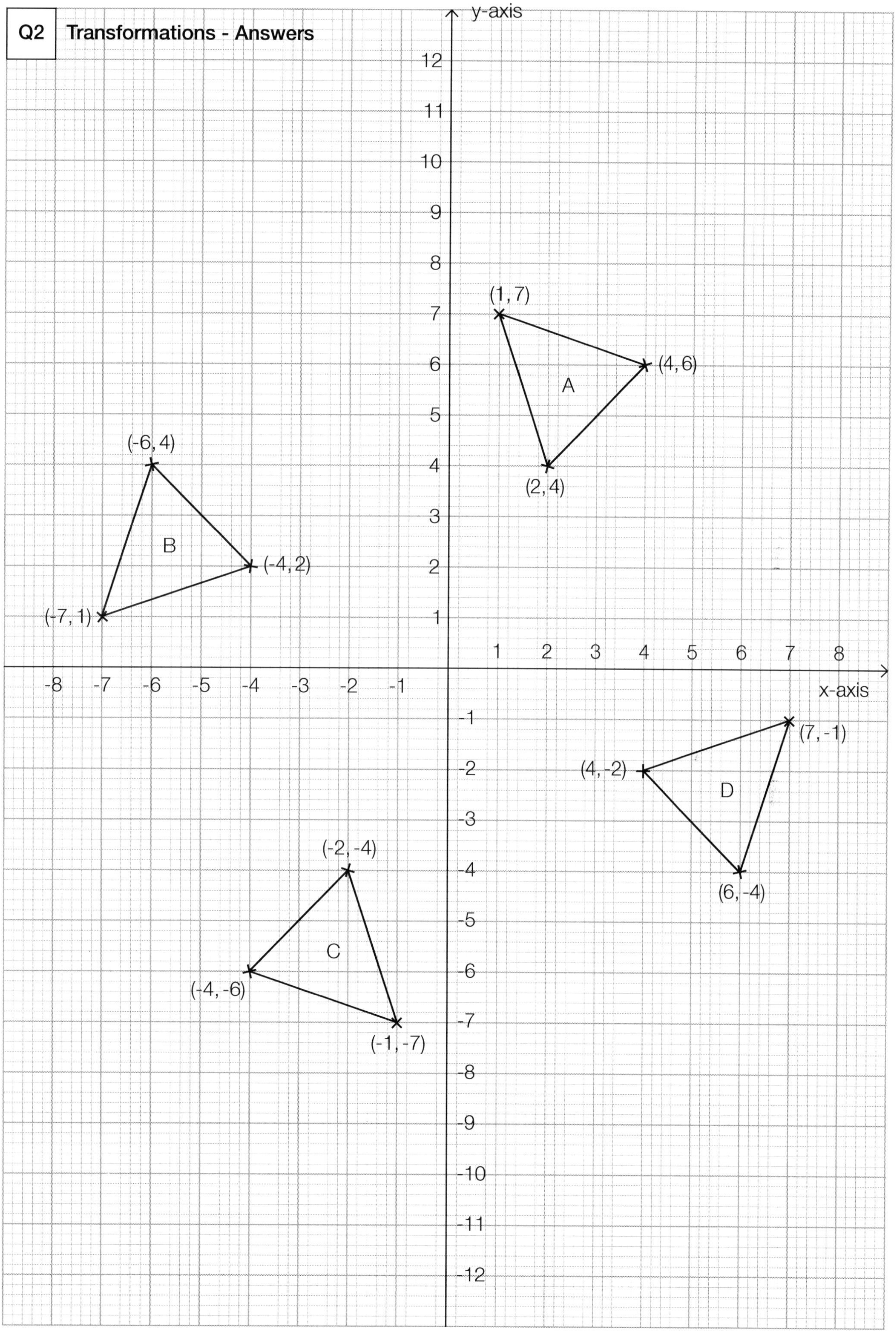

Q5 Transformations - Answers

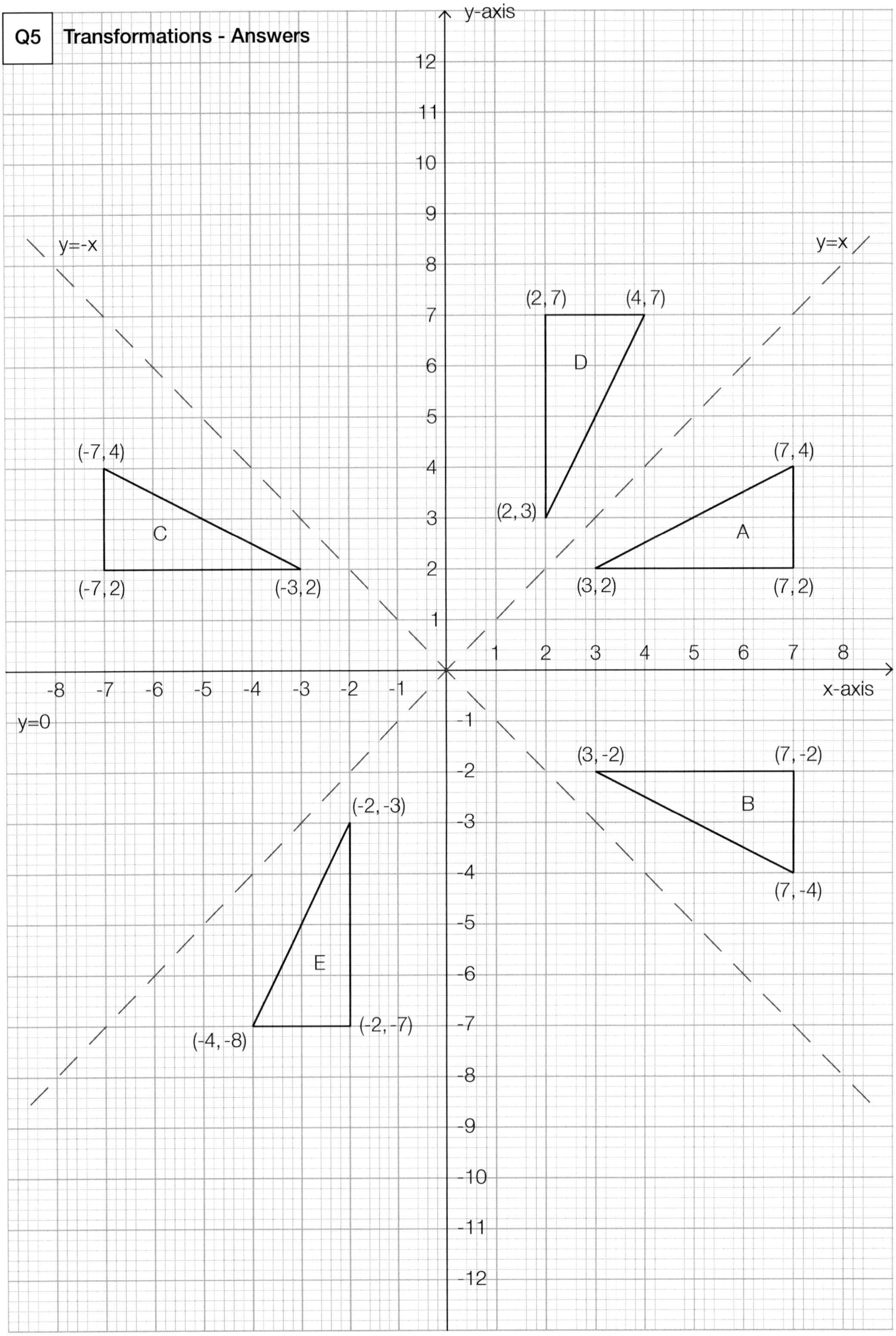

y-axis
x-axis
y=x
y=-x
y=0
A
B
C
D
E
(2, 7)
(4, 7)
(2, 3)
(7, 4)
(3, 2)
(7, 2)
(-7, 4)
(-7, 2)
(-3, 2)
(3, -2)
(7, -2)
(7, -4)
(-2, -3)
(-4, -8)
(-2, -7)

Q7 **Transformations - Answers**

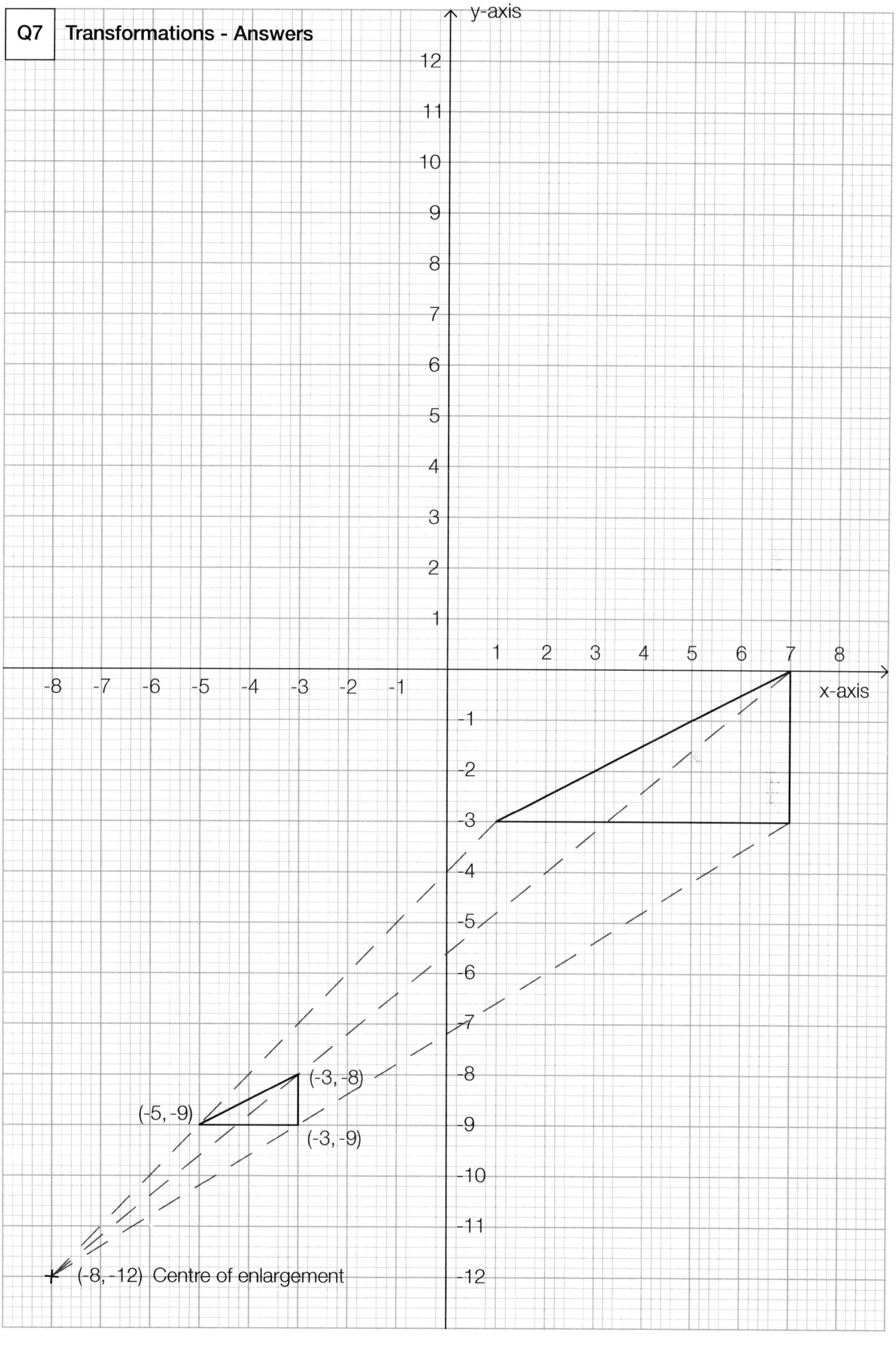

y-axis
x-axis
12
11
10
9
8
7
6
5
4
3
2
1
1 2 3 4 5 6 7 8
-8 -7 -6 -5 -4 -3 -2 -1
-1
-2
-3
-4
-5
-6
-7
-8
-9
-10
-11
-12
(-3, -8)
(-5, -9)
(-3, -9)
(-8, -12) Centre of enlargement

Questions on transformations

Q1 a) The transformation from D to B is a translation by vector $\begin{pmatrix} 3 \\ 12 \end{pmatrix}$

   b) The transformation from D to C is a translation by vector $\begin{pmatrix} -7 \\ 5 \end{pmatrix}$

Q2. See answer on p.288

Q3. See answer on p.289. The single transformation that maps triangle A onto triangle C is a rotation of 180° about the origin.

Q4. a) The transformation that maps shape A onto shape B is **a rotation of 90° clockwise about the origin.**

   b) The transformation that maps shape C onto shape D **is a translation by vector** $\begin{pmatrix} -3 \\ 2 \end{pmatrix}$

   c) The transformation that maps shape E onto shape F **is a reflection about the line y = 0**

Q5. See p.290

Q6. The transformation that maps triangle A onto triangle B is an enlargement of scale factor 2 with centre of enlargement, the origin (0,0).

Q7. The co-ordinates of the diminished triangle are **(-5, -9), (-3, -8), (-3, -9)**

Questions on lines of symmetry and order of rotational symmetry

Q1. Draw in the lines of symmetry on the following shapes and state the order of rotational symmetry for each one:

a Regular pentagon   b Equilateral triangle   c

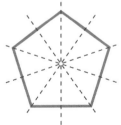

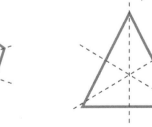

otational symmetry
of order = 5

rotational symmetry
of order = 3

rotational symmetry
of order = 1

d

rotational symmetry
of order = 5

e

rotational symmetry
of order = 3

f

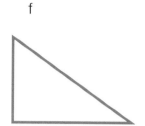

rotational symmetry
of order = 1

g Parallelogram

rotational symmetry
of order = 2

h Rhombus

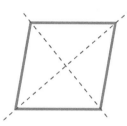

rotational symmetry
of order = 2

i Kite

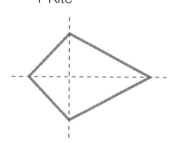

rotational symmetry
of order = 1

Questions on vectors

Q1.   -2 + -3 = **-5**
      4   -2   **2**

Q2.   5 - 3 = **2**
      7 -3   **4**

Q3. $\overrightarrow{AB}$ = **-a + 2b**

Q4. $\overrightarrow{LM}$ = **3c + 3d = 3(c + d)**

Questions on SOH [Sine = $\underline{Opposite}$]
Hypotenuse

CAH [Cosine = $\underline{Adjacent}$]
Hypotenuse

TOA [Tangent = $\underline{Opposite}$] and Pythagoras
Adjacent

Q1   a) $Sin\ x^0 = \dfrac{10}{22} = \dfrac{5}{11}$ $Sin^{-1}(5/11) = x = $ **27°**

       b) $Sin\ 35° = \dfrac{7}{x}$ $x = \dfrac{7}{\sin 35} = $ **12.2cm**

c)   Tan 39° = $\frac{x}{4.5}$ x = 4.5Tan 39° = **3.6m**

d)   Cos 46° = $\frac{x}{18}$ x = 18Cos° 46 = **12.5cm**

e)   Tan 53° = $\frac{4}{x}$ x = $\frac{4}{Tan\ 53}$ = **3cm**

f) $x^2 = 9^2 + (7.5)^2 = 81 + 56.25 = 137.25$
     x = $\sqrt{137.25}$ = 11.**7m** (to 1d.p.)

g)   Cos 78° = $\frac{7.5}{x}$ x = $\frac{7.5}{Cos\ 78°}$ = **36.1cm**

h)   Tan x^0 = $\frac{1}{3.5}$ Tan^{-1} (1/3.5) = x = **15.9°** (to 1d.p.)

i)   using Pythagoras $x^2 = 17^2 - 15^2 = 64$ So, x = **8m**

j)   Sin 29° = $\frac{x}{5}$ x = 5Sin 29° = **2.4m** (to 1 d.p.)

k)   using Pythagoras $x^2 = 12^2 - 6^2 = 108$ So, x = **10.4cm** (to 1 d.p.)

l)   Cos x° = $\frac{7}{11}$ Cos^{-1} (7/11) = **50.5°** (to 1 d.p.)

m)   Sin 30° = $\frac{OC}{6}$ = ½ So, OC = 6 x ½ = 3m

ODC = 45° So, OCD = 180 – (900 + 450) = 450
Therefore, OCD is an isosceles triangle, so OD = 3m
Then , using Pythagoras, $x^2 = 4^2 + 3^2 = 25$ So, x = **5m**

n)   Cos a° = $\frac{adj}{hyp}$ = $\frac{Cos\ a°}{x}$ Therefore, x = $\frac{Cos\ a°}{Cos\ a°}$ = **1m**

Questions on ratios

Q1.   Person 1 : Person 2
          1 : 5   1 + 5 = 6 parts   1 part = £96 6 = £16
          £16 : **£80**

Q2.   Internal angle : Exterior angle
          4 : 1   4 + 1 = 5 parts

Interior angle + exterior angle (of any polygon) = 180° 180° ÷ 5 = 36° 4 x 36° = 144°
          1440 : 360

Exterior angles of a polygon add up to 360°

So, the number of angles/sides of the polygon = 360° ÷ 36° = 10
So, the polygon is a **decagon.**

Q3.   Stephen's share of £16,000 represents 2 parts more than John's share,
       so one part = £16,000 ÷ 2 = £8,000

       John : Stephen : Olivier
            1 : 3
       £8,000 : £24,000 : x
       So, Olivier's share = £88,000 - £32,000 = **£56,000** (7 parts)

Q4.   Perimeter of larger field = 42m
       width = 6m, so length = $\frac{42 - 12}{2} = \frac{30}{2}$ = 15m

       So, area of larger field = 6 x 15 = 90m^2

       Area of Field 1 : Area of Field 2
                  2 : 3
            60m^2 : 90m^2

So, area of field 1 = 60m^2 = L x W = L x 6m So, L= $\frac{60m^2}{6m}$ = **10m**

Q5.   Vol of cone : Vol of cylinder

       $\frac{\pi r2L}{3}$: $\pi r2L$

           1/3 : 1
           1 : 3

Q6   a)   John £90/day Teresa £90 x 1.2 = £108   So, John : Teresa
                                                    90 : 108
                                                    10 : 12
                                                    5 : 6

       d)   John 8hrs/day Teresa 8 x 1.125 = 9hrs/day

            John = £90 ÷ 8 = £11.25   Teresa = £108 ÷ 9 = £12

                  John : Teresa
                  £11.25 : £12
              (x4) = £45 : £48 (x4)
                  15 : 16

       e)   Bangladeshi worker : Teresa
                  £0.24 : £12

(x 100)   £24 : £1,200
£12 : £600
£6 : £300
£3 : £150
1 : 50

Q7.   a)   cost of pens : cost of pencils
£1.40 : £1.15
28 : 23

b)   £1.40 + £ £1.15 = £2.55   £60 ÷ £2.55 = 23.53
So, 23 x £2.55 = £58.65 and change = £60 - £58.65 = **£1.35**

Q8.   a)   Wt. of crisps = 120g ÷ 3 = 40g   Wt. of peanuts = 90g ÷ 2 = 45g

Wt. of crisps : Wt. of peanuts
40g : 45g
8 : 9

b)   120g + 90g = 210g = 0.21kg
10kg ÷ 0.21kg = 47.6   So, **47** guests could be provided for

Q9.   Male : Female : Transgender
16   :   18   :   1
54

There are 54 females, which represents 18 'parts'. So, 54 ÷ 18 = 3 = 1 part

Male : Female : Transgender
16 :   18   :   1
48   54   :   3
48 + 54 + 3 + 8 (prefer not to say) = **113** took part in the survey.

Q10. 190 – 10 = 180   90% = $\frac{90}{100}$ = $\frac{9}{10}$ = 0.9

180 x 0.9 = 162 (identifying as heterosexual)

So, 5% (or 1 in 20) = 9 men identified as bisexual and 5% (or 1 in 20) = 9 men identified as gay.

Heterosexual : Bisexual : Gay
162   :   9   : 9
18   :   1   : 1

Questions on volumes of cylinders, triangular prisms, cones, frustums and square-based pyramids. Take $\pi = 3.142$

Q1. Volume of cylinder $= \pi r^2 h$ $r = 30cm = 0.3m$

So, Vol $= 3.142 \times 0.3m \times 0.3m \times 1.5m = 0.42417m^3 = 424.17L = \textbf{424L}$
(to the nearest litre)

Q2. Volume of prism $= \dfrac{b \times h \times L}{2} = \dfrac{15 \times h \times 20}{2} = 1,200 \ cm^3$

So, h $= \dfrac{1,2\theta\theta \times 2}{15 \times 2\theta} = \dfrac{24\theta}{3\theta} = \textbf{8cm}$

Q3. $1m^3 = 1,000L$ $540L = 0.54m^3$

Volume of water in tank $=$ length $\times$ width $\times$ height
$0.54m^3 = 1.5m \times 0.8m \times h$

So, height of water $= \dfrac{0.54}{1.5 \times 0.8} = \dfrac{0.54}{1.2} = 0.45m$

Height increases by 20% $= 0.45 \times 0.2 = 0.09m$ (9cm)

So, increase in volume $= 0.09 \times 1.5 \times 0.8 = \textbf{0.108m}^3 =$ volume of solid cone

Q4. Volume of a square based pyramid $= \dfrac{B \times h}{3}$ (where B = area of base)

$32 \ m^3 = \dfrac{B \times 6m}{3}$ So, B $= \dfrac{32 \times 3}{6} = 16m^2$

Therefore length of a side of the base $= \sqrt{16m} = \textbf{4m}$

Q5. Volume of frustum $=$ volume of whole cone $-$ volume of 'cut off' cone

$= \dfrac{1 \pi r^2 h}{3} - \dfrac{1 \pi r^2 H}{3} = [\dfrac{1}{3} \times 3.142 \times 20 \times 20 \times 80] - [\dfrac{1}{3} \times 3.142 \times 5 \times 5 \times 20]$

$= 33,514.66' - 523.66' = \textbf{32,991cm}^3$

Questions on density

Q1. Density $= \dfrac{Mass}{Volume} = \dfrac{3,24\theta\theta g}{1,20\theta cm^3} = \textbf{2.7g/cm}^3$

Q2. Volume $= \dfrac{Mass}{Density} = \dfrac{5,000g}{19.32g/cm^3} = \textbf{259cm}^3$ (to the nearest cubic centimetre)

Q3. Density $= \dfrac{Mass}{Volume} = \dfrac{1,\theta\theta\theta g}{1,\theta\theta\theta cm^3} = \textbf{1g/cm}^3$

Q4.   Mass = Density x Volume = 13.56g/cm^3 x 250cm^3 = 3,390g = **3.39kg**

Q5.   Volume of sphere = 4/3πr^3 = $\frac{4}{3}$ x 3.142 x 3 x 3 x 3 = 113.112cm^3

                                                               Mass = 1,009g

Density = $\dfrac{\text{Mass}}{\text{Volume}}$ = $\dfrac{1{,}009\text{g}}{113.112\text{cm}^3}$ = **8.92g/cm^3**

Questions on Distance-Time graph

Q1.   a)   Average walking speed = $\dfrac{\text{Distance}}{\text{Time}}$ = $\dfrac{10\text{km}}{2.5\text{hrs}}$ = **4km/hr**

      b)   Average speed of bus = $\dfrac{\text{Distance}}{\text{Time}}$ = $\dfrac{10\text{km}}{0.5\text{hrs}}$ = **20km/hr**

Q2.

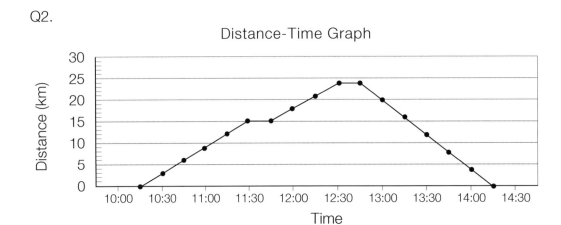

The cyclist arrives back home at **14:15**

Questions on constructing triangles and angle bisectors

Q1.   Using a ruler and a pair of compasses, construct a triangle of dimensions
      AB = 8cm, BC = 6cm and AC = 4cm

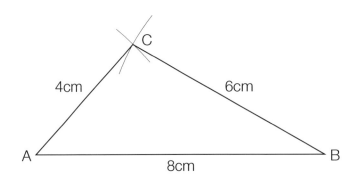

Q2. Construct an angle bisector of the two given lines below:

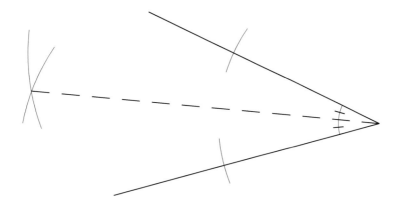

Q3. Construct the perpendicular bisector of the two points P and Q

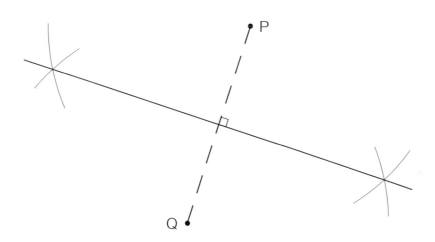

Q4. a) Construct the locus of points that is 3.5cm from the line PQ

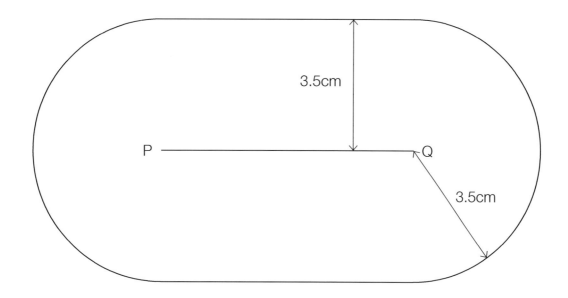

b) Enclosed area = Area of square + (2 x area of semi-circle)

= (7cm x 7cm) + (3.14 x 3.5cm x 3.5cm) = 49cm^2 + 38.465cm^2

= **87.465cm^2**

Q5. Scale 1cm : 4m
         3cm : 12m
      6.5cm : 26m
      2.5cm : 10m

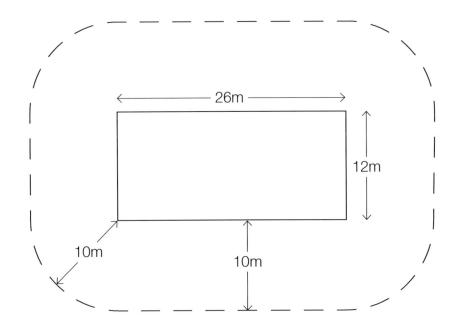

b) Enclosed area between the fence and the plot of land =

= (26m x 10m) + (26m x 10m) + (12m x 10m) + (12m x 10m) + (3.14 x (10m)^2)

= 260m^2 + 260m^2 + 120 m^2 + 120 m^2 + 314 m^2 = **1,074m^2**

About the author

In addition to *GCSE maths (foundation level) for Post-16 learners*, Kevin Norley has authored *Making Britain Numerate (3rd Ed)*, *Making Britain Literate (3rd Ed)*, co-edited *Contemporary Approaches in Education* and been widely published in a range of internationally edited journals and books. He has also presented his papers at a wide range of international education conferences, including as a keynote speaker:

Publications:

Norley, K. (2018), *Making Britain Literate* (3rd Ed), Twentyfivefiftytwo, Cambridge.

Norley, K. (2017), "Mentoring teacher trainees of mathematics for ESL learners in post-compulsory education: reflections and challenges", International Journal of Mentoring and Coaching in Education, Vol. 6 Issue 1. pp. 64–77

Norley, K. (2018), "Factors affecting, and methods to improve, the language development of EAL learners", in Kourtis-Kazoullis, V., Aravossitas, T., Skourtou, E. & Pericles Trifonas, P. (Eds), Interdisciplinary Research Approaches to Multilingual Education, Routledge, London, pp. 79–92

Norley, K. Arslan, H., Icbay, M.A. (Eds.) (2015), *Contemporary Approaches in Education*, Peter Lang, Frankfurt am Main.

Norley, K. (2015), "Technology and Teaching Methods", Published in INTED2015 Proceedings (International Technology, Education and Development 9th conference in Madrid, Spain),International Academy of Technology, Education and Development, pp. 6361–6365.

Norley, K. (2014), "The integration methodology for developing writing skills", European Journal of Research on Social Studies, Vol 1, special issue 1, pp. 88–94.

Norley, K. (2014), "The conversion-integration methodology for developing numeracy skills", in Arslan, H., Rata, G., Kocayoruk, E. and Icbay, M.A. (Eds.), Multidisciplinary Perspectives on Education, Cambridge Scholars Publishing, Newcastle Upon Tyne, pp. 87–94.

Norley, K. (2013), "Language, Social Class, Ethnicity and Educational Inequality", in Arslan, H. and Rata, G. (Eds.), Multicultural Education: From Theory to Practice, Cambridge Scholars Publishing, Newcastle Upon Tyne, pp. 103–118.

Index